New Horizons

SISTERS
OF SAINT LOUIS
HEALING | UNIFYING | TRANSFORMING

New Horizons

The Sisters of St Louis in a Changing World

Jo O'Donoghue

LONDUBH BOOKS

First published in 2012

by Londubh Books

18 Casimir Avenue, Harold's Cross, Dublin 6w, Ireland

www.londubh.ie

1 3 5 4 2

Origination by Londubh Books; cover by redrattledesign

Printed by ScandBook, Falun, Sweden

ISBN: 978-1-907535-26-0

Contents

Foreword

We each have an individual story to tell. Sometimes that story, for a myriad reasons, does not get told. This is a great loss, even more so when it is the story of a large number of women, from different parts of the world, who have chosen to live what poet Mary Oliver calls their 'one precious life' as a family, in a religious community, in this case the Sisters of St Louis. *New Horizons: the Sisters of St Louis in a Changing World*, is our family story, unique to us. We recognise ourselves in it and know that it is about us. In it, Jo O'Donoghue has skilfully captured some of what our experience has been over the past sixty-five years and woven it into a captivating chronicle.

For many years there has been a fear and anxiety among us that something that we sensed was valuable could be lost forever. Successive central leadership teams have attempted to address this matter. Experience and much hard work on the part of some sisters proved that it was difficult for us to tell the story ourselves. We needed the help of external eyes and ears to do justice to the complex decades in Church and state, across the globe, through which we have recently lived. When we asked Jo O'Donoghue, a lay woman, to consider writing our story for us, we were apprehensive. We knew we were taking a risk. What if she did not understand us? What if we did not like what she said about us?

We need not have worried. By using a simple, lively, engaging writing style, Jo blends fact with story and invites us to take a closer look at ourselves and at the historical, social and ecclesial context through which we have lived. By doing this she offers us the opportunity to understand and appreciate ourselves more fully. As we read *New Horizons* we realise that there is no need to be afraid. It is as if we are looking in a mirror and seeing there that the sum of our lives has been and continues to be fascinating and worthwhile. It is appropriate to be proud of how we have responded, on an ongoing basis, to the immense challenges that came our way during vastly changing decades in the Church and the world. Who, in 1947, could possibly have imagined the world, the Church and the St Louis Institute of 2012? We know that these years have not all been easy and Jo is honest and truthful with us. She does not allow us to run away from our collective shadow but helps us to face our darkness with humility, compassion and gentleness.

Jo is a writer, linguist and historian and she draws on each of these skills to fill out the picture for us in an honest and engaging way. She maps out, succinctly and clearly, the journey which the outcomes of successive general chapters, after the post-Vatican II renewal chapter of 1969-70, called us to embrace. Contrary to what we may sometimes have thought as we lived through these years, we can see how these outcomes have built one upon the other in a remarkable and evolving way. We have been women of our time and have made valiant efforts to respond to the external environment and happenings in the Church and in society in appropriate ways, with eyes fixed ultimately on God and on our overall call to *Sint Unum*.

Of course *New Horizons* has its limitations. It would be impossible for any author, any book, to capture in a comprehensive way everything that happened in the lives of many hundreds of women over the course of sixty-five years. Jo used both documents and interviews for her research: internal sources, mainly our Monaghan archives and St Louis publications and external sources such as Church documents, encyclicals and other historical material. We value the sensitivity with which she used this material. She conducted the interviews mainly on a one to one basis, in person or by phone or Skype, with every one of those among us who responded to the invitation to be in touch with her. It follows, of course, that what she heard and recorded and subsequently included in the book was the subjective experience of those with whom she spoke.

Undoubtedly, there are gaps in the story. This reality may come as a disappointment to some. A person or event, pivotal for me, does not even get a mention! This calls us to a great generosity, big-heartedness and realism. Where we have travelled over the past sixty-five years, as the St Louis family, has been influenced by the contribution, whether hidden or visible, of each one of our members. *New Horizons* prompts us to remember this and to give thanks for each one of these women, alive or dead.

Ours is a human and varied story and *New Horizons* manages very well to record our recent history as an institute in a readable way, by effectively weaving different themes. We may well find ourselves laughing and crying as we read evocative stories of pain and endurance, inspirational stories of adversity overcome and humorous stories of contending with new cultures. All these stories are ours. We trust that this our book will encourage us, the St Louis family, to face the future in peace, whatever that future holds, as we continue to embrace the oneness of all that is.

It is our hope that this account will be a faith experience, not only for us, our St Louis associates and others in the St Louis family, but for people of any culture who read its refreshing pages.

Jo, thank you! You are a great woman, a gift and a friend to us.

Uainín Clarke
Donna Hansen
Margaret Healy
Winifred Ojo
Central Leadership Team
St Louis Generalate
Dublin, 2012

Introduction

In 2010 the Central Leadership Team of the St Louis Institute commissioned me to write a history of the institute from 1959, the point at which Pauline McGovern's *God Wills It* left off. Pauline's history marked the centenary of the community's first establishing itself in Ireland. Subsequently the period to be covered in *New Horizons* was extended, backwards, to 1947, as this was the year in which the Sisters of St Louis took the radical step of beginning foreign missionary work, first in Ghana and, over the following two years, in Nigeria and California.

New Horizons is an informal history of the St Louis Institute as it has evolved and reinvented itself from 1947 to date. My brief, in so far as possible, was to base my account on the personal testimony of those who were involved in the events described and, fortunately, several pioneering spirits were in a position to describe first-hand what the sisters experienced when they arrived in Nigeria or Ghana or Juilly after the Irish Sisters of St Louis became reunited with their motherhouse, Les Dames de St Louis, in 1952. I also tried to set the mission and ministry of the institute against the backdrop of the secular history and society of the period.

My aim was to mirror back to the sisters the work they engaged in, what they have achieved and how they achieved it, how they saw and see themselves and what motivated them. I also wanted to provide an account of the different areas of ministry of the institute and its recent history, in Ireland and abroad, for sisters who would not personally have experienced them.

A secondary aim was to put on record the work and life stories of a significant international religious community, which I hope will be of interest to the many women who were educated by the St Louis sisters, to the institute's associates and supporters worldwide and to the public in general.

In many cases the ministries undertaken by the sisters were so many and varied, even in a particular region, that I could do no more than describe a representative sample.

The sisters I met responded to the great Church movements and theological changes of the twentieth century – not just Vatican II but subsequent developments in missiology, personal spirituality and liberation theology – some of them in ways that were radical and that asked a great deal of them personally. This is their story and the story of those who continued in the more traditional ministries of education, healthcare, community service and leadership of the institute but with a new outlook and fresh sense of mission.

A few clarifications: although 'institute' is technically the correct term, I have also used the terms 'congregation' and 'order' throughout this text. When referring to the sisters I normally use their baptismal names and surnames without the 'SSL' that officially designates them. Some sisters who feature in this history predate the reversion to baptismal names and others chose, for various reasons, to retain their name in religion: these, like baptismal names, I use with a surname.

In the interest of simplicity I use the terms 'principal' and 'vice-principal' for these roles in education although in certain situations other terms may be more correct, and in the light of recent St Louis scholarship I use the spelling 'Turquestein' in place of the more traditional 'Turkenstein' for the *fons et origo* of the institute, and 'Brek' (Thérèse) rather than 'Breck'. I have also used 'Asankragwa' in place of 'Asankrangwa', the location of one of the institute's first medical missions in Ghana.

Terms pertaining to religious institutes used in this book include 'CLT' (central leadership team), the team elected at the general chapter to lead the institute, and 'generalate' (the central administration of the institute), where CLT is based. 'Canonical' means something that is in keeping with canon law, the legal system of the Catholic Church, while 'region' and 'province' are territorial subdivisions of a religious institute fulfilling different criteria and with different degrees of autonomy, in keeping with canon law.

Interviews with St Louis sisters took place during 2010, 2011 and 2012. Unless otherwise specified all other quotations are from documents in the institute's archives in Monaghan.

The biblical quotations in the text, *Kings* 4:29 and *1 Peter* 3:15, are from the *King James* version.

Jo O'Donoghue
Dublin, 2012

Prologue: from Turquestein to Monaghan

'It is the sisters who will be the heirs
to the spiritual heritage of the family.'
Louis Bautain (in a letter to Adolphe Carl, 1866)

The St Louis Institute had a complicated, lengthy genesis and it is likely that many of the sisters who entered the congregation in Monaghan in the second half of the nineteenth century and the first half of the twentieth would not have been aware of the full riches of their spiritual heritage. Such awareness came mainly as a result of the exhortation of Vatican II to all religious congregations to re-acquaint themselves with 'the spirit and aim' of their founders. This was easier than it might have been for the Sisters of St Louis because the community had by then been reunited with the motherhouse in Juilly, although there were language difficulties to overcome. It had always been conscious of itself as a French congregation (as had the pupils who attended its schools) but its roots extended far beyond Juilly, both in time and in place. Máirín Barrett was my main source of information on the origins of the St Louis sisters.

The charism that is currently the lodestar of the institute, *Ut Sint Unum* – 'That they may be one' – was adopted as its guiding principle by a group of three individuals who signed a spiritual pact in Turquestein in 1797: Joseph Louis Colmar (1760-1818), Bishop of Mainz and spiritual father to the group; Louise Humann (1766-1836), a philosopher and spiritual teacher; and Thérèse Brek (1755-1825). *Ut Sint Unum* derives from *John* 17:21-26: 'May they all be one. Father, may they be one in us, as you are in me and I am in you, so that the world may believe it was you who sent me.' Significantly, the stated purpose of this union, the prototype St Louis community, was: 'The relief of the sick; the instruction of youth; to reveal the purpose of God in the world.' As a 'mission statement' it sounds quite up to date in its focus, if not in its language. These were the ministries on which the members of the group had already embarked, in the hostile anti-clerical climate of post-Revolutionary France.

Louise Humann was the only one of the three signatories of the Turquestein pact to play a part in the second act of origination: Joseph Louis Colmar had died in 1818 and Thérèse Brek in 1825. In Strasbourg she came into contact with a young Paris-born philosopher, Louis Bautain (1796-1867), whom she helped to deal with a religious and psychological crisis that obliged him to give up his job as a lecturer in the University of Strasbourg. Bautain, who experienced a conversion as the result of the intervention of Louise Humann and a deep reading of the gospels, was her first spiritual son and, with other men and women, both priests and lay people, she formed a loose community or 'family' (a word that the Dames de St Louis continued to use in Juilly) dedicated to the realisation of *Ut Sint Unum*. Some of the women who were involved in Louise Humann's spiritual family in Strasbourg would later form the nucleus of the Dames de St Louis and the Sœurs de Notre Dame de Sion (a 'cousin' congregation) under the leadership of Louis Bautain and Théodore Ratisbonne respectively, while the men formed a short-lived male St Louis congregation.

It was Louis Bautain, by then L'Abbé Bautain, who completed the foundation process, in Juilly, in 1842. In the interim he and his companions had crossed theological swords with the Bishop of Strasbourg and Bautain had to go to Rome to defend himself against charges of heresy. Paris was a more congenial intellectual environment and the Oratorian Collège de Juilly, which Bautain and his friends purchased and over which Bautain began to preside, brought him to that village. The Institute of St Louis he founded included priests and sisters and its purpose was: 'To establish a true spirit of Christian union among the members so that Our Lord's prayer, *Sint Unum*, may be fulfilled in them.' Bautain appointed Clémence, Baronne de Vaux, an aristocratic Parisian philanthropist – Mère Thérèse de la Croix was her name in religion – as the first superior. The male branch of the institute survived only until 1849.

Bautain, although disappointed by the disintegration, was pragmatic. He showed a similar pragmatism ten years later when faced with the obduracy of an Irish bishop. In 1866 he wrote to Adolphe Carl: 'It is the sisters who will be the heirs to the spiritual heritage of the family.'

It may seem strange that in 1859 St Louis sisters should come all the way from Juilly to Monaghan to run a reformatory. This mission had its roots in the economic and social situation in Ireland. The poverty and wretchedness of the country just a decade after the end of the Great Famine meant that there was a great deal of juvenile crime, although much of it was petty by the standards of today. Reformatories, to which juvenile offenders would be committed by law, were a new development. There had been pressure in England for the separate detention of young offenders and in 1854 the government enacted legislation setting up special centres for them. The Catholic bishops, led by Cardinal Paul Cullen, opposed a proposal for similar legislation in Ireland in 1856, fearing that such centres would be under the control of the Church of Ireland and other Protestant denominations and create opportunities for the evangelisation of young people. When the Reformatory Schools Act was finally passed in 1858 it empowered the Chief Secretary to designate certain institutions as suitable for the detention of young offenders – for 'the rehabilitation of criminal and delinquent children': in effect it set up denominational centres with state support.

The Irish connection was strong almost from the foundation of the Dames de St Louis. Irish girls of good family were sent to Paris for their education and some of them, having been educated in the *pensionnat* that was immediately founded in Juilly, stayed on to enter the order. Irish philanthropists like Ellen (Hélène) Woodlock, who had been a sister in Juilly for a time and was keen for the order to establish itself in Ireland, would have seen the reformatory movement in a positive light – and so it was if one considers the alternative of sentencing children to a harsh prison regime in the company of hardened criminals. John Lentaigne, a director of government prisons and reformatories and a native of Monaghan, supported Ellen Woodlock's philanthropic efforts but was anxious that the reformatory should be based in his own home town and not in her home city of Cork. And so it was.

Mère Thérèse, reluctantly it appears, sent as the foundation group in 1859 Geneviève (Mary Priscilla) Beale (1822-78), an English convert from Anglicanism who had previously lived in Ireland, and two Irish Dames de St Louis, Claire (Marguerite) O'Sullivan and Clémence McCarthy. They arrived in Monaghan on 6 January 1859 after a lengthy journey during which little had gone according to plan and found that the accommodation the bishop had promised was not ready.

Further difficulties awaited them, the most serious and troubling being the question of the Irish house's continuing relationship with the order's motherhouse in Juilly. As early as August 1859, when Louis Bautain visited the fledgling foundation in Monaghan, he suspected that relations with the Bishop of Clogher, Charles McNally (1787-1864), would not be easy. He wrote to Mère Thérèse de la Croix: *'Le terrain s'est gagné…mais le diable se retrouve d'un autre [côté]…* '('The ground has been won…but the devil is from another side…') and in a subsequent letter on the eve of his departure for France: *'Il veut, tout simplement, comme tous les évêques de ce pays, être le supérieur des sœurs…'* ('He [Bishop McNally] wishes, quite simply, like all the bishops of this country, to be the superior of the sisters.'). A standoff ensued, which Bishop McNally seems to have won by simple force of inertia (neglecting to reply to the correspondence of L'Abbé Bautain), so that eventually, in a letter of 6 June 1861, Bautain resolved the impasse by instructing the foundation in Monaghan to submit itself to the rule of the bishop: *'Nous renonçons à la direction de la maison de Monaghan…'* ('We renounce direction of the Monaghan house.') He exhorted Geneviève Beale and her community: *'Restez attachées à la maison mère au moins par l'esprit, autant que vous le pourrez…Il faut gagner du temps et l'avenir, qui ne peut pas être bien lointain, sera peut-être plus favorable à l'union.* ('Stay attached to the motherhouse at least in spirit, as much as you can…We must bide our time and the future, which cannot be far off, will perhaps be more favourable for union.') Bautain might have been surprised to know that ninety years would elapse before the desired union came about and then in circumstances no one could have envisaged.

The separation of motherhouse and daughterhouse seems an unfortunate and ironic outcome for the two founders of the institute, L'Abbé Bautain and Mère Thérèse de la Croix, who set such store by the principle of *Ut Sint Unum,* as well as for the sisters in Ireland. We know that, unlike Bautain, the mother superior in Juilly found it difficult to reconcile herself to the independence of the new Irish foundation and the loss of three beloved members of the St Louis family, less than twenty years after the foundation of the institute in Juilly. In the lore of the Dames de St Louis the separation was regarded as a 'schism', according to Juilly-based historian, Máirín Barrett. The theme of unity, separation and reunification recurs in the history of the institute as a whole.

Geneviève Beale, the founder and superior in Monaghan, is described in contemporary accounts as being kind and charitable. She showed humanity towards the children who were committed by the courts to the care of the sisters, beginning with an eleven-year-old Belfast girl in October 1859. Many of the inmates of the Ulster Reformatory for Catholic Girls in Sparks Lane were malnourished and deprived (to use the modern term) and when they improved under her care, she wrote: 'It proves that vice was not a natural instinct with them but the result of ignorance, negligence of parents and bad example.'

She never denied food to the children as a punishment, something that was common practice in institutions and even homes at this time and long afterwards: 'The food the children get is the absolute requisite for their growth and development and we do not consider ourselves justified in changing either the quality or the quantity when the child is in disgrace…'

The reformatory run by the Sisters of St Louis continued until 1903. Bishop McNally and John Lentaigne, with the help of Charles Bianconi, who established the first public coach service in Ireland, and local benefactors, raised the purchase money for the Old Brewery, where the reformatory moved and the convent and school were later built. An industrial school, St Martha's, was established in 1870 as a result of new legislation. The Industrial Schools Act of 1868 was more far-reaching than the reformatory schools legislation, extending the system to children 'at risk' because they had no parental care: children were committed to industrial schools not for criminal behaviour but for vagrancy, begging and homelessness. Industrial schools increased rapidly in number, the Catholic ones being almost exclusively under the care of religious brothers and sisters. The reformatory and industrial school in Monaghan continued in separate premises until a drop in demand led to the closure of the reformatory. St Martha's had its own dedicated building on the Monaghan campus from 1906.

Geneviève Beale must also have been a capable woman. By the time she died in 1878, nineteen years after arriving in Ireland, the St Louis congregation was firmly established in Monaghan and had houses and schools in Bundoran (1870) – although the town was so impoverished and the accommodation so inadequate that the community closed in 1884, reopening on a more solid basis in 1894 – Ramsgrange, County Wexford (1871) and Middletown, County Armagh (1875). The convent there was not long established when the first eight girls were committed to St Joseph's, a new industrial school, on 25 June 1881. Post-famine Ireland was still poor but the Catholic Church was in a phase of growth and the order grew with it. The cathedral of the diocese of Clogher, St Macartan's in Monaghan, dates from this period and is certainly not retiring, being visible from all the main roads into the town. Its foundation stone was laid soon after the arrival of the Dames de St Louis, in 1861, after a long battle by Bishop McNally to acquire the site, although it was not consecrated until 1892.

Under superiors who succeeded Geneviève Beale, the congregation continued to expand, concentrating its energies on secondary education for girls in boarding and day schools as well as primary education. Foundations in Carrickmacross (1888); Kiltimagh (1898); Clones (1900); Rathmines (1913) and Balla (1919) followed; then in Northern Ireland: Newcastle (1920), Kilkeel (1922), Ballymena (1924), Clogher (1933) and Cushendall (1945). Dundalk was the last major foundation in the Republic of Ireland, with the establishment of Dún Lughaidh secondary and boarding school in 1950, and, with the exception of the small secondary school begun in Ramsgrange in 1967, the only such foundation in the Republic of Ireland once missionary work in Africa had begun. The opening of St Genevieve's High School in west Belfast in 1966 was the beginning of the involvement of the congregation in that troubled city.

St Louis sisters also established convents and schools in England from 1912. Redditch, south of Birmingham, was the first foundation; then Great Yarmouth (1920); Bury St Edmunds (1924); Newmarket (1936); Aylesbury (1945); there followed a large number of shorter-term educational, community and social apostolates.

Kiltimagh-Balla had a separate novitiate but reamalgamated with the motherhouse in 1921, a lost story that historian Gabrielle O'Connell restored to the institute's memory with her 2007 book of this title. After this the congregation held a general chapter, which decided that its constitutions should be formalised. This work took four years and in 1926-7 the Holy See issued a decree of approval and the congregation achieved pontifical status as 'the congregation of St Louis, Monaghan (Diocese of Clogher)'. Henceforward it would look to Rome as the ultimate authority and any change of consequence in its rule, such as undertaking missionary work abroad or beginning a medical mission, would require permission from the Vatican.

1

Mother of the Missions

'I brought you here to work.'

Columbanus Greene, 1947

In the decade after the end of the Second World War, a major development changed the focus and ministry of the order: the beginning of missionary work in west Africa and California.

During the same period the consolidation and centralisation of the congregation became complete. After a long separation came reunification, firstly with the order's motherhouse in Juilly, which formally took place in 1952. Although this did not have the same practical consequences as missionary work, nor did it extend the life span of the institute by attracting new vocations, the institute's rediscovery of the spiritual riches associated with the founders of the Dames de St Louis in Juilly and especially the philosophy of Louis Bautain became a significant factor in the revival of its charism and the renewal of its *raison d'être* after Vatican II.

Nor was the amalgamation with Juilly the only reunification at this time. Bishops favoured consolidation and central control – it was the Roman way – something that can be seen in the intervention in support of amalgamation of two bishops as far apart as Georges-Louis-Camille Debray of Meaux (Juilly) and Joseph Staunton of Ferns in the case of Ramsgrange. It had become clear that small independent foundations would not be self-sustaining into the future.

Ramsgrange, one of the earliest St Louis houses, which had its own novitiate and functioned independently of the motherhouse, came into the fold in 1956, as Kiltimagh-Balla had done in 1921 and Middletown in 1927 (Anthony McConville was the last sister to take her vows there in June 1924). Middletown's small boarding school closed in 1948 but the sisters stayed in charge of the primary school and put considerable energies into running the industrial school, which became a statutory service, St Joseph's Training School, under the Northern Ireland Ministry for Home Affairs, in 1952.

There were twenty-six professed sisters in Ramsgrange when the amalgamation took place in early 1956. Two sisters with temporary vows, Loreto Hickey and Sheila O'Shea; a novice, Carmel Mary McCarthy, who later went as a missionary to Brazil; and a postulant, Felicity Hanna, came (the last in tears) to Monaghan. There Felicity joined the 'set' of 1955, at thirty-six the largest in the history of the order. No wonder she was sad. It was said that Ramsgrange enjoyed a more liberal regime than Monaghan and also that it kept some of the Juilly spirit of simplicity: sisters travelled to and from school on a pony and trap, they each received a small sum of pocket money and they were allowed to visit their homes. (Felicity later left the congregation.) Alexis Rynne was the superior sent to Ramsgrange from Monaghan and despite initial trepidation she proved a popular choice with the sisters there until she was transferred to Rathmines in 1962. Mary O'Donovan was the first young sister from Monaghan to make the journey in the opposite direction after her first profession in 1959.

Ramsgrange had a delegate at the order's general chapter that year and by the end of 1956, the whole of the St Louis congregation was governed directly from Monaghan by the newly elected superior general Majella Seery. But it was Columbanus Greene, serving both before and after Majella, who was the great authority figure of the order in the mid-twentieth century.

Brigid Greene was born in 1897 near Fivemiletown on the border of counties Fermanagh and Tyrone, the daughter of a teacher, and attended secondary school in St Louis in Monaghan, entering religious life in 1913. She was first elected superior general in 1944 and initially served two terms, in her first term initiating the missions to Ghana, Nigeria and California and in her second presiding over the reunification with Juilly. But by a twist of fate she was to serve a further two terms in office, something that was not normally permitted by the order's rule.

The general chapter of April 1944 was held prematurely as the serving superior general, Raphael Nugent, who had been elected in 1939, died in office in October 1943. Columbanus, who was mistress of schools (principal) in Monaghan, having occupied the same position in Balla and Rathmines, was elected superior general at the chapter. She was re-elected in 1950 for an allowed second term. Majella Seery, who succeeded her in 1956, died in office on 6 February 1958 and in June of that year, at an extraordinary chapter, Columbanus was again elected superior general. Her final term of office was from 1964 to 1969, a period that presaged the years of great change in religious life ordained by Vatican II.

Columbanus's influence was considerable: she presided over the institute for almost a quarter of a century in the period of its greatest development as a homogeneous, traditional entity before the vertiginous decline in religious life that began in the 1960s. It seems fitting that she had the name in religion of the greatest Irish missionary of all (543-615AD), who is buried before the high altar in Bobbio, and that her successor, Colmcille Stephens, should bear the name of another great missionary (521-97AD), a figure of more complexity according to the chroniclers of the time.

All who came in contact with her describe Columbanus as a woman of deep faith and unshakeable trust in Providence: she appears to have been a woman of action rather than contemplation. 'Discernment' (right thinking or wisdom in judgement) is a word institute members often use nowadays to describe the sometimes lengthy process of coming to a decision on an important matter. It seems from contemporary accounts that Columbanus sought guidance in prayer or wisdom in reflection, then mostly made the decisions herself: Marie de Paul Neiers wrote of her (*Newsletter*, December 1982): 'Many times I have seen her eyes fixed on those quiet waters [of the lake in Monaghan] reflecting the light, as she sat making up her mind about something. There was no rush, no fuss, she would gaze on the peaceful view in silence, a bit remote – then she would turn and speak, simply and without hesitation, with a quality of conviction and faith that touched one deeply.'

In those post-war years and for a long time afterwards, religious life was hierarchical and autocratic and sisters accepted that they would be told what to do and where to go and that they should simply make the best of whatever job they were given wherever it happened to be. Many sisters were sent for third level education, to training colleges for primary teaching or to universities to qualify as secondary teachers. Others slipped through the net and worked at home or abroad in an untrained capacity until they were rescued and sent for further education by Columbanus's successor, Colmcille Stephens, in the early 1970s. In the decades before Vatican II, when thousands of young women and men entered religious life and the Catholic Church in Ireland seemed unassailable, with a strong and overt influence on politics, bishops believed they were always right – or had to behave as if they did – and the same was true of superiors general.

Columbanus Greene managed a large and complicated enterprise with a substantial budget from her headquarters in Monaghan – she was the Irish superior as well as being superior general – with the help of a small council and without the benefit of modern means of communication. The number of personnel over whom she presided continued to increase until the mid-1960s – data from the 1969 chapter shows the highest number ever of finally professed sisters (six hundred and eighty five) although the number of postulants and novices had already started to decline. Columbanus was a woman of her time and her energy and self-belief enabled her to ignore or overcome obstacles that might have deterred a more cautious, reflective leader.

Stories abound of the apparent arbitrariness of Columbanus's allocation of personnel to the different houses in Ireland and missions abroad. It was said that sisters with a degree in Irish were sure to be missioned to west Africa: Maud Murphy and Jane Vereker were two such but Jane says that at least the sisters found Irish useful as a secret conversational code at the time of the Igbo-Hausa conflict in northern Nigeria. Conversely, Eilís Ní Thiarnaigh, who had a BA in Irish and history from UCD, volunteered three times for Africa but Columbanus said to her, when pressed on the subject,

'Sure I can't afford to send you.' According to Eilís: *'Bhí an oiread sin Gaeilgeoirí curtha amach aici cheana féin.'* ('She had already sent so many people with degrees in Irish out' [to Africa]).

Carmel Dodd describes how in August 1952 she was helping Columbanus in her office in Monaghan, standing on a chair to put a parcel on a high shelf. Columbanus asked her where she had been missioned and when Carmel replied that she was bound for Kumasi (Ghana) said she would not be going there, as planned, but to Kano (Nigeria) as 'they needed someone out there for domestic science'. Carmel does not record if she fell off the chair but she certainly began to teach in Kano the following month.

Josephine Fay was sent to California at the eleventh hour in 1953 because she attracted the attention of Columbanus when the superior general came to pray in the chapel in Monaghan. Josephine was helping to wax the floor in preparation for professions (including her own) that were to take place on 12 August. Someone destined for California had fallen ill and when her companion knocked over a bench, Columbanus looked up and her eyes fell on the person she was seeking. When Josephine was summoned to Columbanus's study a few minutes later she feared she would be reprimanded for the incident in the chapel but instead the mother general asked her, cordially, 'How would you like to go to Los Angeles?' and sent her off for her smallpox vaccination. She sailed on the *Mauretania* from Southampton to New York before the end of August, 'terrified out of her wits' and, she says, unprepared for what was ahead of her, and it was 1960 before she saw home and family again. She spent fifty-nine years altogether in California.

Columbanus sent Deirdre O'Hanlon to Juilly even though she had failed French in her Intermediate Certificate and her teacher in Carrickmacross had advised her father that she should give the subject up. Now Deirdre is a *Chevalier dans l'Ordre des Palmes Académiques* in recognition of her services to education and her French is fantastic. Clare Ryan tells a similar story about her own lack of French when she was sent to Juilly in 1952. As to why she was chosen for this mission, her name in religion was Jeanne d'Arc and Columbanus told her later that when she saw the French name she knew Clare was the one: she was finding it hard to get someone and Clare was able to teach music, which was on the Juilly wish list.

She must have done something right – or maybe the calibre of the St Louis sisters was so high that they would have thrived wherever they were planted. In a letter of condolence to the congregation on Columbanus's death in 1982, Claremorris-born Richard Finn SMA, Bishop of Ibadan 1958-74, wrote: 'The sisters sent out by Mother Columbanus were admirably suited mentally, spiritually and academically for the cultural shock and what is one of the most difficult climates in the world.' This was a remarkable achievement given that not one of them could say that she had received advance linguistic or cultural preparation for working in Nigeria.

Joannes Hayes experienced the real Columbanus – convivial with the missionary priests who were their co-passengers and curious about everything she was experiencing – when, in 1947, they sailed together to Takoradi to join the three Ghana pioneers, Joseph Mary Connolly, Bried Mulhern and Sheela Gillespie, who had gone ahead of them:

'MMC was a reserved woman and indeed sometimes in the earlier days she could be sharp and even sometimes hard. But there was in her a wisdom, a breadth of vision, a sense of humour (caustic, mayhap, betimes), a broad humanity, a no-nonsense approach to life and a willingness to take risk that one does not easily meet. Thrown in at the deep end she expected us to swim! The words of *Kings* 4:29 could be applied to her: "God gave [her] wisdom and understanding exceeding much and largeness of heart as the sand that is on the seashore."

'But above all she was a woman of great faith, shown in the actual situation here and in her letters to us. For that we will remember her most.

'Shortly before she died, she told me when she was in primary school she had a primer in which there was a story about brave missionaries, spending themselves for the Lord. She just felt she'd wish to be like them. The good Lord granted her desire in His own way.'

André van den Bronk SMA, who succeeded H.J. Paulissen as Bishop of Kumasi (1952-62), wrote to Columbanus on 8 November 1958, a few months after she had been re-elected superior general because of the premature death of Majella Seery: 'I need not say, however, how happy I am to learn that the Mother of the Missions [is] in Monaghan at the helm of affairs again.' She was not given to effusions but this tribute must surely have pleased her.

Columbanus did not spare herself or any of her community. The Irish of the era of the Great Famine had a reputation (among the English) for laziness and fecklessness, which more tolerant observers tended to regard as 'Celtic' in origin. A century later there was nothing but work for the Irish, at home and abroad. The hundreds of thousands of Irish labourers who began to rebuild war-shattered Britain at the precise moment in history that Sisters of St Louis took the boat for Takoradi and Lagos were famed for their productivity, especially the hardy Connemara men – 'Connies', as they were called – who knew what it meant to survive on the poorest land of all.

Joannes Hayes's story of her first journey through Ghana with Columbanus puts it perfectly. The Ghanaian pioneers were on their way to Kumasi in a mammy wagon (pick-up) with Monsignor Paulissen. When they crossed the River Prah, the monsignor asked them to alight from the wagon as they were now on the holy ground of Ashanti. Joannes, who, according to those who worked with her in Ghana, had a high regard for indigenous culture, recounted: 'In a burst of enthusiasm I said to the superior general, "I would like to die here." She replied tartly, "I did not bring you out here to die. I brought you here to work."' [Joannes remained in Ghana into her old age but despite her wish to the contrary, died in Ireland in 1991.)

The sisters bound for Kumasi and Kano whom Columbanus accompanied on their respective first journeys were witness to her own willingness to roll up her sleeves. Augustine Moane, a pioneer in Kano, had experienced her as stern and strict in Monaghan but saw a completely different side to her in Nigeria. She had the greatest admiration for her (especially as she and her companion Regis O'Donnell had organised the mosquito nets in readiness for

the arrival of the Kano community members) and even came to like
her when she got over being terrified of her.

Once she started the missions to Africa, Columbanus embraced
this work wholeheartedly. Sheela Gillespie, a pioneer in Ghana, said
that Columbanus loved Kumasi best, and this may well be true, as
it was her first experience of Africa. She enjoyed her visitations to
Nigeria and Ghana and, although she may have been ruthless in
assigning sisters as she thought necessary to the great work, she had
a special place in her heart for them. When missioners came home
she welcomed them with open arms and contrived small treats for
them and she kept in touch with many of them until the end of
her life. She entrusted them with a great deal of responsibility and
perhaps their reluctance to disappoint her contributed something to
their achievements.

Columbanus Greene lived to see the order she had led change
greatly in its outward signs and its daily life and to a lesser degree in
its apostolate. In an interview in *Reflections* (1977) she commented
wryly on one fundamental change in religious life: that whereas the
ideal in earlier years was for 'singularity' to be avoided at all costs, it
had become the case that 'uniqueness' was now 'a consummation
devoutly to be wished'. She died in August 1982 and the convent
in Monaghan was full of sisters who came together to celebrate her
funeral on St Louis Day, 25 August. In the years since her death,
although many of the ministries the sisters have undertaken would
not even have existed in her lifetime – and some might even tend to
'uniqueness' – institute members have maintained their tradition of
hard work and commitment wherever their apostolates have taken
them.

2

The Island of Saints and Scholars, 20th Century

'Ireland for the foreign missions'
Edward Galvin, 1916

The period from 1920 to 1960 was the era *par excellence* of Catholic missions overseas. A succession of exhortatory documents from the Vatican emphasised the importance of the evangelisation of the whole pagan world, detailed how best this might be achieved and outlined the pitfalls to be avoided by those engaged in missionary activity. Benedict XV's apostolic letter of 30 November 1919 entitled 'On the Propagation of the Catholic Faith throughout the World' and *Rerum Ecclesiae,* Pius XI's 1926 encyclical on Catholic missions, firmly nailed Rome's colours to the mast of evangelisation.

Pius XI wrote: 'It seems to us that two special objectives ought to be aimed at in all missionary work, both of which are not only timely but necessary and closely connected with each other; namely, that a much larger number than heretofore of missionaries, well trained in the different fields of knowledge, be sent into the vast regions which are still deprived of the civilising influence of the Christian religion; and secondly, that the faithful be brought to understand with what zeal, constancy in prayer, and with what generosity they too must cooperate in a work which is so holy and fruitful.' Thus did the Vatican make the foreign missions the business of all Catholics, religious and lay. It was in this spirit that the Friends of St Louis Missions contributed so much to the congregation's missionary work from the foundation of the organisation in 1950.

In 1951 Pius XII promulgated an encyclical, *Evangelii Praecones,* to mark the twenty-fifth anniversary of *Rerum Ecclesiae.* This reiterated the Papacy's conviction of the primacy of missionary activity, recommending cooperation between different religious when personnel was scarce in extensive areas of endeavour. And there was no missionary area that did not suffer from a scarcity of personnel, so much larger were the African and Asian countries needing evangelisation than the old countries of Europe from which they attracted missionary personnel. Ireland, one of the smallest European countries, contributed far more than its share to the missionary endeavour of the twentieth century.

Historical and social circumstances, no less than religious, placed the Irish Church in the forefront of worldwide Catholic evangelisation. By the time the Free State achieved at least partial independence in 1921, Catholicism was the Church of a fervent majority of the people: well organised, Roman and obedient in outlook and discipline, self-confident, well supplied with infrastructure and with enough personnel to be able to respond to the perceived need for evangelisation, particularly in Africa and the Far East. Irish children of the period read in their history books that their country had once been 'the island of saints and scholars', sending out missionaries to re-Christianise Europe in the Dark Ages and in the process saving western civilisation. It was not too far fetched to imagine that the newly independent Catholic Ireland of the early 20th century might be a second island of saints and scholars.

Bishop (from 1927) Edward Galvin (1882-1956) called on the patriotism of the Irish, founding the Columban fathers with John Blowick (1888-1972). 'Ireland for the foreign missions,' was his call in 1916. He led his first missionaries to China in 1920, declaring, 'I believe Ireland could do wonders among the heathen.' It was a great advantage for missionary work that most Irish people spoke English, the *lingua franca* of the British colonies or former colonies in Africa, India and the Far East. It was also an advantage that they were not themselves British and that the Irish had suffered hunger and oppression at the hands of Britain only decades earlier, so they were able entirely to avoid the taint of a colonial past. The only empire they served was the spiritual empire of Rome.

In the year of independence, Tipperary-born Bishop Joseph

Shanahan CSSp (1871-1943), sometimes called 'the St Patrick of southern Nigeria', led the call for women missionaries in his area to evangelise Nigerian women and girls as he and his confrères had evangelised Nigerian men. Shanahan was instrumental in bringing the Holy Rosary sisters into being under the leadership of Agnes Ryan (Mother Thérèse), who founded the order's first house in Killeshandra, County Cavan, in 1924 and, thereafter, schools in southern Nigeria. The Irish Church of the era may have been patriarchal (and may still be) but missionary Churchmen with practical experience were realistic enough to realise that female missionaries were essential in order to reach families and educate women to become educators of their own children. This was also why Edward Galvin encouraged Frances Moloney to set up a female counterpart to his Columban missionary priests in 1922.

Medical missions were a slightly later development in the Catholic Church. Since 1901 the Vatican had prohibited religious personnel from giving aid in childbirth or attending women in maternity homes and the *Code of Canon Law* (1917) explicitly forbade religious to practise medicine and surgery. The publication of *Constans ac Sedula* in 1936 (after intense lobbying) authorised sisters to engage in midwifery and liberalised the practice of medicine and surgery, opening the way for Marie Martin (1892-1975) to establish the Medical Missionaries of Mary in Drogheda in 1937. Other dedicated orders like the Sisters of Our Lady of Apostles, founded in France in 1876 but strong in Ireland, and the Franciscan Missionary Sisters for Africa (founded by Teresa Kearney in Mount Oliver, Dundalk, in 1952) matched zealous Irish women with locations overseas where healthcare and schools were needed. Healthcare was to become part of the St Louis apostolate from the late 1940s, for the first time since the rupture with France in 1859. Juilly historian Máirín Barrett believes that the nursing apostolate was a rediscovery of the institute's roots in caring for the sick rather than a new departure. According to the Turquestein pact: 'God wills this union for the consolation of the sick and particularly for the education of the youth...'

In 1947, the St Louis apostolate was education, primary

and secondary – including industrial schools in Monaghan and Middletown – and once the order had made the journey from France to Ireland, it had not ventured further than England. It did not immediately respond to the papal call for personnel to commit to the foreign missions. Opting for missionary work required a big shift in outlook and the permission of the Sacred Congregation for the Doctrine of the Faith to amend its constitution. For the institute to commit to missionary work it needed a change in leadership and it acquired the right kind of leader in Columbanus Greene. From the time she became superior in 1944 she was aware that the order was losing vocations to the missionary congregations, especially as she had been mistress of schools in Monaghan. Patricia Moloney remembers her listing off the girls in each year that the order had 'lost' to Killeshandra and the Columbans in particular: always 'our best girls' (the ones who got away). In a later interview (*Reflections*, 1977), she herself gave this loss of potential vocations to her own congregation as her main reason for starting missionary work.

Old perceptions die hard. When Maura Flynn, who had taught for many years in Nigeria, came back to Ireland in 1983 to work in fundraising, the Irish Missionary Union refused her permission to raise money for the missions through the Church and school network. The reason it gave was that the Sisters of St Louis were 'not a missionary order'. Maura had to look elsewhere for funds.

3

The Mission to Ghana

'God, at last, has heard our prayers.'
H.J. Paulissen, Vicar of Kumasi, 1947

It was the Dutch-born Hubert J. Paulissen SMA, then Apostolic Vicar and from 1950 Bishop of Kumasi, who made the first official contact with Columbanus about establishing a mission in Ghana. In the Gold Coast, as it was called when it was still a British colony, there was huge demand for education. There had been no Catholic girls' school when the vicariate was established in 1933; thereafter, the number of pupils increased from 2284 in 1937 to 19,000 in 1947. The necessity for female education had begun to be recognised: 'The harvest is great – and ripe.'

The Sisters of St Louis were to take over St Bernadette's Primary School in Kumasi from French Our Lady of Apostles (OLA) sisters, who had worked there for ten years. A boarding school, it comprised girls up to the age of fourteen or fifteen. The Department of Education initially paid salaries to two of the sisters but the children also had to pay fees. As Ghana was a British colony, and even after independence English continued to be the language of education, the authorities had put pressure on Monsignor Paulissen to find English-speaking teachers for the school: hence his desperate approaches to twelve congregations before Columbanus said yes.

A letter from Monsignor Paulissen, dated 4 March 1947, was addressed to Columbanus from the Catholic Mission, Gold Coast. It refers to 'your kind letter of February 13 in answer to my appeal for sisters to take up teaching work in our girls' school in Kumasi… after so many unsuccessful approaches to different congregations, it would seem that God, at last, has heard our prayers.' On 22 May

1947 the Vatican gave permission to the institute to undertake an apostolate in Africa: *'administrare intendunt scholás puellarum'* ('[where] they intend to run girls' schools').

Monsignor Paulissen, like the Irish SMA bishops, took an interest in the welfare of the sisters facing an entirely unfamiliar climate and it was he who insisted that they wear tropical helmets for the sun, although these must have looked very strange indeed over the tall headdress and veil – the habit was white for the sisters in Africa. In a letter dated 23 May 1947 he wrote to Columbanus: 'As regards your costume, I am of the opinion that at least the headdress must be changed in such a way that you can easily put a tropical helmet on top of the veil. It would be most imprudent to go in the sun between 9 and 4 without this helmet…I feel confident that you are quite justified in making the necessary adaptation at once, try it here and if proved satisfactory ask for permission.' This is the helmet that Nigerian pioneer Augustine Moane described to me and that the sisters were instructed to wear at all costs. Nobody thought of sunglasses, which the sisters realised they needed much more than a helmet not too long after they got to Africa, or of protection against skin cancer.

We know from correspondence the following month that Monsignor Paulissen paid the fares of the sisters, or at least sent them a cheque for £300, 'which, I hope, will cover your fares.' He mentions also putting the convent in decent order against the arrival of the sisters. He was better prepared than Bishop McCarthy of Kaduna, which is why the group of four sisters who were intended for Kano turned their faces instead towards Kumasi. The mission to Nigeria was delayed until early 1948.

Monsignor Paulissen wrote in June 1948, after the mission had been established in Kumasi '…You are aware that the Education Department are making new rules and regulations about the European personnel employed in the schools. It is not yet definitively stated but it would seem that two sisters will receive £350 per annum, a free passage home and free medical treatment. But that passage home must take place every two years: this is a necessary condition for this allocation. All well considered, I think it is a wise regulation.' The situation in Ghana was different from Nigeria, where teaching sisters received no government pay until years later.

From among the many who volunteered, four sisters were chosen for the first foundation in Ghana, all in their twenties and thirties and full of missionary zeal. Joseph Mary Connolly, Bried Mulhern and Sheela Gillespie, the last of whom wrote a detailed account of her experiences, sailed on the liner *Accra*, but its luxury did not save Joseph Mary and Bried from sea sickness. The fourth, Joannes Hayes, travelled with Columbanus to Takoradi on the final voyage of the basic troop carrier *Almanzora*. The three pioneers on the *Accra* had fourteen substantial pieces of luggage, including trunks and tea chests ((big wooden boxes that had been used to ship tea) and a 'fibre' trunk made especially for the trip which did not live up to promise and burst open on the platform in Crewe when they were on their way down through England.

The travellers berthed in Takoradi on 6 October, spent a week in Cape Coast with the Holy Child sisters for a little familiarisation and, Columbanus and Joannes having arrived, went together to Kumasi on the bishop's pick-up on 19 October. Kumasi was happy to welcome the sisters to teach in the primary school – they were the only congregation in the diocese at that time – especially as they arrived in torrential rain. In Ashanti, rain is a sure sign that all will be well, that a blessing has come. Unlike Monaghan in 1859, Kano in 1948 and Barrolandia in 1976, the convent in Kumasi was ready for the sisters and had been well kitted out by the bishop so that the travellers realised, a little to their chagrin, that they did not need all the equipment they had brought half way across the world. The sisters found Kumasi quite pleasant, built in European style, with electricity and running water and plentiful and varied food, especially fruit and vegetables. Conditions in Ghana were better in 1947 than they would be several decades later.

Columbanus spent more than three months in Kumasi, helping the pioneers to get settled in and showing herself to be capable in the arts of home making and especially needlework, before setting off by plane for Kano, where her second group of pioneers had by then arrived. She spent much time unsuccessfully trying to reconcile the helmet and the headdress, eventually opting to keep the headdress as it was, but insisting that her sisters wear the helmet over the headdress even if they were only crossing the yard to the kitchen, a few feet away. Sheela remembers her companion Bried being given a penance 'for going to the kitchen without her helmet'. Columbanus seemed happy in Kumasi: she was probably a missionary manquée herself and it must also have been a relief for her to escape for a while from the heavy day-to-day responsibilities of running the congregation.

As the school year began in January, at least the members of the new community had a chance to find their feet before facing their classes. William Kofi, the local supervisor of schools, gave them lessons in the local language, Twi, and some cultural orientation. The pioneers were proud, and the people of Kumasi delighted, that they were soon able to say a few words of greeting in Twi when they entered a compound.

Columbanus's parting words to the little community in Kumasi show her own common sense and practicality and also provide a neat summary of the St Louis educational philosophy, inherited, although she might not have articulated it then, from Louis Bautain: 'Only when we love our children can we do them any good... remember that as well as teaching them we are learning from them...Stick together. That's fundamental. Don't worry about the future. We must adjust ourselves to a new culture but fundamentally the religious life is the same. All will be well if we observe traditional common sense.'

Her parting gift was a spiritual book entitled *Fear Not, Little Flock* and on the flyleaf she wrote: 'To the little flock in Kumasi, praying to the good shepherd to keep them safe and show them how to lead many souls to his sheepfold.'

Tipperary-born Joannes Hayes commented that the Ashanti people was 'traditional in its views and unwilling to accept anything new' (like secondary education for girls) but she also had a genuine, perhaps rather nationalistic (in the Irish sense), respect for the Ashanti culture: 'We had none of the modern theories about cultural

orientation, but we had a strong determination not to do in Gold
Coast what had been done to us in Ireland – to rob the people of
their culture…we were vultures for culture and attended as many
traditional feasts as possible.' According to those who knew her,
Joannes Hayes had a largeness of spirit that is very desirable in
a missioner, although Kitty Fitzsimons, who taught with her in
Kumasi for seven years, found her maddeningly disorganised. The
early Ghanaian missionaries also noted the Dutch partiality for
'pageantry, acolytes…societies', which were probably unlike the
austere liturgies in Ireland at the time. Then the Ghanaian gift for
celebration and colourful display, singing and dancing made the
sisters' first midnight Mass a memorable occasion.

Sheela Gillespie was charmed by the way all Ghanaians carried
everything on their heads 'with not a hand to it', whether traders
bringing huge basins of fruit to the market or children bringing
their books and pens to school. It was a great novelty to see women
carrying little babies on their backs, secured by a cloth wrapped
around them both (and with a basket of goods on their heads).
Cocoa was the cash crop of Ghana and the sisters, having no car
of their own in the early days, used to get lifts in the cocoa lorries
carrying the crop from the outlying villages to Kumasi in the cocoa
season. Travelling outside with the cocoa, their white habits were
soon the colour of cocoa from the dust of the road.

It took time to get a secondary school up and running in Kumasi,
although it was the earnest desire of Monsignor Paulissen from the
beginning and therefore part of the remit of the founding group.
St Louis Secondary (day) School finally opened in Mbrom on 5
February 1952, with four classrooms and eleven students, and on
1 March the same year a hostel was opened to cater for boarders,
although it was eight years before the sisters could open an official
boarding school. Joannes Hayes was principal from the school's
inception until 1966-7 and many Irish sisters were missioned to
teach there on a long-term or short-term basis (and loved being
there): those I met include Phil McGuinness, Clare Ryan (Juilly),
Mary Jo Hand, Kitty Fitzsimons, who taught the Ghanaian girls to
sing *The Bohemian Girl*, Theodore Lysaght and Triona McGinty, who

was missioned from California. Marie du Rosaire Diver was the last in a line of able and long-serving Irish-born principals.

At the end of Bishop Paulissen's reign he came under criticism for not having done enough for indigenisation and the Ashanti demanded a bishop from among their own people. But another Dutch SMA bishop, André Van den Bronk, succeeded Paulissen in 1952 and served for ten years. The fledgling secondary school in Kumasi was a victim of the controversy when the new bishop was ordained: anti-Bronk pupils deserted it for a period, something that must have worried the sisters greatly. Joseph Essuah, the first indigenous bishop of Kumasi, was consecrated in June 1962.

St Louis Teacher Training College (now St Louis College of Education) opened in Kumasi in 1961, with a staff of three, including Máirín Barrett and a Ghanaian tutor, Hannah Hagan, and a student body of thirty-five. Consilii O'Shaughnessy was principal from the beginning until 1979. Progress was slow: 'little money and a lot of work', according to Consilii. Joannes Hayes wrote that in the early years the sisters in Ghana largely financed the development of the schools from the small number of teachers' salaries they received from the government. The sisters must have lived very frugally indeed to have been able to do this. Archbishop Sarpong of Kumasi confirmed later on that they were major contributors to Ghanaian development, by investing their own salaries as well as moneys they received from the congregation and from fundraising in Ireland. Financial affairs became more rather than less difficult as the 1960s progressed and the country went into economic decline.

Some of the students came to the training college straight out of middle school and others were mothers of families who had finished middle school a decade or more earlier and somehow scraped the money to go to teacher training college and pay someone else to look after children who still needed care. Mary O'Donovan, who taught in the training college from 1967, thinks that these older women had a great steadying and maturing influence on the younger students. At the beginning the sisters taught trainee teachers 'to teach everything': they had 'optimum training' themselves for this kind of teaching because of the teaching apprenticeship they served in the classroom of an experienced sister before going to Carysfort teacher training college or UCD.

In 1963 the new assembly hall in the training college was named in honour of Bishop Van den Bronk and a church was consecrated in 1969. Educational establishments in Ghana were at the mercy of the unstable political situation of those decades: the training college narrowly escaped being closed down in 1974.

It was not until 1965 that the Sisters of St Louis founded a second school, this time on the coast near Takoradi. The Ghanaians got the indigenous bishop they so desired when John Kodwo Amissah replaced English-born William Porter as Archbishop of Cape Coast in 1959. Columbanus wrote to Archbishop Amissah on 29 March 1965: 'When I agreed to send sisters for the school it was on the understanding that Your Grace would provide the convent and schools.' He replied the following month: 'The contractor assures us that it will be possible to start in September this year.' He offered the sisters slightly better terms than at Kumasi 'since the cost of living is a little higher now than when the Kumasi contract was signed.' The land was provided by the Chief of Fijai and the foundation stone laid on 1 August 1965. The Dutch government provided some of the funding and the diocese levied parishes and sought donations for the building.

St Louis Secondary School, located half-way between Takoradi and Sekondi, opened in November 1965. Three sisters, Joseph Mary Connolly, a pioneer in Kumasi, Mary Jude Doherty and Máirín Barrett, taught all the subjects except physical education, with a first intake of forty pupils. There was a good mix of skills, according to Archbishop Amissah: Joseph Mary 'an accomplished musician'; Mary Jude (the principal) 'an eminent scientist and educationalist of vast experience' and Máirín 'an intelligent historian and able administrator'. School construction continued, inconveniently, while the sisters taught in the one completed block. Despite the glowing introduction of Archbishop Amissah, educators are not miracle workers and it took several years of hard work for the sisters to build up the standard of the pupils to O-Level.

Takoradi presented fresh challenges to the small community. The coastal weather was humid and for some sisters not conducive to good health. The people were Fanti, a different Akan sub group with a different language. Even when Ann Concannon went to teach Maths and Science there in the late 1970s the direct road to Kumasi was untarred and it was about six hours' drive, so the members of the two communities did not see one another often.

After Ghanaian independence Kwame Nkrumah (1909-72), who had led the country when it was a British colony, became president. Over a ten-year period he imposed a one-party authoritarian state and economic policies described as 'African socialism', which included collectivisation and massive spending on rapid industrialisation, policies that quickly ruined the economy of a once prosperous and socially advanced country. A military coup removed him from power in 1966 and there followed several decades of military government, coups, counter coups and attempts at democracy. By 1981 the economic situation was so bad that the country was threatened with famine. Sisters who worked in Ghana in the 1980s had a limited diet, of 'bananas, cassava and tinned fish', as Ann Concannon describes it, and came home to their families very slim indeed. It was a difficult situation in which to run a boarding school and feed growing girls. Democracy returned gradually when Jerry Rawlings, the former military ruler, held free elections in 1992, and the economy also returned to a sounder footing.

The school in Takoradi was absorbed into the public system and the sisters, who were in leadership in the school until 1979, changed its name to Archbishop Porter Girls' Secondary School in 1968 to avoid confusion with other St Louis schools. Many sisters and past pupils were disappointed when the St Louis crest was later changed to incorporate bells from the Porter coat of arms and a different motto. Mary O'Donovan was the last Irish sister to leave Takoradi, in 1992.

4

The Medical Mission in Ghana

'As good as any doctor'
Rosalie Corish, 2011 (of Ancilla Fox)

It was Bishop Paulissen who invited the Sisters of St Louis to set up a dispensary at Maase-Offinso, near Kumasi, the birthplace of Peter Kwasi Sarpong, the (arch)bishop of Kumasi who played a big role in the history of the Sisters of St Louis, in 1933. Bishop Sarpong later recalled bringing a St Louis sister, Etheldreda Ryan, to his village when he was a seminarian, to tend to a sick man. The pioneers, Teresa Brett, the first nurse in Ghana, and Philippa Healy, arrived in Maase-Offinso in January 1951 to find that the dispensary they had been expecting to use for local healthcare had no roof.

The pioneers' mission was hampered by tension between the Dutch-led Church and the local chief. The medical staff had to work in makeshift and temporary premises for many months, until gradually, with local, Church and mission funding and contributions from their own modest salaries, they were able to build the skeleton of St Patrick's Hospital: an outpatients' clinic, maternity and post-natal wards and an administration section – all this by 1958. Here the sisters worked as doctors, nurses and administrators – Maura Skelly was a gynaecologist who joined the mission in 1969 – and they also did health visitation in the villages around Maase.

Ide Woulfe came from a family of missionaries and dearly wished to go on the missions herself, but she spent many years in Monaghan as assistant mistress of novices and a period teaching in Aylesbury before training as a midwife in Our Lady of Lourdes, Drogheda, then as a general nurse in Northampton. Her superiors feared that her health would not stand up to the rigours of missionary medical work but she survived it better than many. She was eventually missioned to Ghana in 1951.

Ide was a pioneer in the second medical foundation in that country, established at the request of Archbishop Porter of Cape Coast. Asankragwa is in the south-west of the country, 200 km from Accra; Tarkwa, a mining centre, is the nearest town. Ide's nurse companions were Ancilla Fox, who had spent some time in Nigeria, and Salome Moran, who came from Cahirciveen. Ancilla, from Manorhamilton, County Leitrim, had entered the congregation before missionary activity began and was destined for Sion Hill and home economics but, fortunately for Nigeria and especially for Ghana, she failed the sewing practical. One day, Columbanus asked her out of the blue: 'Did you ever think of nursing?' Ancilla trained in Bury St Edmunds so that she could live with the St Louis community there and did her midwifery in Holles Street, Dublin, after a spell as matron in Balla.

The pioneers in Asankragwa found an area of tropical forest, with trees being cut down to build the hospital. While this was happening the sisters used a small clinic to see patients. They were not paid a salary but the mission (the diocese) supported them a little and gave them a house to live in. Dutch and German doctors who were paid by the mission worked with them but none of them were resident. Small wonder: the hospital had no electricity at the start until, after a few years, it got a generator. And there were problems with water supply, depending on the season. Salome's cousin, Paschalina O'Shea, remembers Salome asking for contributions of hammers and nails and building tools when she was going back to Ghana: on one occasion thirty tea chests accompanied her on the first stage of her sea journey from the North Wall.

Asankragwa was a poor area with high infant mortality, so the sisters felt they were answering a great need for healthcare and they got a warm welcome from the local people. As in Maase-Offinso, Ide, Ancilla and Salome took health to the people, establishing baby welfare clinics in the villages around Asankragwa. Sometimes simple treatments like rehydration were enough to save babies' lives.

Unlike Nigeria where there might be a hospital and a school

or a training college (like Zonkwa or Ado-Ekiti) the sisters in Asankragwa were really out in the bush. They accepted their simple life in this remote place and made do with little, sustained by the 'family' life of their small community. There was a school for boys in Asankragwa but no education for girls at the time of the foundation. Nkrumah promoted education for girls and after independence a secondary school was built there. Ide Woulfe says that this was about the only thing that improved in the years she was nursing in Ghana. In her view, Nkrumah's regime of 'African socialism' and collectivisation destroyed everything that the English had established and people who were creative and talented simply left the country. Traders who were raising money for the education of their families stopped trading when they were forced to join with other traders. The same with the tailor who made the sisters' uniforms, who was obliged to join a tailors' collective.

At first the nurses got home every three to four years; later they came home each year for health reasons. Ide loved the climate and felt that if anything the heat improved her health. She also spent four years in Owo in western Nigeria, but when she came back to Ghana the congregation had decided to leave Asankragwa as it was too far from their other communities. Maureen Smith was the last sister to leave there, in 1977. So Ide worked in Maase; then, after a course in clinical and pastoral care in America, spent a year doing pastoral work in the general hospital in Kumasi. She had to leave Ghana for good in 1983 because her health had deteriorated, not helped by the poor diet that resulted from the food shortages of the early 1980s, and she 'retired' to her next ministry, chaplaincy, in Belfast.

After Asankragwa, Ancilla went on to Maase-Offinso in 1954; there she helped the pioneers to establish St Patrick's Clinic, which in later years became a hospital with a training school for nurses. So well regarded was she in the area that she was named 'Queen Mother of Offinso'. In 1973 she was invited to work as secretary to the Health Department of the National Catholic Secretariat of the Ghana Bishops' Conference in Accra. She handed over to a Ghanaian nurse as matron of St Patrick's Hospital in Maase and later the Sisters of the Immaculate Heart of Mary took over the hospital.

The congregation 'lent' Ancilla to the Secretariat for an initial period of three years from 1 January 1974. In the Secretariat she helped develop the Catholic Department of Health, which she headed for many years. Her job had a wide brief, including advisory, communication, training, recruitment and PR roles, all aimed at strengthening Catholic medical services in Ghana and the link between them, the Bishops' Conference and the Ministry of Health. In 1981 she established the Catholic Drug Distribution Centre and Production Pharmacy, also at the National Catholic Secretariat; this was her own brainchild. A health and humanitarian crisis struck Ghana in 1983 so the health services and pharmaceutical supply came under terrible pressure. To add to the misery of widespread famine, over two million Ghanaians were expelled from Nigeria and had to come back in poverty to their own country. Ancilla, as able an administrator as she was a nurse, spent seventeen years in all working in the two organisations, eventually handing over the leadership of the Health Department of the National Catholic Secretariat to Bernadette Honney, a Ghanaian sister of the Handmaids of the Holy Child Jesus, in 1990. Ancilla was later one of the founding members of the St Louis apostolate in Oku.

In 1988 Rosalie Corish, who had taught in Ireland all her life and never been on the missions, went as bookkeeper to the Drug Distribution Centre in Accra. Like Ancilla, she was paid by the bishops' conference. Ancilla bought the drugs wherever she could be assured of a good quality supply – Holland, Ireland, England, France, America – as a lot of what was on sale in Ghana was not genuine. The hospitals were able to buy the pharmaceuticals at cost or at as near to cost as the drug distribution centre could afford to sell them and Brother James SVD would take the cedi, the local currency, in big denominations, and record all the transactions. Attached to the centre was a pharmacy with a qualified pharmacist, usually Dutch, who made simple medicines, like cough mixture and ointment for skin conditions.

Life in Accra was hard in the late 1980s: the city was dirty, electricity was intermittent, there was almost no public water supply and the house in which Rosalie lived had no telephone so it was difficult to stay in contact with family in Ireland. (Despite this, Rosalie counts her eight years in Ghana 'the best of my life so far'.) When the sisters built a regional house in Parakou, through the efforts of Dorothy Yayock and Ancilla, she lived there with Dorothy and Consilii O'Shaughnessy, who worked in the main finance office of the Catholic Secretariat. Rosalie quickly realised that Ancilla, who had spent decades in Ghana before she arrived, had a huge reputation in the health services: 'Everyone loved her and she was larger than life.' As well as being an innovator, a problem solver and a 'can do' person she was a great nurse and excellent diagnostician: 'as good as any doctor', people said.

Peter Kwasi Sarpong, who succeeded Bishop Essuah in Kumasi in 1970, wrote to invite the sisters to Oku in the Afram Plains region of eastern Ghana in 1991 but it was 1993 before the foundation began. The three pioneer sisters were Ancilla, who came out of retirement for the project, and nurse Esther Adzah, who were to run a clinic, and primary school teacher Helena Owusu Fosua, who had the job of starting a school. Ancilla enlisted the help of the British High Commission (the equivalent of an embassy in a country of the British Commonwealth) which provided funds for the new primary school. Misereor, the German Catholic bishops' development organisation, later financed the building of the clinic, the convent and a junior secondary school.

It was not an easy job to start a school or hospital at Oku. It was hard to get teachers as Oku was remote and difficult to reach, accessible only through Ejura. The climate and geology were inhospitable. In the dry season water shortages became so acute that people stayed by the boreholes days and night in the quest for water – although, at about the time the sisters arrived in Oku, World Vision International had embarked on a borehole programme for the area. When it did rain, more often than not, pupils from the surrounding villages were unable to attend school as the roads were flooded. This meant that parents were often reluctant to send their children to school at all.

When Ancilla felt her time for clinical work was over she decided to become a hermit and established herself in the Turquestein Hermitage in Oku. Stacy Reinemann, who is now principal of Nativity School, El Monte, in California, spent two years in Oku 1995-7 and experienced Ancilla's efficiency first-hand when the latter temporarily emerged from retirement. After a while Stacy became, as she describes it, 'useful' in the medical mission, writing grant applications, organising deliveries of materials and helping with the Tuesday clinic for mothers and babies.

Ancilla left Ghana in 1998 but the hermitage re-established itself – Oku Maria Hermitage – in Middletown, County Armagh, when she moved there. Then the well travelled hermitage and its hermit came to rest in the community in Monaghan. A community of Ghanaian sisters ministers in the impoverished district of Oku to this day.

Carmel Dodd was west African regional leader, based in Ibadan, when Dominic Andoh, Bishop of Accra, wrote to her on 22 February 1984: 'At present there is a need for a sister to do pastoral work in Nima, a slum area of Accra…[which] needs a rather intensive deepening of the faith of our people who have come to live there from practically every corner of Ghana.' Nima was known as an area of ethnic diversity as well as extreme poverty, with people from tribes such as the Ewe, Akan, Dagara, Frafra and Ga. Carmel asked for volunteers for Nima: 'Please pray that in this our response and opportunity as a congregation "to join the poor in their situation" we will do it as generously and as best we can.' Ancilla, who was living in Accra at this time, called it 'a real apostolate of the poor' and much favoured having a ministry there, although it was not, strictly speaking, a health ministry.

Georgina Edwine and Brigid Andoh went to work in Nima in November 1984. Georgina did full time parish work while Brigid taught in the school. The decision to minister in Nima was a response on the part of the congregation to the first statement of the option for the poor at the 1980 general chapter.

5

The Mission to Nigeria

'Isn't it the same God there as here?'

Celine Connolly, 1947

Kano was the first foundation in Nigeria and its story is representative of many others that were established in that country over the years. Gradually foundations were staffed by sisters who had gained experience in other locations in Nigeria but the pioneers who went to Kano in early 1948 must have experienced considerable culture shock. Augustine Moane, the last surviving Nigerian pioneer, remembers feeling a sense of adventure and terror in equal measure. The elation of the congregation and the St Louis pupils who saw them off in Rathmines with 'Go Ye Afar', the missionary hymn of the Holy Ghost fathers, sustained the exiles. They knew that the whole community was behind them, supporting them financially and in all possible practical ways (every classroom then had a missions box to which children donated their pennies).

Like many developments in those more innocent and spontaneous days, the choice of Kano was fortuitous. (Compare the lengthy process of discernment that took place before a decision was made about the latest mission to Ethiopia.) It was Monsignor McCarthy of Kaduna (John McCarthy SMA (1902-75), born in Castlehaven, County Cork; Bishop/Archbishop of Kaduna 1954-75), who requested the foundation. At this time there was one girls' school in Kaduna and none in the big city of Kano, in Monsignor McCarthy's diocese.

This is Patricia Moloney's version of the events leading to the foundation of Kano. On a trip home, Monsignor McCarthy had travelled the whole of Ireland looking in vain for a congregation that would be willing to come to Nigeria, until an SMA priest, P.J. Kerr from Belfast, suggested to him that he try Monaghan, where they had 'oodles of nuns'. (At the time, Patricia was one of seventy in the novitiate, between junior and senior novices.) The two priests came to say Mass one morning and took breakfast with Columbanus and her council, saw the classrooms, the pupils, the nuns and the novices. Then they revealed the reason behind their visit, hoping to persuade the leadership that they could spare sisters to minister in Africa. The vicar (deputy superior general), Gonzaga Reynolds, gave the bishop no hope as she felt that the order needed all the sisters they had to run the schools at home but Columbanus said, 'We'll see,' and put it to her council that they should consider Monsignor McCarthy's invitation. Columbanus carried the day. (Gabrielle O'Connell's official version of this story is that Father Kerr wrote to Columbanus on behalf of Monsignor McCarthy in 1945.)

Sisters and novices at first profession had the opportunity to volunteer for the missions in Africa. In those days Columbanus herself personally matched each sister with her posting. Augustine Moane did not initially volunteer but at the bedside of Celine Connolly, a sister who was dying of cancer in Rathmines, she was 'shamed into volunteering' as she puts it. Celine, who was only just past forty, would have given anything to go on the missions herself. 'What are you afraid of? Isn't it the same God there as here?' she asked, rhetorically, of a trepidatious Augustine, who volunteered forthwith and had more than twenty happy years of primary teaching in Nigeria.

Augustine set off with two companions on 19 January 1948: Isabel Morrin, who had taught Augustine in Kiltimagh and had been appointed superior of the new community in Kano, and Eymard Hartin. Regis O'Donnell, who was Columbanus's secretary, joined them in Liverpool for the journey. Presumably she was needed to travel back to Ireland with Columbanus, as sisters always had to travel in pairs.

Air travel had not yet replaced the great ocean liners and Nigeria was a British colony until 1960, one of many in Africa, so there was plenty of sea traffic with the UK. The Second World War had ended less than three years earlier; Augustine and her companions found themselves on the troop carrier *Empire Bure* that sailed from Liverpool to Lagos, carrying not soldiers but the wives and families of troops stationed in west Africa. Travelling by sea had the advantage of enabling the pioneers to take with them enormous quantities of luggage in tea chests and trunks. As well as their clothing and personal effects – six complete sets of white habits that were specially made in Monaghan – they had to take all their household equipment: linen and delph, and everything in the line of books, stationery, blackboards and chalk they could assemble that might be useful in a school.

When the three sisters arrived in Lagos (Eymard had left the ship in Takoradi to join Columbanus) a priest brought them to an OLA (Our Lady of Apostles) convent and they left by train for Kano the next day, a journey of two and a half days. But when they arrived in Kaduna, Monsignor McCarthy took them off the train to spend another week with the OLA for orientation.

Like the three Dames de St Louis who arrived in Monaghan from Juilly on the feast of the Epiphany in 1859, when these sisters eventually arrived in Kano, on 14 February 1948, their accommodation was not ready for them, despite the delay in Kaduna. The sisters were billeted in Gidan Campbell, the 'compact' two-bedroomed home (*gidan* in Hausa) of a district officer called Campbell who happened to be away. Columbanus and Eymard had already arrived by plane from Kumasi so there were five in the community for a few weeks: three permanent and two temporary. Then they moved to a disused barracks in Bompai, outside Kano, which provided both home and school until the new convent and school were completed in 1951. Knowing that the sisters would need to use a car in Nigeria, Columbanus had sent word back to Monaghan after her own arrival in Ghana that they were to have driving lessons. (The sisters had no car in Monaghan then: a local man, Mr Murray, and his car would be hired if they needed to go anywhere.) Mary Gunn, the sister of a consœur, obligingly came from Clones to provide a few quick communal lessons. When – not without some mishaps – the sisters mastered the car that had been allocated for their use in Kano they didn't know they had to have driving licences (they were not necessary in Ireland then), until a local Muslim policeman went to one of the SMA priests in Kano – there were two: Father Tom Duffy and Father Paddy Balfe – and asked, 'Do you know that your wives are driving around with no licences?'

Although the order's first foundation still had no permanent home, Columbanus and Regis travelled nearly four hundred miles on a reconnaissance mission to Ado-Ekiti, in Ondo diocese in western Nigeria, where the next foundation had already been approved, before they went back to Ireland. This was at the request of Monsignor Thomas Hughes (1891-1957), a Mayo-born SMA, who was consecrated Bishop of Ondo in 1950. Hughes and other SMA priests came to Ilorin to fetch the reverend scouts and the foundation began just a few months later, as planned, in October 1948.

Establishing the schools in Kano was neither as speedy nor as straightforward as the pioneers might have imagined before they left Ireland. There was only a handful of girls in each class in the Catholic primary school, so no 'feeder' for the secondary school that the sisters planned to open. At first Augustine, Eymard and Isabel went to teach in the existing coeducational school, then the sisters separated the girls and built up the girls' school until they had full classes and the numbers to sustain the first year in the boarding school in Bompai. Numbers were low at the start, as Kano was largely a Muslim state, and at this stage the Muslim girls were not being educated at all.

The first communities in Kano, Ado-Ekiti and Minna maintained the strict Monaghan rule but sisters tended to have more practical freedoms on the missions, such as driving a car and travelling on their own. The convents were small and isolated at the beginning, as there were no other religious at a convenient distance with whom the sisters could socialise. They were sustained by a pioneering spirit, by the challenge of making do with what they had and gradually building up to something better and by the conviction that they were doing the most important work of the Church on the missions. Sisters and past pupils often comment on the St Louis 'family' spirit, which was a strong aspiration of the original foundation in Juilly, and the communities would have needed this kind of interpersonal bond to sustain the members.

Patricia Moloney, destined to spend most of her working life in Nigeria, sailed to Lagos on the last voyage of the Elder Dempster Line's *Accra* in December 1950, and Carmel Dodd on the spanking new *Oriel* in 1952. Seven other sisters sailed with Carmel but she was the only one bound for Kano. She arrived there at the beginning of the weekend, finding a community of four, and had been assigned various tasks in the school and compound by Monday morning. Carmel taught cookery and food science in rudimentary kitchens – but then many rural homes in Ireland would have had neither electricity nor running water at this time.

For sisters who had never left Ireland Nigeria was exotic. Acculturation or ethnography were not strong points of the congregation, or any other congregation at the time – it would be years before anyone even studied sociology. Under British rule life was easier in Nigeria than it subsequently became: trains were comfortable and the telephone service worked at least some of the time. Carmel Dodd and Patricia Moloney remember the pleasant smell of groundnuts (peanuts), which were one of the main exports of the colony: groundnut oil was produced from them in Liverpool. Port Harcourt, the cargo port, was seven hundred miles from Kano and in the interval between the harvest and the transportation of the crop to the port by rail or road, bags of ground nuts would be built into enormous pyramids that seemed as impressive to them as the Pyramids of Giza. Kano was a great traditional metropolis and Bompai, outside the city, where the convent and school were located, a halting point for Tuareg traders from Libya, who crossed the Sahara bringing salt and other goods and sold or bartered them for leather from the Kano region, a trade they had carried on for two millennia. Caravans of camels came in the dry season, essential given their cargo of salt, and grazed on the few available blades of grass. The camel drivers, wearing muslin across their mouths to protect their lungs from the sand, rested the animals for two weeks before continuing west to the coast at Sierra Leone. A century earlier slaves would have been among the goods they traded.

The climate in Kano is extreme, with rainy and dry seasons (October to March) but the rainy season can be spectacularly fertile, with two crops often harvested. Patricia Moloney did not come home for five years and when she set foot in her home in Feakle, County Clare, her family thought she was like a skeleton: the effect of heat, a different diet and hard work. Before too long all the sisters came home more often for the sake of their health.

Educational foundations followed Kano in swift succession. First came Ado-Ekiti on 16 October 1948, led by Finian Cullen, with Leone Keegan and Chrysostom O'Daly. It was the first contact this area of the country had ever had with female religious. Bishop Hughes personally supervised the airing of bedclothes and the provision of curtains for the sisters' convent – it still wasn't quite finished, although habitable. But the school building was ready and children of all ages eager to start so the sisters got that off the ground once they had mastered some Yoruba.

In August 1953, immediately after completing her BA and Higher Diploma in Education, Mary Jo Hand was appointed principal of Mary Immaculate Teacher Training College, Ado-Ekiti, which had been established to train women for Catholic primary schools in Ondo Diocese. This was a big step forward but a daunting ministry, as, overnight, the sisters needed to enable students to prepare notes of lessons, schemes of work and visual aids, as well as imparting teaching skills. The four-year course also had an academic side and although the students had not completed secondary school, they became excellent teachers, always scoring highly in the practicals. Laboure McTeague soon followed Mary Jo, with many creative ideas from her experience of Mount Pleasant Training College, Liverpool. The team also included Maeve Dolan, Rose Neeson (who, sadly, was killed in an accident on the road from Lagos), Clare Ryan, Anne Kelly, Augustine Moane and Priscilla Lee.

When Mary Jo arrived for the first time in Ado-Ekiti compound, in the company of Chrysostom O'Daly, an ace driver, she saw Bishop Hughes on the roof of Maria Assumpta Hospital, nailing down the new 'pan' (corrugated tin) roof against the fierce tornadoes of the rainy season. Although true to form for Bishop Hughes, it was the first time Mary Jo had ever seen a bishop in such a position. Early days in Ado were also the first time she was presented with corn on the cob, difficult to eat in a ladylike way while wearing the St Louis headdress.

The college in Ado produced musicals, to the great enjoyment of missionary priests and other expatriates who had very little entertainment available to them. The sisters had ample props and wardrobe for these, as Leone Keegan had returned from Ireland to Ado-Ekiti with forty-five tea chests of all kinds of everything collected from wellwishers when she was on home leave. These came by boat and Father Luke Carney drove the diocese's mission lorry the three hundred and fifty miles from Akure to Lagos to collect them at Apapa Wharf. A long wooden crate containing a statue of Our Lady was missing but arrived safe and sound some weeks later, with Our Lady's head protruding through the open end of the box, miraculously unharmed.

When enough women were trained to staff the girls' primary schools in the diocese, Mary Immaculate in Ado-Ekiti merged with St Peter's (men's) Training College, Akure, and the training college buildings turned into a secondary school for girls. Mary Jo presided over this transition before being transferred to Kumasi four years later.

At one stage there was a community of eight Irish sisters in Ado. There was little scope for recreation and they celebrated feast days with a drive to the nearby waterworks at Effon, where there might be a patch of grass where they could sit and have their flask of tea and a chicken sandwich. On the occasion of Maire Blair's final vows, the group was entertained by Mary Murray and Mary Jo Hand who, suitably attired (thanks to the props cupboard), danced around on the cement floor of the sitting room while delivering an adapted version of the travellers' song from John B. Keane's *Sive*, complete with topical references.

Minna, in the diocese of Kaduna, was the third foundation in Nigeria, on 25 August 1952, led by Dominic Joyce with Cronan

McNicholas. Owo in Ondo diocese followed in November 1952, led by Finian Cullen from Ado, with Winifred Egan.

In December 1953 Chrysostom O'Daly was one of the founders of Ondo community, sixty five miles away from Ado, with Una Lafferty and Felicity McEnnis, and became the first principal of St Louis Secondary School as well as being superior of the community. At the end of July 1959, not long after returning from a home visit to Ireland, she contracted blackwater fever and died within a few days despite having had medical attention in the congregation's own hospital in Owo. She was the first St Louis sister to be buried in Africa. Health was always an issue for the sisters, especially the ever-present danger of malaria. According to Sheila McGovern, who contracted the illness shortly after she arrived in Kano in 1955, the saying was that you were not a missionary until you went down with malaria. Truly they were intrepid women. Sheila taught in primary and teacher training in Kano and Zonkwa for twenty-six years.

Between 1960 and 1976, St Louis sisters founded eleven further ministries, mostly in western Nigeria. Many combined education and health ministries, including teacher training (such as Zonkwa in 1960) and midwife training as well as second-level schools of various kinds, grammar and technical: Jos and Akure in 1960; Ibadan, the seat of Nigeria's first university, in 1961; Ikere-Ekiti (1962), a St Louis School in Owo in 1963; a secondary school in Zonkwa and a vocational school in Oye-Ekiti in 1965; Bida (1968); Ikare-Akoko (1969). At this stage there were more than a hundred Irish sisters working in Nigeria.

The last community established by Irish sisters (in 1976) was Kontagora, where Leone Keegan and Colette Corvin taught in the college of education. Later, in response to the needs of the community, Colette focused instead on adult literacy and training programmes for catechists in rural areas, a different kind of educational service. Iseyin (1978) was the first St Louis community in Nigeria to be founded by Nigerian sisters – Juliana Nwabuzo, Isabel Mann and Cecilia Adeniran. Their apostolates were the hospital and the government secondary school. Sisters of St Louis are still involved in the hospital and in a primary school in Iseyin.

After Nigeria gained independence from Britain, in January 1960, the Hausa and Fulani peoples of the north, much more numerous than any other tribe, held sway not only in their own region but in the central government in Lagos. Anti-northern unrest, which had been simmering since independence, came to a head with a coup in January 1966, when army officers from the Igbo region in the east of the country assassinated not only the federal president but the leaders of the northern and western regions, Hausa and Yoruba – five leaders in all. But the Igbos were not confined to the east of the country where their safety might have been assured when the inevitable backlash came. There were many Igbo pupils in the boarding schools in Kano (where their parents had migrated to pursue trade and business), Jos (where their parents worked in the tin mines that were big local employers) and Zonkwa. Jos was particularly vulnerable because of its location between the Igbo homelands and the northern state.

All during 1966 trouble was brewing and anti-Igbo feeling growing in the north and centre of Nigeria: there were checkpoints and harassment, provocation and persecution of Igbos, who bit by bit went back to their own region. Eustace O'Gorman, who was principal in Kano, recalled Hausa boys coming to the school to visit their sisters, full of the news that all the Muslim students in Nsukka University in the east had been killed – news that was completely false. She was horrified when she realised that these Hausa could see no wrong in killing Igbos.

Patricia Moloney, then principal in Jos, remembers vividly a pupil's father who was a miner coming to her office just before the pogroms. Girls from the first intake in 1961 were preparing to sit the West African School Certificate, the equivalent of the Irish Leaving Certificate. This man had come to take his daughter home to the east. Patricia pleaded with him to leave her in school as she was a bright girl ready to take her examinations and she felt that the sisters would be safe and would be able to protect the Igbo pupils. He left 'without saying goodbye' and was killed at the railway station the next day along with nine other men. His daughter later reached home safely by train.

The sisters who were in Kano, Jos and Zonkwa describe vividly the horrors of the massacres of Igbos that began at the end of September 1966: keeping vigil night after night in the compound in Bompai, hiding fleeing Igbos in the rafters and the organ gallery in the chapel, finding the bodies of Igbo staff outside the compound after a night of killings; trying desperately to put the students on the Red Cross trains – the last such train left Kano on 4 October – or on planes chartered by European employers that would bring them home to the east. There were thirty-three Igbo student teachers in Zonkwa, whom Maura Flynn managed to evacuate through Kafanchan, as well as six student nurses in the care of Nuala McCluskey.

It was an extraordinary situation in which to have become involved and the sisters had to rely entirely on their own small communities, as they were often cut off from news of the outside world. Eventually Archbishop McCarthy, some SMA priests and an official from the Irish embassy in Lagos came to Kano to check on the welfare of the community there as telephone lines were down and communication was difficult. From the point of view of the sisters at home, the poor communication was really a mercy – and there was no television to bring live pictures of horrors. Nor was there any talk then of post-traumatic stress, or counselling to help sisters to recover from the trauma of living in an atmosphere of violence and murder.

The following year the Igbo east seceded from Nigeria, styling itself Biafra, and the Biafran war with its attendant famine lasted for three years before the country was reunited in 1970. Fortunately, unlike other Irish missionary congregations, the St Louis sisters had no foundations in the east of Nigeria. In 1967 Columbanus wrote a letter to Eymard Hartin, which concluded: 'If you feel the sisters are in danger, don't wait for instructions from me: *éirigh as* (give it up)' But *éirigh as* was never part of the St Louis lexicon. The last Irish-born St Louis sister (except for Colette Corvin) did not leave Nigeria until 2009. And it was not fear or danger that caused her to leave.

6

The Medical Mission in Nigeria

'In those days you just rushed out and did what you could.'
Proinnsias McKiernan, 2011

St Louis sisters began to work in healthcare in Nigeria when they arrived at Maria Assumpta Hospital in Ado-Ekiti in Ondo state on 25 August 1949. What started as a small dispensary developed into a maternity hospital and then into a one hundred and fifty bed hospital. By 1954 Teresa Brett, who had previously served in Maase-Offinso in Ghana, and Theresa Kerley had opened a school for midwives as the need for maternity care was pressing and by having a training school the sisters acquired student nurses to work with them as well as providing for the future.

The second health foundation was when Philomena Dolan went as matron of the government general and maternity hospital in Minna in Niger State on 25 August 1952. She also began to travel to 'bush clinics' among the Gwari and Fulani people, to villages like Bosso and Beji, Egwa and Fuka. People from the villages also came to the mission health centre in Minna itself. Philomena later served in Ado-Ekiti and was principal of the school of midwifery in Zonkwa.

A hospital had been built in Owo by SMA priests and in November 1952, Finian Cullen and Winifred Egan were the foundation team there. As in Ado, this clinic had a maternity hospital which included a training school for midwives. Ancilla Fox joined Finian and Winifred the following month. She remembers that when she arrived in Owo, after having been seasick all the way to Lagos, the most prevalent disease was yaws, an infectious skin condition, which in its tertiary stage destroys bones and cartilage. She would never have seen that in Ireland, or even in Bury St Edmunds, where she trained as a nurse. The treatment was intramuscular injection of oily penicillin. As with many events in the lives of St Louis sisters, her leaving Nigeria and being missioned instead to Ghana was fortuitous. She contracted hepatitis, flew home to Dublin to recuperate and never again worked in Nigeria.

Monsignor William Lumley SMA, Prefect Apostolic of Jos 1934-53, came to Ireland on leave in 1953 and visited many convents in the hope of getting sisters for Shendam, in the Plateau Province of northern Nigeria. All his efforts were in vain until finally, on the advice of Bishop Hughes of Ondo, he came to Monaghan. Columbanus agreed to his request, promising to have some sisters ready to move there before the end of the year. Monsignor Lumley could not believe his good fortune and sent word back to his priests in Shendam to begin preparation for the sisters' coming.

Cronan McNicholas, Margaret Fox, sister of Ancilla, and Osyth Gomersall, an English sister, were chosen as the first community for Shendam. Margaret and Osyth were both trained nurses – a hospital was nearing completion at Shendam. Cronan was to be in charge of the convent. They sailed from Liverpool on the *Aureol* on 3 December 1953. They had the company of Monsignor William Porter SMA of Cape Coast and Columbanus as far as Takoradi as she was going on visitation to Ghana. From Lagos they went to Minna for Christmas, then to Jos on 4 January 1954 and Shendam on 27 January. The hospital was part mission and part government, which meant that the government paid salaries and funded medication and the mission ran the hospital. Bríd Costello arrived to join the team in June 1955. In 1961 Shendam Hospital was handed over to the government and the sister nurses' appointments were terminated in 1964. The convent stayed open until January 1965; then it was handed over to OLA as the order's Nigerian novitiate. Now it is a house of the Sisters of Our Lady of Fatima, a Nigerian diocesan order.

In Zonkwa, in southern Kaduna, Nuala McCluskey, newly arrived from Ireland, established a clinic on 9 February 1955. The parish priest, Eric White, had already opened a dispensary in the

village but it was totally inadequate for demand. Kafanchan was
the nearest hospital and although the distance was not great the
condition of the road was such that few seriously ill patients could
be expected to survive the transit. There were no white people,
nothing but a few little huts in Zonkwa when the first sisters came.
The priests had arrived before them; they were spread thinly in
the huge diocese of Kaduna but where they built a church, a little
settlement would grow up around it. Gradually the compound
grew, to include a secondary school and a teacher training college.
Precisely because there was so little else in the bush village of
Zonkwa, it became known among the sisters as 'Zonk City' and
sters who travelled to Zonkwa or through Zonkwa by train describe seeing the twinkling lights of the compound appearing out of
the darkness as they approached. When Mary Clerkin was missioned there in 1952, the year after foundation, she and her companion
'were looking out for the lights of Zonkwa', once they left Kaduna.

Nuala McCluskey and her sister Eithne were the third generation
of girls of their family from Inniskeen to go to school in Monaghan
and they both became St Louis sisters. Eithne, the elder, spent
her whole life in primary education in Ireland, north and south,
supporting from afar the apostolate of her sister. Nuala spent
thirty years in Zonkwa, working in the hospital and also in outposts
in the bush. She had trained in nursing in Belfast and midwifery in
Holles Street, Dublin, where she got the gold medal for first place
in her class in midwifery. She also studied for a diploma in the
London College of Pharmacy to allow her to dispense medicine
in a hospital, as the sisters would not have been allowed to open a
hospital without a pharmacy. When she arrived there was nothing
but the barest minimum of equipment; she effectively created the
hospital: according as she got the money together she would build
another ward, then another. Brother Murphy SMA organised the
construction work for her. 'We were young; we thought nothing
of it,' Nuala says. Caritas and the German organisation Misereor
provided funding and there were some generous benefactors in
Ireland, including family doctors who knew what was needed.
Eithne helped in the background, packing tea chests with equipment

and supplies, ready to travel back to Nigeria with Nuala or another sister returning from holidays.

Nuala was the entire hospital staff in Zonkwa for a year. Her first patient, a woman, was a victim of domestic violence. There was a big demand for maternity and neo-natal services and the priests who were evangelising the villages in the region would bring women who were having problems in labour into the hospital in Zonkwa in their pick-ups or Land Rovers.

Sheila Finnegan trained for nursing in Bury St Edmunds and did her midwifery in Holles Street. Her first missionary posting was to Maase-Offinso in Ghana with Philippa Healy and Etheldreda Ryan, before she was transferred to the hospital in Minna. She did a tutors' course in UCD, then spent sixteen years in Zonkwa from 1963, replacing Anne (de Britto) Hayes, who had founded the school of midwifery in 1961. Sheila began the school of general nursing in Zonkwa in 1965. When she left Africa she worked as a tutor in Dublin hospitals.

Dorothy Yayock, the first St Louis postulant in northern Nigeria, was a student in this midwifery training programme. After she qualified she entered the novitiate for the 'African sisters of St Louis, Kaduna Diocese' which had just started in Zonkwa under the direction of Roseanne Byrne. She was the first Nigerian directress of novices and she became matron of the hospital in Zonkwa, then moved into regional leadership in Nigeria and Ghana.

Later a rural health programme was established in Zonkwa with the help of Oxfam. It was under the supervision of Bernadette Smyth and had the services of volunteer doctors from Canada (Canadian University Services Overseas, CUSO). A special training programme to qualify girls to work in rural health centres and clinics was initiated, with the emphasis very much on preventative medicine.

After Nuala McCluskey had spent a year running the hospital in Zonkwa on her own, she got help from Dutch doctors, who worked in the hospital in a system organised by Dutch SMAs. Instead of doing military service in Holland, they would opt for this kind of humanitarian work and stay for two or more years. Germans likewise had to do military or humanitarian service so a few German doctors worked in Zonkwa. Nuala is gratified that these doctors did so well when they went back to their own country and that some of them visit her in Dundalk to this day.

The education of doctors is lengthy and expensive but superior general Columbanus was aware what a great advantage for the congregation it would be to have some of its own doctors to work with the nurses in Nigeria. There was the added complication that at least two sisters would have to train simultaneously. Proinnsias McKiernan and Carmel Garvey were the first sisters to qualify in medicine in UCD. Proinnsias has no idea why she was picked to study medicine in 1950. 'The Holy Ghost,' she supposes. But she had a natural bent for the sciences and might have become a nurse if she had not entered. In her pre-med class, there were nine sisters, all from missionary orders.

After completing their course and interning in the Mater in Dublin, Proinnsias and Carmel set off for Lagos on the *Accra*, taking with them anything they thought might be useful in a hospital. After a dreadful storm at sea, during which the ship's rudder broke, they arrived in Lagos on Christmas Eve 1958. A taxi driver whisked Proinnsias off the boat, took her on an adventurous ride through Lagos and put her on a plane to Kano. Carmel was left with the thirty pieces of luggage until Mary Jo Hand collected her.

For Carmel's first car journey in Nigeria that Christmas day, her driver was Bernard, from Maria Assumpta Hospital, Ado-Ekiti. He was known for speeding and nothing got in his way. Mary Jo tried to get him to abate his speed, using the plea that Sister Baptista (Carmel), being new to the country, might 'go die' from a speed of 70mph on a very bad patch of road. In a flash, Bernard replied, 'But I go sleep at forty.' When they pulled in for petrol at a makeshift service station in Ibadan, they were regaled by the Christmas message of Her Majesty the Queen to her Commonwealth from a nearby transistor radio, the first of many incongruities the new missionary would experience. They were just in time to hear the strains of sung Benediction from the little convent oratory as they drove into the compound in Ado later that Christmas evening.

Maria Assumpta Hospital, Ado-Ekiti, had started as a maternity clinic but when male patients arrived the sisters had to cater for them too. There was a demand for surgery, which Carmel met as best she could, although at this stage with only basic surgical skills. Eventually the hospital was able to get help from Italian, Dutch and German doctors through Misereor.

In recognition of her services to the health of the Yoruba people Carmel Garvey had the great honour of being made a chief by the king (Ewi) of Ado-Ekiti. Carmel, dressed in colourful and regal Yoruba costume and headdress, received, according to Yoruba custom, a chief's title unique to her: 'Awemoye', meaning 'one who bathes the child to life', is both poetic and entirely appropriate to her life in medicine.

Proinnsias got to Kano in time for midnight Mass and a few days later went by small plane to Jos. She was to go to Shendam to get experience with a German doctor who had a good reputation. But when she arrived in Shendam on the Saturday evening, the doctor put his bunch of keys on the table and said, 'I'm off to Jos for a week. Over to you.'

No sooner had he left than the district officer came to the hospital looking for a doctor. A body had been found in the bush and she was required to do a post mortem. Cronan McNicholas, who was superior in Shendam, and Margaret Fox went out with her to the scene of the crime, carrying a tilly lamp. It was dark and hot. They quickly realised that the man had been stabbed, so the cause of death was not difficult to establish. It was Proinnsias's first post mortem.

The German doctor returned and Proinnsias stayed in Shendam until April, working with him and learning a lot about African illnesses. Shendam is low lying and humid. It was remote and there was a long distance to travel even to a letter box. Then she went to Zonkwa. Nuala McCluskey had been there for a few years by then and had set up a maternity ward and an outpatients' clinic. The sisters had built two new wards in anticipation of Proinnsias's arrival, as well as a basic theatre. She says her first tour was not the happiest as the hospital didn't seem to draw in a big clientèle. People

Regis O'Donnell fed the ducks by the lake in Monaghan every day after lunch.

'Go Ye Afar': the Ghana pioneers on the Accra in 1947.
From left: (Mother General of Whitby Anglican congregation, Holy Rosary sister),
Joseph Mary Connolly and Bried Mulhern.

'Sacred Memories': Conception Murphy in St Louis, Monaghan.

Joseph Mary Connolly, J. Van den Bronk SMA, brother of Bishop André Van den Bronk of Kumasi, Columbanus Greene, J. Obdam SMA and Joannes Hayes, Monaghan, July 1970. Columbanus is holding the Papal decoration, 'Pro Ecclesia et Pontifice', that she received that day.

The three McNicholas sisters from Kiltimagh with their mother.
From left: Cronan, Perpetua and Mochua.

'Oodles of nuns'. The novitiate in Monaghan, with postulants, 'white veils' and 'black veils', 1954-5.

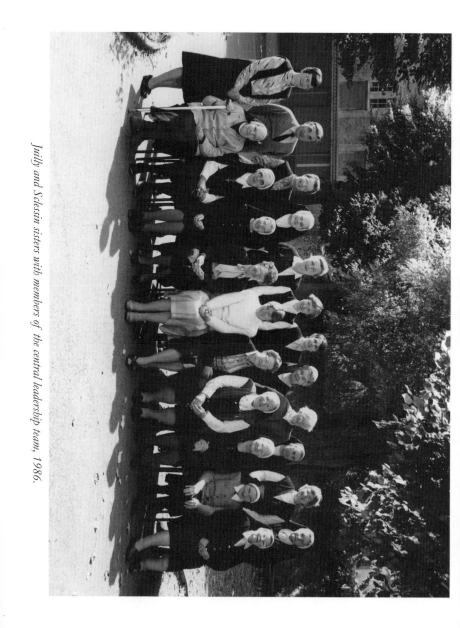

Juilly and Sclessin sisters with members of the central leadership team, 1986.

The novitiate in Akure in the 1970s. Standing, from left: Maureen Ezeani, Cecilia Adeniran, Clare McKeever, Patricia Ebegbulem, Clare Ikediashi, Maeve O'Sullivan, Bernice Broohm. Seated, from left: Anita Morley, Monica Adeya, Columbanus Greene, Augustine Moane, Martinian Bergin, Isabel Mann.

The community of La Cañada, 1957.
Standing, from left: Dolorosa Minogue, Mary Gibbons, Rita McCormack, Catherine Foley, Moira Conheady.
Seated, from left: Ronan McDonnell, Majella Seery, superior general, Ignatius Keegan, Julie Conole.

were reluctant to engage with western medicine: they were scattered in the bush all around and they had no money to pay even the small fee they were charged. Nuala had set up leprosy clinics in different places and once a month they would visit and see the lepers. Even in this area the uptake was not all that great, as there was a great distrust of anything foreign.

Shortly before Proinnsias arrived the sisters had opened a girls' primary school in Zonkwa. The priests in their various missions would collect the girls who were interested and bring them in to board. Then the teacher training college took the best half of the crop from the primary school. Education spilled over into all facets of life: when the people had a little education and enough English to understand what was being said to them the clientèle of the hospital grew. Proinnsias never learned a native language as there were so many different languages. Zonkwa, like Shendam, was in the middle belt and there was a multitude of small tribes. She did pick up a little Hausa but feels it was a mistake not to go to Hausa school and learn it properly. But, 'In those days you just rushed out and did what you could.'

Proinnsias came home to Ireland in May 1961, as did Carmel from Ado-Ekiti, and they both undertook a diploma in tropical medicine. A sister from the Medical Missionaries of Mary advised Columbanus that the doctors should do a postgraduate qualification in surgery before going back to Nigeria so they spent four years studying for the fellowship in general surgery and took the Irish and English exams. While Proinnsias was away the mission in Zonkwa employed an Italian doctor.

By the time she went back to Zonkwa in 1966, the student nurses from the midwifery and the general nursing school were providing the hospital with essential staff. Nuala had also started clinics throughout the bush. The priests who were evangelising in the villages were part of the medical service: they would hold clinics on a particular day and Proinnsias and Nuala would go out and tend to people. Eventually some midwives they had trained were able to service the clinics in the local area.

On Proinnsias's second tour the service they provided became effective. They started an under-fives programme and a prenatal programme. Those clinics made a big difference to the survival of small children. At the beginning it was common to find as many as five dead babies on the verandah in the morning, the deaths caused by malnutrition or the malnutrition of the mothers.

Proinnsias stayed in Zonkwa until 1979. She liked the climate there. People used to say that Jos was up (on the plateau), Shendam was down and Zonkwa was 'neither up nor down'. She loved the people once they got to trust the doctors and nurses and found the experience rewarding. Any idea she had going to Africa that she would be preaching the gospel flew out the door as soon as she arrived and religion never entered the heads of the medical missionaries from then on. They just did what they could to help.

When Proinnsias came home in 1979 she had a problem with her eyes and never went back to Nigeria. Instead she worked for some years in the Royal Hospital in Donnybrook.

Nuala was moved to Iseyin, a hospital run by the Daughters of the Holy Spirit, where St Louis sisters had already served, to replace the matron. She worked there for two years. In 1986 she received a telegram from congregational leader Dorothy McCloskey asking her to 'come immediately'. She wanted her to upgrade a medical unit for sisters in St Louis House in Monaghan and have it registered with the health authorities. Nuala says that she knew no more about running a nursing home in Monaghan than she had about Africa when she came to Zonkwa in 1955 but, ever adaptable, she went and took over the unit in Monaghan and ran it with the help of other medical staff.

Nuala would have loved to go back to work in Nigeria but the moment had passed. She did revisit Zonkwa for the golden jubilee of the foundation in 1998. The big hospital and training school are run by Nigerian sisters of St Louis but the town is still small, a light in the darkness of the bush.

In 1977 when Hannah Boylan, a nurse, was missioned to Ado-Ekiti, it was a thriving hospital with a good ante-natal clinic in which Hannah worked. Carmel Garvey and an Egyptian doctor she had trained were on the staff. But in 1984-5 the government decided it would take over all the missionary hospitals. The sisters were not allowed to charge anything, no matter how little, and gradually the hospital declined. When the government handed it back to the congregation it was on a much smaller scale. Michael Fagun, bishop of Ekiti when that diocese was created, arranged for Sisters of Saint Michael the Archangel, an indigenous congregation he himself had founded, to run the hospital in the place of Sisters of St Louis.

The final medical foundation by Irish sisters in Nigeria was in Ikire, in south-western Nigeria, in 1967. When Theresa Kerley and Neassa (Mary) Clancy arrived, it was no more than a dispensary but they built Oke-Ola up to a fifty-six bed hospital in the service of the people of Ikire. The OLA sisters later took over management of this hospital.

7

Formation and Structure in Nigeria and Ghana

'Eager to integrate the African sisters of St Louis into our congregation'
St Louis General Chapter, 1975

As long ago as 1926, the encyclical of Pius XI on Catholic Missions, *De Rerum Ecclesiae,* declared: 'We call your attention to the importance of building up a native clergy. If you do not work with all your might to attain this purpose, we assert that not only will your apostolate be crippled, but it will become an obstacle and an impediment to the establishment and organisation of the Church in those countries.' And *Evengelii Praecones* (1951) in the papacy of Pius XII, stated: 'The object of missionary activity, as all know, is to bring the light of the Gospel to new races and to form new Christians. However, the ultimate goal of missionary endeavour, which should never be lost sight of, is to establish the Church on sound foundations among non-Christian peoples, and place it under its own native hierarchy.'

Nigeria is an enormous country and as the sisters were concentrated in two areas – in what was then called the north/central belt and in the west of the country – there were originally two novitiates, one in Zonkwa and one in Akure.

Archbishop John McCarthy opened a novitiate for the African sisters of St Louis, Kaduna Diocese, in 1962. The sisters were to be a diocesan congregation trained by the Irish sisters of St Louis. On 25 March 1963 four postulants were received in the presence of Columbanus and Archbishop McCarthy: three grade-three teachers and one midwife, Dorothy Yayock. All four were past pupils of Zonkwa. The following year, 1964, five girls entered the postulancy and two entered in 1965. Some of these postulants were past pupils of Kano and Minna. Roseanne Byrne was appointed novice mistress and a few months later, in December 1964, a novitiate building was opened in Zonkwa. All four postulants of 1963 completed two years of novitiate and had their first profession and some of the others made first profession but only Dorothy stayed in the congregation.

On St Louis Day 1963 the Bishop of Ondo, William Field, opened the novitiate for the African sisters of St Louis (a diocesan congregation for Ondo diocese) in Akure. This arrangement had been the subject of discussion and negotiation between him and Columbanus. Ten days earlier Anita Morley's name had been read from the changes list: to her surprise she was appointed the first novice mistress in Akure. Anita, a primary teacher, had spent just three years in Nigeria, in the classroom in Jos. On 24 August she boarded a plane for Ibadan and when she arrived in Akure she found every sister in western Nigeria in the compound scrubbing, cleaning and polishing the newly built novitiate against the official opening the next day. On the day of the ceremony rain came down in torrents and the unpaved area between the convent and the novitiate, recently a building site, became virtually impassable.

At this time religious vocations for girls were practically unknown outside the east as Yoruba culture had a strong expectation that girls should be mothers. Additionally, education raised the value of girls on the marriage market: the bride price of a girl with GCSE qualifications would be high. At the beginning girls came and went as the idea of religious life was so foreign to their culture and they confused the desire for religious life with their desire for education. Roseline Okiti and Magdalena Obiafor were the first two postulants in Akure. They had already spent some formation time with Felicity McEnnis in Ondo but neither stayed with the congregation. Formation was a difficult process, not just because it demanded a great deal of the postulants and novices but because so much of the formation was totally foreign to their culture. Patricia Ebegbulem and Cecilia Adeniran were the first long-term postulants in Akure.

Although the culture of the Akan peoples is matrilinear and the concept of religious life is foreign to this kind of society, Ghanaian girls showed an interest in joining the congregation soon after the arrival of the sisters in Kumasi. Sheela Gillespie recalls that Bishop Paulissen arrived at the convent one evening 'after trekking in the bush', announcing that he had brought with him fifteen year old Lucy, who wished to become a sister. Having consulted (by letter) with Monaghan and received the blessing of Columbanus, the sisters took Lucy to live with them and educate her. She stayed about a year and a half and Teresa, a young girl from the same village who also joined the community, left after six months. The sisters were not too sad to see these girls go as they really did not feel ready, nor did they have the womanpower, to take on formation work. As Sheela said, 'We felt we needed to know the people and their culture well before embarking on such an important apostolate.'

It was later decided to combine formation for Ghana and western Nigeria. Bernice Broohm was the first postulant in Kumasi, and with Bernadette Essien, she joined the novitiate in Akure. The two Ghanaians had the blessing of Bishop Sarpong of Kumasi, although, like the Nigerian postulants and novices, their canonical status was unclear.

Gradually the numbers in Akure rose. By the time Anita finished her eight year term as mistress of novices there were six junior professed, one novice and two postulants. Seven of this number took final profession. Martinian Bergin took over in formation in 1971 and Davnet McGreal in 1977. It was a matter of concern to the formation personnel and to the leadership that there was, canonically speaking, confusion about the designation 'African sisters of St Louis'. Technically the western sisters belong to St Louis African Sisters, Diocese of Ondo, but Dorothy Yayock belonged to St Louis African Sisters, Archdiocese of Kaduna, and Bernice and Bernadette to St Louis African Sisters, diocese of Kumasi. In Zonkwa, there were no new postulants between 1971 and 1979, when Bridget Agum and Margaret Yusufu entered. In 1979 Dorothy Yayock, who had made her final profession in 1975 and studied abroad, was put in charge of postulants in Zonkwa.

The African sisters' situation was anomalous: they wore St Louis habits, their constitutions were based on the St Louis constitution and they looked on Columbanus Greene and later Colmcille Stephens as their superiors general but they knew that their respective bishops had a proprietary right over them.

It was the 1969 general chapter that decided on the new role of regional superior for west Africa. This was in keeping with the theology of religious life that came from Vatican II, with more consultation and collegiality, less authoritarianism and governing from the top. The west African regional would have the assistance of three councillors, each with responsibility for one of the three areas of Ghana, northern Nigeria and western Nigeria. Patricia Moloney was the first west African regional superior.

The African sisters and the Irish sisters who worked in formation were conscious that the existing situation was not desirable and petitioned through Patricia Moloney that their case be discussed. It became essential to reach clarification of the canonical status of the African entrants to the congregation. Ghana presented a particular problem as there were so few Ghanaian novices at this time and there was a question mark about admitting this small number of Ghanaians into a European congregation: the Ghanaian novices were in the Ondo novitiate but did not belong to the Ondo diocesan congregation and it was assumed that they would return to Ghana and form the nucleus of a new diocesan congregation in Kumasi.

Breda O'Hanrahan began her duties as regional superior in succession to Patricia Moloney on 1 January 1973 and took up the issue of the status of the west African sisters. She observed from a meeting of the African sisters that they felt closer to Sisters of St Louis than to any African congregation. But it took a long time for the process to complete itself. It was a period of confusion for some of the African sisters who wished to serve their own people in the best possible way but saw the advantages of belonging to an international institute with canonical status rather than an indigenous or diocesan order over which the local bishop might try to wield influence. Some of the bishops favoured their remaining diocesan sisters, although Bishop Field of Ondo, who had founded the diocesan congregation of St Louis in Akure, gave his full support to their joining the Monaghan congregation from an early stage. Throughout the process the African sisters involved had the canonical right to opt for a diocesan order instead of becoming part of the integrated community.

It took years of discussion with local Churchmen and with Rome before the situation was resolved. Some bishops were slow to yield control of these growing groups of African sisters but Rome threw its weight behind integration in the person of the Pro-Nuncio, Archbishop Pignedoli: although the Vatican in general favoured indigenisation, there was some concern about the number of native congregations that were growing up quickly.

Winifred Ojo entered the order in 1973. She says that before she met the late Cecilia Adeniran, who was a student at the time, 'I didn't imagine that Yoruba people could become religious.' Sure enough she had to convince her father that she was doing the right thing. There were about twenty Nigerian sisters in the institute when she entered and she always had the sense that she was entering an international congregation, not one that would be under the control of a local bishop, although this was the period when there was uncertainty about the canonical status of the west African sisters. She would have felt 'stifled in a diocesan order'. There were still many Irish sisters in the north of Nigeria, where she went to work after teacher training, and she felt very much at home with them.

The 1975 chapter cleared the way for integration from the institute's side by declaring 'that it was not merely open but eager to integrate the African sisters of St Louis into our congregation, recognising in their existence the special work of the Holy Spirit and the opportunity of furthering the international dimension of our missionary endeavour in west Africa.'

Eventually the African sisters, both Ghanaian and Nigerian, opted for amalgamation rather than remaining diocesan congregations or becoming independent indigenous communities. In 1976 they requested to 'be integrated as full members of the international congregation of St Louis Monaghan'.

On Pentecost Sunday that year superior general Colmcille Stephens received fifteen Nigerian sisters and three Ghanaian into the institute. Each in turn expressed her desire for integration before Bishop Field of Ondo. At the ceremony Breda O'Hanrahan spoke of how the occasion deepened the congregation's understanding of *Ut Sint Unum*: 'So, as we repeated together the act of spiritual union of L'Abbé Bautain, used by the Fathers of St Louis in 1832 and based on the Turquestein Pact of 1797, our horizons were enlarged and we caught something of that vision that inspired our founders.' Bishop Field described the integration as 'the crowning glory of the work of the sisters' on the missions.

After a process of discernment the Ghanaian sisters decided that they wished to become a region of the St Louis international institute with their own regional superior and the Nigerian sisters announced their wish to become a province. Isabel Mann, the Nigerian regional leader at the time, became provincial leader and Patricia Ebegbulem was the first elected provincial superior. Nigeria is the part of the institute that has most new life and vigour. Ghana, although usually with a smaller number of vocations in keeping with its smaller population, also has a young and vibrant sisterhood.

On 7 January 1995 the Ghanaian region was inaugurated. Anne Kavanagh, the congregational leader, emphasised the continuity of the congregation's charism: 'These structural changes do not, in any way, weaken the unity we cherish.'

8

The Mission to California

'Certification, a driver's licence and naturalisation'

The United States went from the Depression of the 1930s into the Second World War and out of war into the boom era of the 1950s, which produced a baby boom, in contrast to the years of contraction of the birth rate before the war. California, as well as states on the east coast, saw a rapid rise in population as a result of migration from other states and an influx of immigrants from many countries. A contributory factor was the GI Bill of 1944, which eased the return to civilian life of almost eight million ex-servicemen, offering them low-interest loans to buy homes and start businesses as well as provisions for education. Suburban United States dates from this period and nowhere was suburbanisation more widespread than in southern California. With the exception of one foundation in Sacramento, for several decades the St Louis mission to California was a mission to the archdiocese of Los Angeles.

The Archdiocese of Los Angeles was created in 1936 under the leadership of Limerick-born John J. Cantwell. He opened many schools and churches for Hispanics but it was after his death in 1947 and the succession of the New-York born Irish-American J. Francis McIntyre (1948-70; Cardinal from 1952) that the major expansion of the archdiocese occurred, catering for Americans who moved to California or were born there and a huge wave of immigrants of all nationalities, Asian as well as Hispanic. Between 1948 and 1963, eighty-two parishes were opened in the archdiocese and the number of Catholic schools increased from one hundred and forty seven to three hundred and forty seven, which means that an average of one new school a month was established for fifteen years.

The St Louis mission to California began against this background. In the 1950s, the period of greatest growth for the mission, there was a virtually limitless demand for educational personnel and clergy. Ireland, which had a surplus of religious, both women and men, was able to meet this need, and Irish teachers and priests were much in demand. The sisters' first parish, Nativity, had an Irish pastor, Denis Ginty. The parish of the Nativity had been in existence for a quarter of a century but the school was only two years old and had been run by the Missionary Sisters of the Sacred Heart. Los Angeles's third archbishop, Cardinal Timothy J. Manning (1970-1985), was born in Ballingeary, County Cork, although educated for the priesthood in California, and he became a good friend of the sisters; he and his chancellor were competent financial managers and, with the generous contribution of parishioners throughout the diocese, put the new schools they continued to found on a stable financial footing.

In 1949 when the mission to California began at the request of Cardinal McIntyre, sisters were missioned there without volunteering. They had no expectation that they would ever see their homes again and California was almost twice as far as the east coast of the US, where most Irish emigrants had settled. The first eight St Louis pioneers, the 'Forty-niners' as they are often called, accompanied by the superior general, Columbanus Greene, and Kathleen McNally, sailed on the *Queen Elizabeth* from Southampton to New York, thence by train from Penn Station via Chicago and Omaha to Nativity parish, El Monte. The sisters had Mass at noon in the convent chapel on the day of their arrival, St Louis Day, 25 August 1949.

The pioneers were the superior, Ronan McDonnell, an important influence on the development of the mission, Colm Moran, Natalie McNally, Kilian Eaton, Antonia Byrne, Claudine McEnnis, Carmela Dunleavy and Maura Byron. Ronan and Colm had been teaching in Rathmines Infant School and the whole of Williams Park in Rathmines was caught up in missionary fervour and fundraising. As well as the Irish trained sisters, two of the pioneers had received teacher training in England.

One of the pioneers, Maura Byron, remembers her arrival in California: '… the vastness of the ocean and of the continent that separated us from home; the extraordinary quality of the sunlight… the warmth and loving acceptance of all kinds of people. And always the sense of challenge – children to be loved and educated, parents to be worked with, parishioners to be served, new things to be learned, to be done, to be made part of the new expression of our old St Louis ways.' Wherever they went, hard work was the norm for the sisters.

With the exception of Louisville Woodland Hills, a high school of distinction, all the foundations of St Louis sisters were grade or elementary schools. The buildings, school and convent, were supplied by the diocese and were usually in the same compound as the parish church, and sisters were paid small stipends by the parish, with no provision for retirement. All Catholic schools in America are private, dependent on fee income and support from congregation or church, as, with the exception of some federal programmes for pupils with learning or language challenges, they do not receive government support.

Although the culture shock associated with California was not as great as would have been experienced in Ghana or Nigeria, Los Angeles was still very different from Ireland of the 1940s or 1950s. The extent of the city, for those who had been used to Monaghan, or even Dublin, the heat, the smog, the mixture of nationalities, the extremes of affluence and poverty, the difference in vocabulary and educational terms, the pledge of allegiance to the flag, the collecting of fees – all these must have taken getting used to. The classes were big – sixty or more pupils – but this was also the norm in Ireland at this time. Religious communities in Los Angeles, such as the Columban sisters and fathers, the Holy Child Sisters, the Immaculate Heart of Mary (IHM) sisters and the Sisters of St Joseph of Carondelet (CSJ) were generous in the welcome and support they offered the pioneers – a support that continued from the parishioners in the founding schools and the parents of the American-born sisters. Maura Byron recalls that on the night of their arrival in El Monte in August 1949, the sisters went to the Columban sisters in Westminster for dinner.

For the first ten years of the California mission, new sisters were missioned every summer, so that their total number reached a hundred by 1959, as 'part of the growth of the educational system of the archdiocese [of California] and to collaborate in ministry with the priests and people of the newly established parishes,' as Maura Byron puts it. Most of these were immediately put to teach in whichever schools had a vacancy, with an experienced and qualified principal and other staff members. Many of them were untrained when they began to teach, although their Irish Leaving Certificate was recognised as the equivalent of a year of college in California and the custom in the novitiate in Monaghan, that novices would serve a sort of 'apprenticeship', by accompanying and helping an experienced sister in the classroom, stood to them. Sisters got their education and certification in teacher training colleges such as Immaculate Heart College and Mount St Mary's College (Sisters of St Joseph of Carondelet), during weekends and part of the summer holidays, while continuing to teach. It was a busy life and it was said, tongue in cheek, that the aim of a sister missioned to California was threefold: certification (as a teacher), a driver's licence and naturalisation (US citizenship).

Sisters tell stories of being missioned to California on St Louis Day, 25 August, and being sent to stand in front of a class the day after they arrived. School reopened on the Tuesday after Labor Day, the first Monday of September. Michèle Harnett says that this was one thing they should have done differently: 'They should have given us some time to be acculturated when we went out. I arrived on 4 September 1963 and I was standing in a classroom of fifty six third graders on 7 September.' There was no talk of jet lag (once sisters started to go by plane: the first group to fly in 1953 included Canice Durkan, later Californian regional superior) or readjustment, let alone acculturation. The climate was much hotter than Ireland but there was no relief from the full black habit. The work was hard. On Maura Byron's first morning in Nativity School, El Monte, in September 1949, she faced a class of sixty five fifth grade boys and girls. Josephine Fay spent six years in St Mel's, Woodland Hills, where Mary O'Driscoll was principal, after her initial posting in El Monte. It was then a rural area with orange groves, in the process of development, and the population was predominantly ex-army. Such was the demand for school places that she taught a double session 8.00-12.00 and 12.30-4.30, with sixty children in the morning session and sixty seven in the afternoon.

Under the new superior general, Majella Seery, 1957 was a year of exceptional growth. In that year alone three new communities were founded and thirteen extra sisters were missioned from Monaghan that summer. Majella visited California in the spring of 1957 and seemed eager to accede to any request for sisters. St Anthony Claret, a new school in Anaheim, was staffed by three St Louis sisters that September, as was the brand-new elementary school of Holy Name of Mary, San Dimas-La Verne. The third new foundation – St Robert, Sacramento – was further afield: Majella inspected the new school and approved the plans for the convent during her spring visit and four sisters made the four hundred mile journey to Sacramento by the night train on 1 September 1957, staying with Mercy sisters in the parish until their own convent was ready. This was the only St Louis foundation outside southern California at the time and sisters worked there until 1975.

The number of St Louis foundations in California indicates the extent of the involvement of the sisters in the educational apostolate of the diocese. Except for Nativity School, which predated the sisters' arrival in 1949, all the schools in which sisters taught, up to and including Louisville Woodland Hills (kindergarten in 1958), were founded by them. These schools still serve the educational needs of the Catholic parishioners and some continue to incorporate the St Louis charism and educational philosophy. From 1958, sisters assumed administration or teaching responsibilities in established schools, including St Mel's in Woodland Hills.

San Miguel was one of the last educational foundations under-taken by the Sisters of St Louis, in 1987. It was in inner city Los Angeles, a lower income area, and the choice was deliberate, in keeping with the option for the poor that had been adopted at the 1985 general chapter. The ministry there ended in 1990.

The location of the congregation's most durable foundation in California, which also became the site of its novitiate and its largest remaining community, was, like many other aspects of the mission, fortuitous. The Los Angeles chancery invested in an extensive property in the San Fernando Valley which it sold to the community in 1957. La Manzanita (a local evergreen shrub named for its berries), had a ranch building, hills, canyons, shrubberies and white-painted corrals. The ranch house became the convent and regional house and a kindergarten was opened. The sod was turned for the high school in February 1960 and miraculously, despite a building strike, the school, under the principalship of the dauntless Ronan McDonnell, accepted its first ninety freshmen students in September 1960.

Science teacher Triona McGinty was missioned to California as a young sister of twenty-four and arrived in time for the opening in 1960. She describes the first year of Louisville as 'a comedy of errors' but says that nothing fazed Ronan. The first day they had no screwdriver for necessary adjustments – or water in the school buildings. Triona was delighted with the extensive grounds so she took the girls down the canyon where they came in contact with poison ivy. She didn't know any better and nobody had time to hold her hand. Maura Byron, who succeeded Ronan as principal, remembers: 'Indeed there was no paved road on Mulholland Drive, but there was tethering space outside the gate for Moby Dick, the large white horse Marilyn Riggs rode over the hills to school each day.'

The sisters in California looked to the congregation's well re-garded schools in Ireland, semaphoring by their choice of uniform that, although Louisville was a great ocean and a continent away from Monaghan, Carrickmacross and Balla, it was continuing a great tradition. Maura Byron comments on this sense of continuity: 'I remember, too, the blue of school jackets, sweaters and berets worn by the ninety-two new freshmen. It is the same "St. Louis blue" worn by legions of students down through the years in schools all over the world, and was for us pioneer sisters here at Louisville, Woodland Hills, a special link with an illustrious past.'

The first Louisville graduation was in 1964: the graduates included Margie Buttita, who has served for many years in Brazil. Bridget Ehlert and current congregational leader, Donna Hansen, are also past pupils of Louisville and Donna is known to have sung a solo in Gilbert and Sullivan's *Patience*. The Sisters of St Louis, whether at home or abroad, were unrivalled for productions of musicals. Bridget Ehlert, who graduated in 1966 and later served as principal, remembers the excellence of the Irish sisters as educators: that they had a particular interest in each pupil, the ethos of the high school was person-centred and they put all their energies into making the school the best possible. Bonds between the sisters were strong, probably because they were living so far from home and cut off from their families of origin. The family atmosphere that originated in the motherhouse in Juilly came to the fore in the community again under these circumstances, especially as the St Louis sisters in the early years of the foundation were one of the few non-American religious groups in the diocese.

Accustomed to continuing education, receptive to renewal and eager to embrace change, sisters based in California attended summer school in the Catholic University of America, the University of Chicago, Berkeley and Spokane to study the new theology of Vatican II. Then all the sisters would go on holiday to the ocean and those who had just come home from summer schools shared what they had learned with the others. In addition to informal exchanges, formal renewal programmes, many of them initiated and presented by Bridget Clare McKeever, made an important contribution to the spiritual life of sisters.

As time went on, sisters with the requisite degrees taught a variety of subjects in a number of diocesan high schools, such as Mater Dei, Santa Ana; Saint Anthony, Long Beach; Crespi Carmelite, Encino; and Bishop Amat, La Puente. Others taught at third level, including Bridget Clare McKeever at St Meinrad's Seminary, Patrice Benson at St John's Seminary, Maureen Kelly at Mount St Mary's College, and Bríd Long at the Catholic University of America in Washington DC. Several sisters, including Catherine Foley, Margaret McGrath, Monica Quigley and Bridget Ehlert, worked as supervisors (inspectors) of elementary and high schools in the diocese. As well as teaching at third level, Bernadette Murphy was Director for Educational and Formative Services for the Archdiocese of Los Angeles.

The first postulant came to the Californian region as early as 1955. In 1962 the congregation decided to start a juniorate in Cushendall, County Antrim, to educate girls specifically for the California novitiate: they would accompany American postulants and novices in their formation. Like so many other ideas the brainchild of Ronan McDonnell, this was envisaged as a means of integrating the sisters in the two countries, rather than sending only professed sisters to California as had been the custom. Antonia Byrne was put in charge of the school in Cushendall and the aspirancy sent the first six postulants to Woodland Hills at the end of August 1964 for formation with the American postulants. Maura Clerkin is a Cushendall girl and Margaret Hosty attended the juniorate in Clogher when Cushendall closed in 1965, before entering in California in 1967. More than fifty girls had entered the Woodland Hills novitiate by 1980, although many of them decided that religious life was not for them and there were no new vocations after this time.

The California region founded a community in Barrolandia, Brazil, in 1976, in response to the call of the Vatican for each congregation to send personnel to Latin America, a mission that was rejuvenating for the sisters who took part and for the region as a whole. A small number of sisters still minister in Brazil.

9

Les Dames de St Louis

Les deux congrégations formeront un seul corps…
Sacred Congregation for Religious, Rome (1951)

Juilly is a village north-east of Paris in the flight path of Aéroport Charles de Gaulle (and the Concorde when it flew), with two venerable Catholic secondary schools. One is the large Oratorian Collège de Juilly, which dates from the seventeenth century and was in the 1840s the headquarters of Louis Bautain's group of St Louis fathers. Across the square is the Cours Bautain, a primary school and *collège* attached to the original convent of the Dames de St Louis, without which none of the history recounted in these pages would have taken place.

In January 1950 Mère Véronique Cazaux, Superior General of the Dames de St Louis, wrote from Juilly to Columbanus Greene, superior general in Monaghan, requesting the amalgamation of her community with the Sisters of St Louis in Ireland. This was, according to Columbanus, a 'pathetic appeal to save St Louis of France'. It was not the first approach on the subject: a letter had already come from the Vicar of Meaux to request the reunification of the congregations.

The minutes of the general council meeting in Monaghan on 12 February 1950 report: 'A letter from the Mother General of St Louis Convent, Juilly, France, asked earnestly and humbly if our Mother General would consider the amalgamation of their houses in France and Belgium with Monaghan. The council decided to ask for full details regarding numbers, finances, etc., before giving any definite reply.'

The amalgamation was discussed at the general chapter of 1950 and at a council meeting of 26 May 1951, Columbanus suggested that 'the only possible way to extricate them from their difficulties is simply to take them in. In charity we cannot do anything else, they are our own.' In the subsequent secret ballot, the vote was unanimous for amalgamation with Juilly. The formal amalgamation took place on 29 November 1952.

Although the two congregations had parted company in the early years of the foundation in Monaghan when Louis Bautain, the founder of the Dames de St Louis, had reluctantly ceded authority over the new community to the Bishop of Clogher, there had been regular contact between Juilly and Ireland over the decades. The archives in Monaghan and Juilly provide evidence of friendly correspondence and willingness to cooperate, Louis McGrath, who founded Mount Carmel High School in Kilkeel in 1922, was an ardent francophile and francophone and had photographs of the graves of the founders taken in Juilly. But, not unexpectedly, there was a difference in emphasis between the two branches of the order, in their apostolate, in their respective rules and in their daily life.

Máirín Barrett is the source of much of the following inform-ation about the situation in the French motherhouse at the time of *la fusion*.

As well as Juilly, there were small St Louis foundations in nearby Meaux and far distant Labastide d'Armagnac in the Landes. In Belgium the two communities of Sclessin-lez-Liège and Thier-à-Liège were involved in primary education but as the Belgian government paid the salaries of teachers, their situation was more favourable. There were thirty sisters in Juilly and nineteen in Sclessin, with the remaining nine sisters distributed among the other foundations; Meaux and Labastide were, in fact, closed before the amalgamation took place because of shortage of personnel.

The desperation of Véronique Cazaux was caused by the shortage of vocations – the youngest member of the community, Marie Pierre Bourlier, who still lives in Juilly, was twenty-two and had entered in 1947 – by the fact that the community was ageing (the oldest sister was seventy-eight) and by the decline of the school, which meant that the sisters were poor. There were fifty pupils in the *pensionnat* (boarding school), an orphanage with twenty-five children and a small parish school. The political climate in post-war France was left-wing and *laïciste* (secularist) and it must have seemed inconceivable that government finance would ever come the way of Catholic schools. As it stood, all expenses had to be paid for from pupils' fees.

In retrospect it seems likely that the Dames de St Louis never recovered from the effects of the legislation of 1903-5 that closed all Catholic schools in France run by religious orders. The early governments of the Third Republic (1870-1940) were strongly *laïciste* in tendency and the laws of 1881 and 1882 which established free, mandatory and secular public education are associated with Jules Ferry (1832-93), who spent several periods as *Ministre de l'Instruction Publique* and also as premier. *Laïcisme* peaked with the law of 7 July 1904, passed by Émile Combes (1835-1921) which decreed: '*l'enseignement de tout ordre et de toute nature est interdit en France aux congrégations*' ('teaching of any level or kind is forbidden to congregations in France').

Although the Dames de St Louis, an authorised congregation that ministered to the poor, the sick and orphans, maintained ownership of the motherhouse in Juilly, there was nothing for it in 1905 but to close the school, the main source of income. The foundations at Sclessin and Thier-à-Liège dated from this period as the Belgian diocese invited sisters to open houses and run schools there. Even the novitiate was transferred to Sclessin for a time. Some of the sisters came back to Juilly after the First World War ended in 1918, when the political climate was more favourable, and reopened the pensionnat under the name Cours Bautain, while the order maintained its foundations and personnel in Liège.

The years of the Second World War, 1939-45, were a period of great privation and insecurity for the Dames de St Louis in Juilly. In early June 1940 the whole village, including sisters and orphans, fled before the invading German forces in what became known as the 'exodus'. They returned when the French president, Philippe Pétain, negotiated an armistice with Germany, which came into effect on 25 June. Four years of German occupation followed until Paris was liberated by the Allies in August 1944.

When vocations ceased in 1947 the local Bishop of Meaux bluntly told the sisters in Juilly that they would have to amalgamate either with Monaghan or with another congregation in France. Monaghan was presumably the lesser of two evils, although it must have been difficult for Véronique Cazaux to go, cap in hand, to her counterpart in Ireland, knowing that amalgamation would have consequences not necessarily agreeable for her sisters. The Belgian houses in Liège did not favour the amalgamation – as sisters were paid teachers' salaries by the government they were not suffering financial hardship like the community in Juilly – and a number of them left the congregation at this point, as was their canonical right.

The two branches of the congregation had been separated for almost a century and each side maintained its myth about the other: the Irish felt that Mère Thérèse de la Croix 'didn't like the Irish' while Juilly accused Genevieve Beale of not trying hard enough to avoid the separation, the famous 'schism'. As well as the canonical amalgamation and the transfer of Irish personnel to Juilly, Pauline McGovern's centenary account, *God Wills It* (1959) helped to heal the breach by emphasising the French roots of the order and the philosophy of the founder, Louis Bautain.

Máirín Barrett points out that the apostolates of the two branches of the order differed no less than the respective rules. The Juilly and Belgian communities were involved in youth work, running a club called the 'Patronage' ('Patro'). Sisters took the young people on outings and taught them handicrafts. The sisters in Belgium ran another group called 'Joyeuses' and Thérèse Marie Mutsers took the children camping in the summer, something that would not have been allowed under the Monaghan rule. Nor were the French and Belgian sisters so exclusively involved in education ministry as the Irish. Some of the sisters had nursing qualifications and acted as district nurses, holding clinics and visiting the sick in their homes, a service that was highly valued by the people of Juilly, as the village had neither doctor nor pharmacy in the 1940s. Gilberte Delpèche did her sick rounds on a bicycle for twenty years, something that would not have been countenanced by the

Monaghan rule. Bicycles did not come to Juilly again until after
Vatican II.

When the two communities were amalgamated, canon law,
through the Sacred Congregation for Religious, decreed that the
French and Belgian Dames de St Louis should accept the Monaghan
rule and customs.: *'L'union est telle qu'à l'avenir les deux Congrégations
formeront un seul corps sous le titre et gouverné par les constitutions des
Sœurs de St Louis a Monaghan. Cette union s'applique à tous les droits et
toutes les obligations...'* ('The union is such that in the future the
two congregations will form a single body under the name of
and governed by the constitutions of the Sisters of St Louis in
Monaghan. This union applies to all rights and obligations...')
In practice this meant that the communities of Juilly and Sclessin
would have Irish superiors and that Irish sisters would be missioned
to help their French consœurs in their ministry. The Monaghan
habit was to be the habit of all the St Louis sisters, at home and
abroad.

Both sides had to adapt: the French would lose some of their
freedoms, of which the loss of the right to go home on holidays
every three years was the most grievous. The change of headdress
embarrassed the sisters in Belgium just at a time when Belgian
orders were beginning to wear simple veils and show a few
centimetres of hair. On the other hand, a few of the elderly sisters
continued to wear the old bonnet, as they were allowed to.

The Irish sisters who came to Juilly, who were mostly young,
had to acquire mastery of a language which in its spoken form was
almost unknown to them and adapt to the more formal French
customs around food, drink and *politesse*, like addressing all the
sisters as 'ma sœur'.

On 5 September 1951 Clare Ryan, along with Emilian McKenna
and Mercedes Eardley, arrived in Juilly from Ireland. Rome gave
permission at the end of 1952 and when formal amalgamation took
place on St Louis Day, 1953, Mercedes became superior in Juilly
and Emilian was sent to Sclessin as superior. Cours Bautain badly
needed the injection of young sisters who were gradually missioned
from Monaghan and who helped in the boarding school, did

whatever domestic tasks were required and taught as soon as they were able or qualified. Clare Ryan was put to teach as soon as she arrived, although she had no French. Pauline McGovern, who was studying French in UCD, spent part of the summer of 1952 in Juilly and remembers some of the awkwardness of *la fusion*, although the sister who presided over the gloomy subterranean kitchen produced a 'great French dinner' for St Louis Day.

Deirdre O'Hanlon came to Juilly in 1956 and found that the community had little of anything, even meat, and few pupils, no more than three or four in most classes. When Noreen Murphy joined her a few years later, it was still a life of (relative) privation, even for those accustomed to no-frills religious life in Ireland. Food was simple and far from abundant, as was hot water, and baths were rationed. The building was dilapidated and comfortless. There was a lot of physical work in the convent and boarding school, there were no labour saving devices and there was the added discomfort of wearing the full habit in summers much hotter than the temperate Irish weather to which the sisters were accustomed: the hard linen was also a hardship to the French sisters, who were used to a softer headdress. No wonder the fingers of Irish sisters were crossed that Juilly would not be their posting when the changes were read out in August. The village is still a quiet, peaceful place, although close to Paris, and it was much more isolated then, when the rule was strict, when money was so scarce. At least in Monaghan there might be a musical to look forward to or the possibility of meeting religious from another order and always plenty of company of your own age in the novitiate.

En revanche, Noreen Murphy was in the Sorbonne in *mai soixante-huit* (May 1968) and saw plenty of excitement during that revolution as well as having her science exams not so conveniently deferred. After Vatican II, Juilly's proximity to Paris meant that members of the community could participate in conferences, study sessions and intercongregational meetings, as its annals relate. Sisters based in Belgium were able to avail of similar opportunities in Liège and Brussels.

Educating the Irish sisters who came to Juilly after first

profession but before going to college at home was not always straightforward. Máire Muldowney remembers Colmcille arriving in Juilly in 1970 and saying to them, 'What are you all doing here not trained?' A number of sisters went home in 1970, like Máire herself, who then qualified as an art teacher. Before that Marie de Paul had encouraged her to paint and Deirdre O'Hanlon had organised a correspondence course for her in Paris, the tutor of which said to her, '*Ma sœur, vous avez de l'âme.*' ('Sister, you have soul.') Máire remembers that Colmcille 'brought a bit of humanity into the place', ordaining that it wasn't necessary for the sisters to get up quite so early in the morning. This was the stage at which discipline and the monastic regime had begun to change in Ireland.

The Irish sisters in Juilly had no choice but to master French, usually after months of listening in silence. But the French sisters did not tend to learn English, which meant that integration was one way only. Nor, in the earlier years, did they visit Ireland, so they had no experience of how life was lived in Monaghan or other Irish communities. This must have made things all the harder for them. When the parents of Irish sisters visited and stayed in the Villa (one of the 'perks' of Juilly), they were kind to them but, for the most part, communication was not easy. Neither in France nor in Belgium were there any enduring new vocations so there was never really a sense of the Irish and French/Belgian branches being grafted together to bear new fruit. (A Belgian, Annie Ferson, entered the novitiate in Monaghan in 1963 and was professed in 1966. She was assigned to Sclessin but left the congregation some years later.)

Pauline McGovern's *God Wills It*, Bríd O'Doherty's research for her PhD on Louis Bautain in the Sorbonne from 1964 to 1968 and the studies of Luxembourg-born philosophy teacher Marie de Paul Neiers were what really reignited the link with Juilly: a community of the mind rather than one of physical proximity. Bríd O'Doherty defended her thesis, *Le Chrétien du XIXème Siècle selon Louis Bautain*, in December 1968 and was awarded her doctorate *summa cum laude*. It was of vital importance that she and other St Louis scholars were able to access the archives in the convent in Juilly and also in the Collège de Juilly across the road, where Louis Bautain and his male disciples had been based. How providential that these archives had survived two world wars as well as the Franco-Prussian War of 1870, even though Juilly was in the path of the invading German armies. Equally providential was the fact that the amalgamation made the archives available to the congregation as a whole, which would not have been the case had the Dames de St Louis chosen to join some other congregation after the Second World War. Access to its origins was the greatest gift amalgamation bestowed on the congregation.

The work of the early scholars was consolidated by Bríd Long, who served as archivist in Juilly and who researched the theological thinking and educational philosophy of Louis Bautain for her PhD, and archivist and historian Máirín Barrett, who continues her research and teaching there. Bríd's work bore fruit in the charism chapter of 1984 and in the continuing attachment of the order to the guiding principle of *Ut Sint Unum* and Louis Bautain's ideal that Christianity is a force that can 'heal, unify and transform' the world.

10

The Renewal General Chapter of 1969 and 1970

'Controlled and some uncontrolled experiments...'
Columbanus Greene, 1969

At the time of writing it is almost half a century since the Second Vatican Council began in October 1962 and its pronouncements and their implementation are still the subject of debate and controversy. In the popular mind the council and the renewal of the Catholic Church are associated with the papacy of John XXIII, who succeeded Pius XII in 1958 and announced the convening of the council the following year. But this most popular of modern popes died in June 1963 only eight months after the council began (he was eighty-one), and it was in the reign of his successor, Paul VI (1963-78) that the key conciliar documents were published in 1964 and 1965 and gradually implemented, or not implemented, by the Church.

In contrast with the dramatic changes of Vatican II, the previous decades look like a blank canvas but it is not true that nothing changed in the Church in the long papacy of Pius XII (1939-58). To give just one example, in *Sponsa Christa (Bride of Christ,* 1950), Pius acknowledged the need for change: 'We find in the institutions of religious women elements which are, of themselves, unnecessary and bring no advantages but being merely external and of historic interest, are due to circumstances in the past that are now fundamentally altered. These are no longer of use, and may even impede a greater good: there is no reason for their preservation...' The pope asked for the revival and reanimation of minds and wills, 'to grapple as soon as possible with the new ways of life of our time'. This sounds like the renewal proposed by Vatican II but the pope's urgings seem to have fallen on deaf ears, not just in Monaghan but in all the other congregations of women. A more general Church renewal was necessary to bring about real change.

As with the papacy, so with the congregation: it is not true to say that nothing changed, as the beginning of missionary work did contribute to an improvement in the situation of the sisters vis-à-vis their families. Gradually, sisters who were missioned to California and Africa came home more frequently, partly for health reasons in the case of Africa, or to comply with government regulations. In 1958 there was an explicit loosening of regulations on home visits (up to this visits home were allowed only 'at the request of a dying parent'): 'Sisters will have permission to visit their homes in case of the serious illness, death or funeral of an immediate relative, or for other serious or compassionate reasons and so judged by the mother general. Also at the discretion of the mother general, other visits may be allowed.' One wonders how the mother general, who then managed a congregation of six hundred sisters, would have had time for such minutiae. And on the whole the monastic regime prevailed: the severe discipline of formation; the 'great silence', that prevailed from after supper in the evening until after Mass the next morning; the large institutionalised communities.

The general chapter of 1964 re-elected Columbanus Greene as superior general for her fourth and final term. The minutes of the chapter contain a reference to a change in the habit, the first of many over the decades that followed, when it became, if not a burning issue, certainly a perennial one. The degree of discussion that would be necessary is already palpable in this account from the chapter: 'It was proposed by Mother General that the habit, although revered, and itself attractive and distinctive, would be modified according to modern standards of convenience, hygiene and economy. A number of suggestions followed and it was finally agreed that sketches for a new habit would be sent to Mother General by sisters holding diplomas in art and expert in dress design. When the question arose of discarding the black cross attached to a moire ribbon, Mother General remarked, "Our foundress brought it to us from France." The whole assembly with one voice responded,

"It must remain."' (It is difficult not to be reminded of Pius XII's comment about institutions of 'historic interest'.)

The stiff, square headdress, which was unique to the congregation, made way for a softer, simpler veil in the experimental habit adopted at Easter 1966. In the same year the much disliked prohibition on sisters attending the ordination of their brothers was lifted.

'Open the windows and let in the fresh air.' The second Vatican Council ended in 1965 but it took a while for the winds of change to blow *aggiornamento* or modernisation into the corridors of the St Louis motherhouse in Monaghan. Sisters had begun to study the documents of Vatican II and institute theologians like Pauline McGovern and Brid O'Doherty gave month-long summer renewal courses to their consœurs but it was not until the chapter of 1969-70, the 'renewal chapter', that the institute really began to face the future.

Vatican II issued sixteen documents on topics from theology to liturgy; other documents of interpretation and clarification, classified as 'post-conciliar', followed. *Lumen Gentium* (*Light of Nations*, November 1964) and *Gaudium et Spes* (*Joy and Hope*, December 1965) had important consequences for religious life and for the Catholic laity. *Lumen Gentium* affirmed the universal call to holiness: all baptised members are called to holiness and no one way of attaining that holiness is more sure, more perfect than another. For many religious this required a major re-evaluation as they had been encouraged to believe that religious life was inherently superior to the secular state.

Gaudium et Spes articulated the proper concern that should be the business of all Catholics: social justice: 'The council, considering the immensity of the hardships which still afflict the greater part of mankind today, regards it as most opportune that an organism of the universal Church be set up in order that both the justice and love of Christ toward the poor might be developed everywhere.'

When the smoke of Vatican II had cleared, Paul VI rearticulated and expanded this exhortation in *Evangelica Testificatio* in 1971.

Some theologians and Churchmen, who took these two documents seriously or even literally, used them as the basis of liberation theology and the option for the poor from the late 1960s onward.

Perfectae Caritatis (Of Perfect Charity), the decree on the up to date renewal of religious life, was issued by the final session of the council, in October 1965. It urged religious orders to renew their commitment to the 'spirit and aims of each founder' and to give priority to 'spiritual renewal': '...it must be seriously and carefully considered that even the best-contrived adaptations to the needs of our time will be of no avail unless they are animated by a spiritual renewal, which must always be assigned primary importance even in the active ministry.' But the document did not give any concrete advice on how to achieve this and it is no wonder that years of confusion and a great diversity of theological and liturgical approaches ensued.

Perfectae Caritatis threw down the gauntlet of practical adaptation in a comprehensive and open-ended way. The rigidity and conformity of the past, restrictive but secure, were blown away and the apostolate, ideological framework and leadership of the religious orders were all open to re-evaluation: 'The manner of life, of prayer and of work should be in harmony with the present-day physical and psychological condition of the members. It should also be in harmony with the needs of the apostolate, in the measure that the nature of each institute requires, with the requirements of culture and with social and economic circumstances. This should be the case everywhere, but especially in mission territories.'

Before Vatican II had even started Pope John XXIII wrote a special letter to women religious, encouraging them to pray and prepare, so that their 'response when the enactments of the council are made will be prompt and generous'. It was precisely because women religious like the St Louis sisters were so obedient to the rulings of Vatican II that they embarked at the end of the 1960s on a journey of such radical change: it may have been exhilarating for the young and the brave but it must have been terrifying for many who had spent all their adult lives in a rigid, hierarchical and authoritarian system. As Miriam Commins wrote in *Link* of summer 1989, 'The trouble with us is that our novice mistresses did their job too well.' Now the Vatican was suggesting that what sisters had internalised, often painfully, over the course of many years not just of formation but of community life and discipline, was no longer 'in harmony with the needs of the apostolate'. But what would replace it?

One of the rulings of Vatican II was that all religious congregations were to hold a 'special general chapter for the renewal and adaptation of the religious life' as soon as possible after the end of the council. Columbanus got permission to postpone the St Louis renewal chapter for two years, as an ordinary general chapter was due in 1970, to allow various internal commissions to carry out preparatory work, both spiritual and practical, on the life of the congregation. Each sister received a copy of *Perfectae Caritatis*. Retreats and lectures, as well as reading and prayer, facilitated reflection on the form renewal should take: in the words of Columbanus, 'in various aspects of community living, controlled and some uncontrolled experiments have been made, with in many cases promising results.'

In letters Columbanus sent to the sisters in advance of the renewal chapter, one gets the sense of someone trying to rein in a galloping horse. Her characteristic wry humour is evident in a letter of 17 September 1968: (back to the habit) 'In sending some guidelines for controlled experimentation with the habit, may I repeat a quotation from *Perfectae Caritatis*…"Since they are signs of a consecrated life, religious habits should be simple and modest, at once poor and becoming…" To avoid expense and the appearance of worldliness, no one sister is to wear more than one experimental habit…I would like to get a snapshot of the experimental habits and of course the wearers. It is not envisaged that every sister would rush to discard her present habit for something or anything different and start dressing up.'

She tried her best to set a middle course, acknowledging the anxieties of some, the anticipation of others, in a letter of 15 November 1968: 'Some are understandably anxious, doubtful about the future…We must be intelligently measured, act prudently and with good judgement in all the initiatives undertaken [to realise our adapted renewal].' And on 30 November 1968: 'As this kind of chapter is a new experience, we are not finding it as easy as we expected – no one knows all the answers.' Nor did the congregation find all the answers over the course of the following months – or even years.

The renewal chapter, from which so much was expected, opened on 26 June 1969 with seventy-two delegates. For the first time there was outside input, all male: Cecil McGarry SJ, Michael McGough OMI, Seán Fagan SM and Seán O'Riordan CSSR were advisers.

In her final report as superior general Columbanus told the chapter that although there were six hundred and eighty five finally professed sisters, the number of novices and postulants had fallen: there were twenty novices in Monaghan and fourteen in California; five postulants in Monaghan and nine in California. The house in Thier-à-Liège had closed and the numbers in Belgium continued to shrink as the community in Sclessin aged. The congregation needed more sisters for Africa but a shortage of personnel was already beginning to make itself felt: this was partly a result of the badly planned introduction of free education in Ireland in 1967, which greatly increased the numbers of secondary school pupils overnight.

From 7-26 July the renewal chapter sat in general assembly and the commissions reported: a slow, painstaking process of discussion, preparation of texts, amendment, redrafting.

This and subsequent general chapters had an unnamed informal chronicler (not a minute taker), who in this instance reported that the vexed question of religious dress was an obstacle to progress: 'This matter of dress has taken up at least five hours of the assembly's time so far, not to mention the hours spent by the commission in coping with some seventy-five amendments, the largest number submitted on any topic that has been dealt with – and amendments continue to come in, one of the main issues now being whether the sisters shall wear a plain cross, an ordinary crucifix, or a specially designed crucifix incorporating the words *Sint Unum*.'

On Sunday 29 June came the excitement of the election of a new superior general, the first since 1958, which now seemed like a different world. Colmcille Stephens (b. 1926), from Ballyshannon, County Donegal, a science teacher and vice-principal in St Louis High School in Kano, was elected to lead the congregation. Although the choice of Colmcille seems to have been a complete surprise to the chapter, the sisters present had the impression that Columbanus supported her election. She knew Colmcille well, as she had been a pupil in Monaghan when Columbanus was mistress of schools there, and probably felt that she would be a safe pair of hands but young enough at forty-two to be able to move with the times. But it was certainly a departure from tradition that a sister should be elected to office who was not a delegate at the chapter. (Eymard Hartin, one of the pioneers in Nigeria, was the delegate from Kano.)

There are many accounts that relate Colmcille's astonishment (or horror) when the news of her election arrived in Kano, where, the story goes, she was unpacking burettes in the Science labora- tory. 'Are they all gone mad in Monaghan?' she is reputed to have said before, no doubt, recollecting *Dieu le Veult* and bowing to fate. 'Come at once,' the telegram instructed her. Because of the complexities of travel from Nigeria, even with the first-class ticket that her colleagues in Kano persuaded her to buy, Colmcille did not arrive back in Dublin until late on Thursday night, 3 July.

Only on her way through Heathrow did she have access to a telephone and then her protests of her own unsuitability and un- preparedness fell on deaf ears (Columbanus's): 'Not at all, it's all fixed, everyone knows, bishop, communities, your parents, it's in the papers.' And anyway, 'There's no clause for saying no!' (This reconstruction of the conversation courtesy of Gabrielle O'Connell, *Seo agus Siúd*, October 2008) The order's first sight of Colmcille was in Rathmines, where Michèle Harnett, whom she had taught in Dundalk, remembers her being relieved to see a familiar face. Colmcille appeared with Columbanus before the chapter in Monaghan on the afternoon of Friday 4 July. The anonymous chronicler describes her as 'quite calm and courageous in the face of her great new responsibilities.' She was probably still in shock. As she describes it herself: 'It was a difficult time and I didn't know how I would cope with it at all. I didn't feel I had enough experience or knowledge.' Colmcille's experienced council, which included Augustine Moane and Pauline McGovern, gave her some degree of reassurance, but those who knew her well believe that the shock of her appointment took its toll on her health. Máire Cannon remembers tears flowing down her face as she greeted individual members of the community in Monaghan the day after her arrival.

The first session of the renewal chapter ended on 11 August 1969 and the new superior general and her council sent out copies of the acts of the chapter, with commendable speed, on 15 August. Colmcille's accompanying letter urged the sisters to have faith in the future, to 'believe that religious life has the capacity to renew itself' and 'not to waste time in hand-wringing'.

Among the significant changes introduced by this chapter were that 'sisters shall be given the option of returning to their baptismal names, using surnames, where necessary' and 'The sisters may adopt the initials SSL after their names', a practice that has endured to this day. Many sisters had been given names in religion – Derinella (Patricia Moloney) and de Brébeuf (Máire Muldowney) are two that come to mind – that were at the very least unappealing to their recipients. Patricia Moloney recalls that the novices were warned in advance not to cry when they received their names from the mother general at reception, no matter how unwelcome they were. Mochua McNicholas, at the age of ninety-four, remembers 'crying her eyes out' at receiving her name, which turned out to be the pet name of the Irish saint Cronan, her own sister's name in religion. However, Mochua chose not to revert to her baptismal name when the opportunity arose.

Other provisions allowed for free seating in the refectory (greater flexibility and less hierarchy), for sisters to receive and send their letters sealed (greater privacy), for sisters 'to wear special dress for medical studies or for activities like geographical and scientific outings and for physical education' (greater practicality) and for 'community discussion monthly on an experimental basis' (greater democracy). Once they were given permission to think for themselves, sisters were not long in realising that it was not really necessary for an apostolic congregation like the Sisters of St Louis to have such a monastic discipline: one severe constraint, the great silence, was no more.

On the perennially engrossing topic of habit, it was decreed: 'three habits chosen by majority vote of the chapter [which had been modelled and discussed on 20 July] to be worn experimentally during the following year, except in Africa, where three different habits, also chosen by vote, were to be worn experimentally.'

Vatican II encouraged religious orders to reconsider their apostolates and this chapter declared: 'That the special areas of apostolate of the congregation are educational and medical services and that the congregation intends to remain faithful to these works…' but that this commitment 'shall not exclude the possibility of allowing individuals to work in other areas, in which their talents and inclination fit them to give a true apostolic witness.' It took another decade for the congregation to start moving systematically away from the education apostolate in Ireland.

At this chapter the congregation also made the first moves towards a more delegated leadership structure, as urged by Vatican II, establishing the west African region by consolidating three existing areas, northern and western Nigeria and Ghana, with Patricia Moloney as the first regional superior.

Colmcille was accurate in her summary of religious life after Vatican II: 'Our sisters find themselves nowadays in such new situations that legislation covering some areas and individuals is quite unsuited to others. The resulting lighter structures and greater freedom of decision and action mean a tremendous challenge to personal maturity and responsibility.'

A new entrant to the institute, Siobhán Dillon, saw the practical difference for herself between 1968 and 1969. Novices used to have to 'do the top corridor' (make the beds of sisters) in St Louis House in Monaghan, something that was, in reality, 'finding work for novices to do'. This all changed in 1969: the new reality that there would no longer be 'oodles' of postulants and novices needing occupation meant a change in the hierarchical structure of the institute, which, even though it traditionally thought of itself as a family with no lay sisters, had its own pecking order. Michèle Harnett, veil-less in the convent in Dundalk in the summer of 1969, encountered Columbanus, who said to her, 'Sister, put your proper habit on!' Another sister, who heard the rebuke, reassured her: 'Don't worry, she'll be out of office in a week.' And so she was – and Michèle was in Rathmines to see the arrival of Columbanus's successor, who had far bigger things on her mind than veils.

The renewal also had effect outside Ireland. On 27 September 1969 three bicycles for 'recreational use' arrived in the convent in Juilly. This was the Juilly equivalent of the revolution of *mai soixante-huit* in Paris. The annals report that when, earlier on, the local people saw the sisters appearing in their abbreviated habits they thought a new order had moved into the convent.

The second half of the renewal general chapter opened in Monaghan on 7 July 1970. The directives on habit that were issued at the end were more liberal than the previous year's three options. Now all that was asked was that sisters should wear: a St Louis crest (silver) as an identifying emblem; all black (navy blue for California and white for Africa); formal outfit of dress/suit; informal outfit of skirt/pinafore/jerkin/blouse; that knees should be covered when seated; that the veil should fall over the shoulder and be retained by a soft white band…' and that, 'Those who choose to wear the traditional habit should have the support of the community.'

More autonomy was granted to individual communities and their superiors and to individuals within communities. There was much more emphasis on the individual as unique and on the role of each individual in the community. This meant that there was less emphasis on obedience, something that, a number of delegates feared, would lead to indiscipline and difficulties for the superiors of communities. No doubt this fear was realised at times.

The chapter reiterated the priority of the educational and medical missions for the congregation but, significantly, allowed for other apostolates in social areas and mentioned the mission to South America, although without reaching a definite decision on it. On the renewal side, there was an emphasis in both chapters on formation and ongoing development, including missiological studies (on sabbatical) for sisters working on the missions and on retreats, courses in spirituality and theology and renewal programmes. For the first time the formation of junior professed sisters would include a year's theology in Mater Dei Institute or Maynooth University.

Mary Jo Hand remembers that sisters put 'an extraordinary amount of energy' into renewal at this time, participating in courses – some of them intercongregational – in spiritual direction, retreat direction and behavioural sciences, as well as theology, while doing their best to give time and attention to the 'being' or quiet side of their lives in the midst of all the changes.

What is notable about the two chapters of 1969 and 1970 is the amount of work done by the commissions and the assemblies. To be able to produce a coherent volume of acts by 15 August of 1970 is a considerable achievement, even if some of them were tentative. For the changes were only beginning.

11

Change and More Change:
Eoin McCarthy and the General Chapter of 1975

'A superior general is not superhuman.'
Colmcille Stephens, 2011

The 1975 general chapter was held in Kilkeel from 17 July to 4 August with a much smaller attendance than that of 1969-70 – forty delegates. On 26 July the reluctant leader, Colmcille Stephens, was re-elected superior general. A new leader in waiting emerged when Dorothy McCloskey was elected vicar. So far so predictable.

But general chapters were no longer the rubber-stamping affairs they had been up to 1969 and before this chapter academic Eoin McCarthy from Trinity College, Dublin, made his appearance in the life of the institute. One of the characteristics of Colmcille Stephens that made her an appropriate leader for this early period of great change was her willingness to seek guidance and outside help. After the chapter of 1969-70, McCarthy, a consultant in organisational management, was commissioned to review the life and work of the institute. He visited every community, at home and abroad and produced an interim report at the end of 1973, then began a programme of consultation, conferences and training sessions for delegates in preparation for the 1975 chapter.

Eoin McCarthy's interim report provided much food for thought about the situation in the institute three years after the end of the renewal chapter. He commented on the great dedication and generosity of sisters but also observed deep divisions in attitudes to community life and spirituality, as well as generational divisions. Many sisters distrusted their superiors, had little understanding of the management process (if at this stage it was a management process) and were too ready to feel victimised or misunderstood. On the other side, there was little or no training in leadership for local superiors. Several sisters commented to me with a mixture of humour and remembered frustration that Columbanus sometimes appointed sisters as local superiors because she could not think of any other useful job for them to do. Many of her appointees were still in office in the 1970s.

According to McCarthy, sisters were ignorant of the world outside the community's walls and even of the way religious practice had changed in the wider world. Older sisters were resentful and perplexed by the endless and, as they saw it, inconclusive discussions of the younger sisters, which they labelled 'immaturity' or 'inadequate formation'. McCarthy found communities insular and lacking in contact with other houses, with no real concern for their own consœurs who were working abroad as missionaries. There were few sisters ready to make decisions, take the initiative or hold office and he found that sisters had little idea how to reverse the serious decline in vocations.

Eoin McCarthy also commented on the dearth of publications by St Louis sisters, despite their high levels of educational achievement. Even now some sisters claim that the institute was 'anti-intellectual' and that sisters who were academically gifted were not encouraged to make the most of their gifts. It is true that some able sisters spent their lives as teachers and did not get the chance to do higher degrees but it has long ceased to be the case that those who sought educational opportunities were denied them. In any event, such issues must be judged by the norms of Irish society as it was thirty, forty, fifty or more years ago when educational opportunities were limited for everyone and career opportunities for women very limited indeed. Even a glance at the bibliography of this book, with its extensive list of publications by institute members about the institute's history and theology, will help to lay this belief to rest. An earlier St Louis author was Kathleen O'Sullivan who published *A Way of Life: A Human-Spiritual Growth Series for Lay Groups* (1987) and *Light out of Darkness* (1993), a book of prayer and meditation she developed from her retreat work.

In 1975, although there were still more than six hundred finally professed sisters worldwide, other figures reported to the chapter were ominous. There were no novices anywhere in the order and only four postulants, three in Monaghan and one in California. There had been no postulants between 1970 and 1974. These were the grim realities of entry to the order; then there were the exits: sixty sisters had left since the previous chapter. Declining numbers of sisters and rising numbers of secondary school day pupils had led to a great deal of curtailment in the period since 1969: the closure or planned closure of boarding schools at home along with the opening of the first community schools; withdrawal from schools in England and withdrawal/Africanisation in Nigeria. Secular change was conspiring with the directives of Vatican II to change the sisters from a monolithic teaching order into something much more fragmented and vulnerable. The headquarters and beating heart of the institute, Monaghan, had already lost the generalate (the administrative centre of the congregation), which moved to Grosvenor Road, Dublin, in April 1973. It would soon lose the boarding school that had begun in 1861, two years after the arrival of the Dames de St Louis from Juilly.

All in all, there was a great deal of loss and perhaps not enough time or attention given to grieving. For, as Colmcille pointed out in her opening speech to the chapter, it was still an order devoted to work and now it had all the work of change and renewal to see through as well as sisters' everyday labours, professional and domestic. Colmcille, too, had visited all the communities in the previous five years and observed their strengths and weaknesses: 'a high degree of dedication, cooperation and loyalty' but 'a lack of acceptance of one another…a certain preoccupation with success and efficiency in work and a consequent lack of time for and appreciation of reflective living'. She echoed Eoin McCarthy's criticism: 'We suffer also from an immaturity in the exercise of personal responsibility.' Was it any wonder that sisters emerging, dazzled, into the 1970s, who had been trained and disciplined to work and to eschew personal responsibility in favour of unquestioning obedience, would 'suffer' thus? The wonder was that they were as open and positive and adaptable as they proved themselves to be.

Up to this the superior general was the person in charge at chapters. One of the innovations that Eoin McCarthy introduced in 1975 was that the chapter should have different voices and that a different face of the institute should chair the sessions. For this role he chose and inducted two sisters, Anne Murray, from Ireland, and Kristan Schlichte, from California, who were both under the age of thirty. Anne remembers his instructions that they should be ' intentional' and make it clear to the delegates that it was a new system, even including 'traffic lights' to limit the interventions of delegates. She and Kristan were urged to establish their authority on the gathering, lest it 'descend into pre-Vatican II hierarchy'. The first person to break the rule by not stopping at the end of her allotted time was former superior Columbanus. Anne Murray, in the chair at that moment and no doubt quaking in her shoes, had to say to her, 'Mother, stop speaking, please.' Nobody present had ever heard anyone, let alone a young sister, talk to Columbanus like that. Kristan Schlichte remembered that – naturally enough – Columbanus's presence 'continued to be a focal point for the congregation': 'I found myself drawn to her expression for some clue to her opinion on a given topic.' And she had many opinions on the changes, sometimes expressed to Colmcille, especially in the period before the generalate moved to Dublin, in exasperated comments such as: 'Have we to do everything the Jesuits do?'

The chapter considered many possible changes and recommendations, including Number Eight from Eoin McCarthy, which is remembered, ruefully, as a bridge too far: that sisters 'would spend, subject only to limitations of health, a period of up to two months each year formally absent from their communities' in order to experience real life in a variety of social settings. Although the general chapter agreed in theory with this, Anne Murray saw no sign of its being implemented so she and another sister decided that they would go inter-railing and youth hostelling through Europe during their summer holidays, starting off their budget trip by hitching a ride from an obliging cross channel meat lorry, and submitted the proposal under Recommendation Eight. But the aspiring travellers got a letter back from Colmcille that 'regretfully she felt the proposal was unsuitable for consecrated women'. The meat lorry mode of transportation was rejected on grounds of modesty and propriety. Recommendation Eight was never fully implemented.

Among the acts of the chapter of 1975 was a decision to experiment with smaller communities, again in accordance with Eoin McCarthy's interim report and a further report he submitted in May 1975. The motherhouse community in Monaghan was transformed into several smaller communities from the late 1970s and the Wakefield and Sacred Heart communities in Grosvenor Road, Rathmines, offshoots of the very big convent community, date from the late 1970s and early 1980s. The habit was liberalised further: the veil dispensed with for informal occasions and inside the house. Blue was permitted as an alternative to black and beige as an alternative to white. The duration of home visits was to be decided 'at local level'. Sisters in Africa were to make a visit home every two years and from California every three years. In a major departure for sisters trained to believe that a vow of poverty meant having no personal money at all, there were proposals for implementing a personal budget – an annual sum that sisters would receive and from which they would disburse all their expenses: 'It would seem then that action is called for to promote all-round personal maturity, by providing opportunities for added knowledge and experience.'

There was to be a focus on promoting vocations and better management of finances: the potential cost of every decision was to be established before the decision was acted upon (something that, according to Eoin McCarthy, had been noticeably missing in the institute up to this). Gone were the carefree days of Columbanus's or Majella Seery's decisions about Kumasi, Kano or Los Angeles on the basis of faith (or fate) alone. An Irish region was to be established and Ivan Toolan, who had been assistant mistress of novices 1958-70, was chosen for this position, which she fulfilled ably from 1976 until her death in a car accident in April 1980. Some of her major preoccupations were the continued break up of larger communities into smaller, the care of the sick and ageing and educational policy. The English region was established at the same time with Philomena O'Higgins as the first regional superior.

The 1975 chapter presaged the option for the poor that the 1980 and 1985 chapters explicitly adopted by bringing the concept of social justice to the fore – 'That we deepen our understanding of the implications of social justice in the light of the Gospel, the signs of the times and the statements of the magisterium' – and endorsed the imminent establishment of a mission from California to Brazil. Liberation theology, a philosophy no less social and economic then theological, that had its basis in the Vatican II document *Gaudium et Spes* (1965) but especially in the Medellín Conference of 1968, had taken root in Latin America and its influence was beginning to be felt throughout the Catholic world.

What the acts of the chapter do not convey – and what Eoin McCarthy for all his insight and dynamism could not prescribe a practical cure for – was the serious divergence among sisters about the meaning of religious and prayer life and how it should be ritualised. It was difficult to implement change while preserving unity and, according to Anne Murray, who served in regional leadership in the 1980s: 'We developed among ourselves different theologies and spiritualities and it became increasingly difficult for the people who had moved ahead and the people who hadn't moved ahead to talk about these things.' In the 1970s she lived in communities where the Eucharist became a source of division rather than unity: whether it could be celebrated in a circle or always had to have a priest at the top of the church. 'It was difficult to sustain mutual care and respect unless you were willing to give up your point of view and most of those who gave up were the innovators. The principle of compassion for older people influenced the younger sisters as we felt we couldn't deny them the comfort of their belief system in their old age.' There was disagreement about language, about the model of Church, the model of congregation and people's expectations of leadership. Different sisters were at different stages in the journey from before Vatican II – when the Church and the congregation were in reality mediaeval, cloistered and compliant – to after Vatican II. It was a difficult journey for many of them.

Colmcille could not have known that the decline in religious life over which she presided in the 1970s was terminal. She thought that things would stabilise, that numbers would improve when people got used to the new way of doing things, that religious life 'would rise up again'. Democracy is difficult for people who have spent years living in an autocratic system, as the post-communist world has shown us. The revolutions of the 1960s in the US, in Paris, in Prague, in Northern Ireland – and in the Vatican – brought a new political consciousness. Colmcille's style of leadership and her personality were different from those of her predecessor: she was by nature a person conscious of her own fallibility, who consulted and sought consensus: 'A superior general is not superhuman.' Managing changes that were both wide-ranging and profound while keeping the St Louis ship afloat was the challenge of her time in office. Dorothy McCloskey went a step further in the 1980s, challenging the institute in different ways.

12

Liberation Theology and the Mission to Brazil

When your ship
begins to put down roots
in the stagnant water by the quay:
put out to sea!
Hélder Câmara (1909-99), 'A Prayer for Every Day'

Vatican II, especially the conciliar documents *Lumen Gentium* (1964) *and Gaudium et Spes* (1965), opened the door to liberation theology, although the Churchmen who drafted them could have had little idea how wide open this door would blow. The 1960s were a decade of revolution and opposition to injustice in many parts of the world, including countries of South and Central America. But Brazil had a military dictatorship from 1964 to 1985, after a left-wing government was overthrown by a coup. In other Latin American countries, as in Francoist Spain, the hierarchy supported right-wing dictators and upheld the status quo: in Brazil many theologians and bishops and their followers became revolutionaries in the name of Christ.

A key development was the conference of Latin American bishops, held in the Colombian city of Medellín in 1968. In their statement at the end of the conference the bishops unequivocally took the side of those who 'hunger and thirst after justice', asserting *that* the Christ was made flesh 'to liberate everyone from the slavery to which sin has subjected them: hunger, misery, all oppression and ignorance, in a word, that injustice and hatred which have their origin in human selfishness. Thus, for our authentic liberation, all of us need a profound conversion so that "the kingdom of justice, love and peace," might come to us.' The conference declared: '…it is indispensable to form a social conscience and a realistic perception of the problems of the community and of social structures...This task of *concientización* and social education ought to be integrated into joint pastoral action at various levels.' (Brazilian educator Paolo Freire had coined the word 'conscientisation' two years earlier in his hugely influential *Pedagogy of the Oppressed.*)

Almost three decades after religious orders adopted the preferential option for the poor – a phrase itself derived from liberation theology – it is hard to imagine how revolutionary these prescriptions were and how dangerous they sounded to more conservative Churchmen. Works by the Peruvian, Gustavo Gutierrez, especially *Teología de la Liberación* (*A Theology of Liberation: History, Politics, Salvation*: Lima, 1971), which named the concept, and Brazilian theologian Leonardo Boff (among others), provided the analysis, biblical underpinning and intellectual perspective of liberation theology, which was as much a mass Church movement as a theology. Cardinal Arns of São Paulo and the poet-Bishop of Recife, Hélder Câmara, were two members of the hierarchy who put the theories into practice. Not all religious in Brazil adopted liberation theology: there were still traditional orders with private, prestigious schools, that were close to the rich and powerful. Boff claimed that the roots of what he taught were in the Vatican II document *Lumen Gentium* (1964) but before too long liberation theology went too far for the Vatican, whose spokesmen called it 'Marxist', silenced some theologians and began to replace the radical bishops with safer men.

The newly elected John Paul II attended the Puebla (Mexico) conference of 1979 and his opening speech attempted to stem the tide of political 'rereadings' of liberation theology, which he said were erroneous: 'Christ as a political figure, a revolutionary, as the subversive of Nazareth, does not tally with the Church's catechesis.' At the end of the conference liberationist theologians produced an alternative set of documents reasserting the validity of liberation theology, thereby diluting the impact of the official consensus. The names Medellín and Puebla are often on the lips of devotees of liberation theology.

While Margie Buttita was in school in Louisville, Woodland Hills, California, she decided to become a missionary to Latin America and intended to join the Maryknoll congregation, which had a wide mission outreach. Ronan McDonnell and other sisters in Louisville assured her that the St Louis congregation would in the future have a mission in South America. Margie joined up, went to college, taught in three grade schools and waited until 1976 for the mission to start.

When Brazil was eventually named as the area of new mission for the California region, the most eager aspiring missionary was incredulous. New York born, of Italian extraction, she had learned Spanish and assumed that with the great choice of countries in Latin America, a hispanophone region would be chosen. Antonia Byrne from the Californian community had done some research on Columbia and Peru – but Portuguese-speaking Brazil it was to be.

Margie is still not sure why Brazil was chosen but thinks it was as a result of the Irish genius for connection. Three sisters had brothers serving as priests there: Joan Kavanagh, Breda O'Hanrahan and Teresa McMahon. The Bishop of Miracema, the diocese in which Barrolandia, the first foundation, is situated, was a Kerry-born Redemptorist, James ('Dom Jaime') Collins. Later she was glad the mission was to Brazil as liberation theology had originated there and at that time it had the most radical hierarchy in the Catholic world. The need for missionaries in education, parish work and basic Christian communities was enormous. Everything about Brazil was (and is) vast: its size, its population, its cities and the gap between rich and poor, city dwellers and remote rural villages.

Founding a mission in Brazil was certainly discussed at the general chapter of 1970. According to Triona McGinty, at that time a science teacher in Louisville, Catherine Foley, who attended the chapter, told her that although Californian sisters wanted to start a mission in South America they were instructed at the chapter to send sisters to Africa instead as there were already missions there. It seems likely that the congregation as a whole had too much on its plate, implementing the *aggiornamento* prescribed by Vatican II while losing personnel, to have corporate energy for a new mission. Triona was missioned to Ghana and taught science and religion in Kumasi, 1971-3. It was not until the 1975 general chapter that the mission to Brazil was agreed by the congregation as a whole. Gradually the ties that bound the congregation tightly in on itself were loosening: this was evident in the new regional structures, the break up of large communities and the greater degree of personal autonomy that began to be allowed around this time. California was given its head. Canice Durkan became regional in 1975 and it was she who did the final organisation and the missioning of the sisters who left for Rio de Janeiro.

Thirteen sisters volunteered for Brazil and three were chosen, one American and two Irish: Margie, Catherine Foley, who was to be the superior of the foundation, and Maura Clerkin, who had been through the juniorate in Cushendall and entered in California the same year as Margie. They were all teachers – Catherine had been a school principal – and had no pastoral experience or formation as ministers. The only theology they knew was what they had learned during their own formation. Not to mention that they had not a word of Portuguese between them. But they would learn everything quickly in Brazil.

The three pioneers left Los Angeles on 29 November 1976. They planned to minister not in a big city but in the small town of Barrolandia in Tocantins, the north-central region of the country, 1000 km due north of Brasilia, on the edge of the Amazon basin. After two months of familiarisation with Portuguese and their new apostolate (although, in keeping with tradition, the convent was not ready) they went back to Rio de Janeiro for the four months initiation course for missionaries from abroad in CENFI (*Centro de Formação Integral*), along with sixty other missionaries from all over the world. The centre is run by the Latin American Episcopal Conference (*Consejo Episcopal Latinoamericano*).

At CENFI the sisters learned Portuguese and had lectures on history, economy and politics, on basic Christian communities, on conscientisation, on teaching the Bible – all from a liberation theology perspective. As part of the programme they stayed for a while with a Brazilian family. What Catherine, Margie and Maura learned from their training in liberation theology was that they should work with the people, not dominate them, not work out of their own experience and try to impose it, go in humbly and listen to the people's own story, including their indigenous culture. They were to become 'inserted' or 'inculturated' in the reality of the people.

The pioneers opened the new convent in Barrolandia on 25 August 1977, to scenes of huge celebration and *festa* among the local people. Barrolandia was poor and the sisters' life there was simple, but simplicity – the poverty of the Church – was also a requirement of liberation theology. Electricity supply was intermittent; there was no television, no newspapers, no banks, no telephone in the house, only short-wave radio. The school had oil lights. Water was scarce in the dry season. For the first five years they were more or less cut off from the outside world, even after they got a car, but they were sustained by the faith, spirituality and hospitality of the rural people and their enthusiastic commitment to liberation theology. The bishop gave the sisters permission to do baptisms and marriages and one Sunday a month crowds of people would come to be married or bring babies to be baptised, although in that *machista* society they had to get used to women having such a big role in the Church.

Maura and Margie especially wanted to be involved in pastoral work, empowerment of women, basic Christian communities: the last thing they wanted to do was teach. Maura had taught in the prosperous parish of Pacific Palisades before she came to Brazil and felt called to something more challenging than education. But teaching was what the people of Barrolandia wanted of them – no fees involved – so all three sisters went back to school. There was one school for a town of five thousand people and it was populated day and night; by night the adults came after their day's work. The school, not the church, was, the sisters discovered, the centre of the parish: for meeting, for planning, for courses, for training of lay ministers. Margie taught for nine years and Maura was director of the school for six. Catherine was the secretary until she went back to California four years later and all three were involved in training teachers, some of whom had little education themselves. Some salary was paid by the government, little and often late, and much of the funding for the mission came from Adveniat, a German Catholic charity for Latin America, and the Latin American Relief Organisation, as well as the congregation and Friends of St Louis Missions at home.

Coming from gender conscious California it was a shock to be in such a *machista* society, liberation theology or not. Margie, who had thought of becoming a Maryknoll sister, had her wish when she worked with them for a period in São Paulo. The Maryknoll sisters were 'good at feminism' she says, and she was also influenced by Brazilian ecofeminist theologian, Ivone Gebara, whom she heard speaking several times.

In the 1980s the Catholic Church saw the main source of injustice in Brazil as land ownership. Lack of land was creating exclusion and marginalisation and contributing to the exodus from rural areas and the growth of *favelas* (shanty towns) around the cities. Maura Clerkin became involved on the ground, accompanying the local people as they fought for their land, many families living in roadside campsites awaiting their *terrinha*. She became a member of the Catholic bishops' Pastoral Land Commission (CPT) and made herself unpopular with the mayor and the people of property in Barrolandia. It was, says Maura, 'a marvellous time to be Church without being Church'. For her and her consœurs in Brazil, the option for the poor of the general chapter of 1985 was 'absolutely appropriate'.

After a sabbatical in Berkeley in spirituality and liberation theology, Maura returned to Brazil and was invited to work in CENFI, which had moved to Brasilia. Her six years there were a rich experience. She chose to go back to active ministry in Brazil after spending some years in Ireland for family reasons, working in prison ministry and the Pastoral Land Commission for a further five years.

Ann Matthews taught in Monaghan for twelve years and like Maura Clerkin felt keenly the systemic inequalities of traditional education, something that called her to liberation theology and the example of Katey Dougan and Anne Staunton, who preceded her on the mission to Brazil. She counts among those who had a strong influence on her theologian Eamonn Bredin, who taught her in

Mount Oliver, and his book *Disturbing the Peace: the Way of Disciples* (1985) and among her heroes Hélder Câmara and Pedro Casaldaliga, bishop of São Felix do Araguaia, the next diocese to Miracema, who had a price on his head because he was involved in the land war and whom she considers an uncanonised saint. It was Ann who quoted the lines by Câmara at the top of this chapter.

What she remembers from her period in CENFI in 1990 was feeling marginalised and powerless because she could not speak Portuguese, which she says was a good training for working among the disempowered. She spent six years in Barrolandia, mostly working in the parish, doing liturgies and giving the sacraments, and some time in the other two houses, in Colméia and Goiânia. It was the period when the mission was strongest, with twelve sisters. She remembers Carmel Mary McCarthy, who came to Barrolandia from California in 1980, as having a particular gift for bringing leaders on, which must surely be one of the key skills for the implementation of liberation theology. Carmel Mary died in 2001 after returning to Ireland. Maureen Smith, a nurse who had spent twenty years in Africa, came to provide healthcare and training in Barrolandia, where there was no resident doctor at the time. Maureen returned to Ireland in 1984 and died in 1985. The Brazilian mission suffered more than its share of loss, with the deaths of Katey Dougan in 2010 and Helen Regan in 2011, as well as Carmel Mary and Maureen.

The second St Louis foundation in Brazil, established by Margie Buttita, Carmel Mary McCarthy and Judy Dieterle in 1981, was in Colméia, 100 km north of Barrolandia, and the work there was in catechesis, developing leadership and basic Christian communities. Several sisters continued to work in land agitation. This community closed in 1992 and that same year Helen Regan moved to São Paulo. In March 1988 Brazil became a region of its own, which facilitated sisters from all parts of the institute coming to work there. Katey Dougan and Ghanaian sister Bernice Broohm opened a community in Palmas, a new city which had attracted a huge inward migration but without the infrastructure or services to cater for them. There was not even a parish at the beginning, and the city did not belong to any diocese. It was truly pioneering work in which the sisters journeyed with the local people, trying to improve their living conditions, health and education and facilitate the empowerment of women. This house closed in 2004.

Judy Dieterle came from Barrolandia and Margaret Hosty from California and opened a house in Vera Cruz, on the outskirts of the city of Goiânia, in 1986. It was conceived as a formation house for the two Brazilian novices at the time, Elenice Natal de Lima and Raimunda Bispo, both teachers: as it was near a big city it was hoped that they would have better opportunities for intercongregational formation and continuing education. The novices joined in the sisters' pastoral, education and health ministry and some associates came to live and work with the sisters in Vera Cruz for a time.

At a deeper level, the logic of liberation theology is that lay people can do the work of the Church so the goal of religious should be to make themselves redundant as soon as possible. This tension may well have worked against vocations in Brazil but the scarcity of native sisters was more likely a result of the *zeitgeist*. Several postulants started out with the sisters and at one time there was hope for a strong and growing native sisterhood in Brazil, a necessity for the long-term survival of the mission. Raimunda left the congregation after two years. Suely Marinho de Sousa made her profession in 2002. She spent two years between Nigeria and Ghana, where she had to adapt to a totally different system of Church and religious life, without the liberation theology, hoping in vain that some west African sisters, who were youthful and energetic, might go out to Brazil to form a community with her. Suely spent more than seven years with the congregation before leaving in 2004.

Margie Buttita's opinion is that the congregation delayed too long and the sisters were too old by the time they began the mission to Brazil. It takes time and personnel to build up vocations and do formation and as the experience in west Africa shows, vocations can be slow to establish and there can be fallow periods. None of the congregations in Brazil, even the native ones, have many vocations.

In 1995 Margaret Hosty founded the AAVE group in Goiânia: AIDS: *Apoio, Vida, Esperança* – AIDS, Support, Life, Hope – an

NGO in solidarity with carriers or people living with carriers of HIV/AIDS. The group offers counselling, literacy education and services to approximately three hundred families, all of whom have at least one carrier of the virus and sometimes more. It also took on preventative work – 'to get there before the virus'. The bishops' conference asked it to coordinate the hierarchy's AIDS pastoral programme in the central western region of Brazil and to train leaders to carry on the work of the programme.

Helen Regan was a real pioneer, as her account about her early days in a shanty town of the crowded, polluted, dangerous city of São Paulo attests. She first went to Brazil in 1989 but, even after spending several years in the poverty of the interior state of Tocantins, it was hard for her to adjust to the precariousness of life in São Paulo with its guns, drug crime and casual violence. One of the biggest cities in the world, it has unimaginable extremes of wealth and poverty but Helen wanted to go where no one else wanted to go and minister to those among whom nobody wanted to be. She lived alone in São Paulo and worked with children who were carriers of HIV/AIDS, then established a HIV/AIDS project called *Bem-Me-Quer* (Care Well for Me) in 1996. She coordinated this project until shortly before her death, as well as doing parish work and catechesis in her own impoverished area of the city. She left Brazil because of a serious illness and died in Ireland on 10 September 2011.

Other sisters came from Ireland, England, California and Ghana to work in Brazil for shorter periods. It did not suit everyone and by this time there was no question of sisters simply being missioned somewhere without consultation, as happened earlier on with California, and having to make the best of it. Liberation theology asked a lot of those who ministered in Brazil, and while this was also true of the missions in Africa and California, in the earlier missions sisters were supported by community, by a strong sense of tradition and by the structures of the Church, which were not all that different whether one was in Monaghan, Kano or Woodland Hills. To thrive in Brazil, one had to be self-reliant, physically robust and committed to *la linea* of liberationist thought.

Máire Muldowney was moved by the option for the poor to

volunteer for Brazil in 1986, feeling that more was being asked of her than teaching art in the comfort of St Louis High School in Rathmines. She spent three years in Colméia at a time when the mission was strong and there were several houses but found she was not cut out for preaching to basic Christian communities and teaching English to large numbers of adults in a school without electricity. Máire's life in Colméia was not made any easier by the fact that she broke her ankle by falling over the dog the night she arrived. If there is one thing liberation theology requires it is mobility: necessary for insertion and inculturation, not to mention bringing the Church to the people. After her return to Dublin Máire taught art to second-chance students in Youth Horizons and worked in chaplaincy, as well as devoting time to her own painting, a process that culminated in her successful exhibition of 2011.

When Bláthnaid McCauley took early retirement as primary school principal in Newmarket, Katey Dougan, who had belonged to the English region, suggested that she go to Brazil. Bláthnaid had been involved vicariously in Katey's apostolate through fundraising. Wisely she went on a trial period of three months and spent some time in all the houses that were then open. But she had a health problem that flared up when she was in Brazil and her doctor advised against her staying there. She admits that she was relieved at some level to have to come home and find her own ministry, which turned out to be chaplaincy in the universities in Brighton: 'I wish I had gone to Brazil years earlier and maybe then I could have worked with Katey among the poorest of the poor.'

When the sisters left Barrolandia, feeling that their work there was done, there were eighty lay people working in the parish. An Irish priest, who came to minister there after they left and who did not agree with their approach, said that it 'took him two years to dismantle the structures they had created'. The same thing happened in other areas of the country: Hélder Câmara in Recife was replaced by a conservative bishop; Ivone Gebara was silenced by the Vatican for a period. The long papacy of John Paul II was not favourable to liberationist thought, nor, it seems, is that of his successor.

13

The Preferential Option for the Poor

'A conversion of minds and attitudes'
Evangelica Testificatio

Colmcille Stephens's final report as superior general, to the 1980 general chapter, told a continuing story of attrition, this time the ageing of the congregation manifesting itself in the fact that thirty-one sisters had died since 1975, while nineteen had left. Ireland had only one novice, while Nigeria had nine in formation between postulants and novices. Consultant Eoin McCarthy had helped with implementation of the acts of the 1975 chapter, until his sudden death at the age of fifty-one in December 1977, and Colmcille paid tribute to his significant contribution to modernisation.

Liam McKenna SJ and Luis Dolan CP, an Argentinian who worked with the Better World Movement, also contributed expertise. The BWM had its origins in the theories of Italian Jesuit Riccardo Lombardi in the 1950s; by the 1970s it had become part of the post-Vatican II renewal movement of the Church, broadening its remit to issues of participation and justice and creating pastoral projects for young people, families, ministries and religious institutes.

Jack Wilcox, an American priest who was also involved with the BWM, was the consultant for the chapter and the thirty-nine delegates met in Maynooth in July and August 1980. Elizabeth Moran SSC was facilitator. It is in the documents of the 1980 chapter that one can read explicit reference to *Evangelica Testificatio* (*Evangelical Witness*), Paul VI's apostolic exhortation of 1971 ('on the renewal of the religious life according to the teaching of the Second Vatican Council'). As well as *Perfectae Caritatis*, *Evangelica*

Testificatio built on the conciliar document *Lumen Gentium* which advocated 'love for the whole mystical body of Christ, especially for its poor and sorrowing members and for those who are suffering persecution for justice's sake' and *Gaudium et Spes* ('that both the justice and love of Christ toward the poor might be developed everywhere').

The Berger Methodology of Prospective Planning was the chosen *modus operandi* of the 1980 chapter and, in part, of the 1985 chapter, and sisters were offered training in the system in advance. This methodology, devised by the French philosopher and development consultant Gaston Berger in the 1950s and 1960s, was popular among religious congregations in the 1970s and 1980s, especially those facilitated by consultants of the Better World Movement. It avoided extrapolating the future on the basis of present reality, instead visualising a desired future and, working backwards, determining the steps to bring it about. For religious orders at the time it was a useful and positive technique: instead of concentrating on decline and more decline (extrapolation from the present) it focused the gaze of the membership several steps ahead (a desired future). At the very least it had the effect of making congregations feel that they were more in charge of their own destiny.

The general chapters of 1980 and 1985 changed the focus of the congregation from gloomy prospects of decline, curtailment and contraction to a radical counter cultural mission. The acts of the 1980 chapter, under the heading 'Our Desired Future', include a policy statement, 'a preferential option for the poor': 'In response to the Church's call to answer 'the cry of the poor', this chapter resolves: 'that we have, and are seen to have, a preferential option for the poor. This call requires of us [quoting from *Evangelica Testificatio*]: "a conversion of minds and attitudes…a liberation from all temporal encumbrances". It is a call to love; that we inform ourselves of the "personal distress and collective misery of the poor"; in our daily lives we give proof, even externally, of authentic St Louis poverty.' In the years between the 1980 and 1985 general chapters, the new superior general made repeated reference to the congregation's 'desired future', doing her best to keep the memory of the chapter and its policy statement alive in the congregation: 'What we are trying to do is to find ways of building a bridge between the present and the possible, not only dreaming of the possible but getting there.' (*Newsletter*, June 1984)

Dorothy McCloskey (1929-1990), who was elected superior general in succession to Colmcille at the 1980 general chapter was a Dubliner from a comfortable middle class background and an only child. She inherited from her parents a great love of music and she was a gifted cellist, pianist and organist. It was as a music teacher that some sisters had their first encounter with Sister Ambrose, as she was known in religion, in Kiltimagh. She was personally reserved and private, not warm, charismatic or persuasive in the usual sense of those words but she had courage, determination and vision in abundance and sisters who lived or taught with her in the community in Kiltimagh recall her responding enthusiastically to the call to renewal of Vatican II in both intellectual and practical ways, a course of action, of 'being Church' in which she never wavered. Hugh McTigue, who became the first lay principal of Kiltimagh, marvelled at her vision of leadership of the institute in 1980: 'the clarity with which she saw the future and the logic with which she had organised her anticipation of it'. Not only did she have vision, she had equipped herself with skills for management and organisation by studying for a Master's Degree in Organisational Behaviour in the Irish Management Institute (IMI). She was an intellectual, with an intellectual's logic and rigour.

Many sisters struggled with the option for the poor even after the 1985 chapter reiterated it, unsure of how to apply it to their own lives. But the leadership of the congregation took it seriously and it influenced policy decisions from 1980 onwards: to move to Colméia in Brazil for community ministry; to open a novitiate in Goiânia 'to train Brazilians to respond to the needs of the poor'; to establish a community in Jobstown, a burgeoning public housing area in Dublin, in 1985; to begin a community in the impoverished suburb of Nima in Accra in 1984 and to work with the destitute in Majidun, Lagos. The idea of having associates came from the 1980 chapter:

again this is a 'desired future', the continuation of the charism of the congregation by lay people. America was the first region to begin an associate movement, in 1984, something that pleased Dorothy greatly. The desirability of a strong associate movement was emphasised again at the 1985 chapter.

After the 1980 general chapter, an apostolate reorganisation committee (ARC) was established in each region. Anita Muldowney chaired the Irish committee, which prepared a report dealing with issues such as the curtailment of various education apostolates and the development of management structures in secondary schools, parish ministry, the formation of new communities and formation training. The priority was the insertion of sisters into parishes and communities although the congregation, even then, did not have enough womanpower to fill all the roles on which they focused.

On her visitations to all the regions during her first term as superior general Dorothy repeatedly urged the congregation to continue to 'work for justice, peace and freedom', declaring that the sisters were being faithful to the order's charism by doing this, asserting that they were addressing the evils of their era just as Louis Bautain (and Mère Thérèse de la Croix) would want to 'address the evils of his time'.

Dorothy challenged the sisters in many uncomfortable ways, not least about the jobs they were doing in traditional ministries. In June 1984, when a recession was raging in Ireland, with public indebtedness rather than bank indebtedness at its core, she asked the sisters in the *St Louis Newsletter*: 'Are we holding on to works where there are redundancies? If so, are we sure that what we bring to these works is an added dimension of hope and strength for the future that could justify our being there?' She acknowledged in the following issue of the newsletter that this challenge had been met by 'puzzlement – even anger'.

Conversion has the connotation of a Damascene bolt of lightning but in reality, like all human change, and particularly when systemic change is in question, it is more likely to be a gradual, maybe lengthy process. Dorothy had a qualification in organisational change but it seems that in her decade at the helm she was impatient for conversion and did not always succeed in bringing the membership of the institute with her. In earlier decades sisters were missioned to supply the teaching needs of the congregation's schools but in the 1980s they were challenged to move in the opposite direction. It is small wonder that some sisters, trained for the education apostolate and envisaging it as their lifetime's work, were resistant to this challenge. This policy, arising from the 1980 and 1985 general chapters, in combination with falling numbers and ageing personnel, hastened the exodus of sisters from schools in Ireland. Teaching was seen as a job that a lay person could just as easily undertake, while parish work in a remote town like Barrolandia or in a leprosarium in Akure might still demand the dedication and self-sacrifice of a religious.

For many Irish educators and parents, the premature departure of religious of all congregations from the educational apostolate was a great loss. Over and over again past pupils and sisters themselves remarked to me what wonderful teachers the Sisters of St Louis were, and many sisters I spoke to confirmed that they loved teaching, at whichever level they practised it. Winifred Ojo says, 'We were founded for education but after 1985 it seemed as if everyone had to move out of education, as if we were not for the poor if we were in education. Some of us didn't see it as either/or. Now there is a better reconciliation.'

Anne Jordan, who worked as a teacher during this period, thinks that Dorothy McCloskey 'did not fully understand how locked into education we were.' Some sisters wished to remain teaching and considered it a valid ministry – and, after all, do the poor not need education too? For Anne, 'the fact that we were trustees of the schools was a huge tie and it has taken until very recently to divest ourselves of this role [through the Le Chéile trust].' But it seems more likely not that Dorothy lacked understanding (of this or of any other issue) but that she believed that a different type of ministry, more in keeping with the option for the poor, was a matter of congregational choice and personal agency.

The focus of the general chapter of 1985 was: 'How can we, Sisters of St Louis, confront in a relevant, creative, Gospel way, the issues and evils of today?' and the practical thrust: 'We want to move much further and more fully into the living out of the mission statement of 1980, with the following development in the 1980 chapter plan: 'How we live: our lifestyle has strong monastic roots. We need to try to allow a religious lifestyle to evolve (to foster it too) that is more in keeping with the mission of an apostolic congregation: communities that are open and available to those whom we serve.'

The venue for the 1985 chapter was Kilkeel, where Dorothy had been principal until she was elected vicar in 1975. Her preparation for the 1985 chapter shows her to have been phenomenally industrious and efficient; she seems to have organised everything personally, down to the catering and photocopying. Noel Kerins SSC, Elizabeth Moran and Sylvia Diamond OP acted as consultants to central administration and also at the chapter itself. Elizabeth Moran facilitated the chapter.

The letter of convocation specified that the methodology to be used was a combination of the prospective method (used for the 1980 general chapter), focusing on apostolic mission, and social analysis, 'a systemic way of examining a local or regional situation, in order to discern that situation for the purpose of apostolic vision'.

Social analysis originated in the Latin American context as a means for ordinary and disempowered people to gain power in oppressive situations. It is usually part of a facilitated group process to enable the group to make important decisions for action. The steps of social analysis involve collecting data – historical, geographical, economic, cultural, political and social – in the area being studied, then reflecting on the discoveries in the light of the Gospel, while allowing oneself to be touched and converted so that the outcome is experiential rather than theoretical or academic.

Dorothy McCloskey was re-elected superior general on 2 August 1985. The concept of a central leadership team originated in the 1985 chapter and the team assembled in January 1986: the superior general, two assistants, a general bursar and a general secretary living and working together in the generalate in 5 Grosvenor Road in Dublin. It was decided that the term of office of the superior general and council would revert to six years to allow more time for planning and implementation of the mission and to alleviate pressure on the leadership and expense for the congregation.

There is a reference in an informal account of the general chapter to the preferential option for the poor which was mandated in 1980 chapter but 'was either disowned or ignored after no attempt was made to implement the concept' – the view of an unnamed chronicler for whom the pace of change was too slow. In other areas too, there was frustration: the Californian sisters expressed most clearly their sense that the Church had not adopted the collegial model that Vatican II had espoused but was continuing in the male hierarchical tradition, with priests and bishops feeling threatened by educated female religious. Sisters in California at this time were leaving the education ministry and, with the great variety of courses on offer in the US, studying theology, spirituality and psychotherapy.

After much discussion and many drafts the following mission statement was eventually accepted unanimously by the forty-three delegates at the chapter: 'We sisters of St Louis pledge ourselves to live God's love for the poor and to stand in solidarity with them. In fidelity to the Church and to our founders, we challenge ourselves to respond to the radical call to conversion which is at the heart of the Gospel, and so to growing freedom, courage and resourcefulness in answering the cry of the poor. Through all our ministries, old and new, we resolve to become agents of change in struggling to transform unjust structures and to promote reconciliation. Listening to Christ in each other, we become a household of disciples, a community in the service of the mission entrusted to Him by the Father.'

In September 1985 the enactments of the general chapter as well as revisions to the constitution and directory were circulated. The enactments were contained in a slim document of six pages carrying the mission statement and another document entitled, 'The desired future statement from the 1980 general chapter modified in the light of our mission statement (1985)...Our communities where, in faith, we have freely chosen to live together in honesty, trust, love and mutual acceptance are centres of continual renewal. Speaking the truth in love, we challenge one another to respond to our vocation.' This is the Berger methodology in action.

The new constitution was accepted by Rome in 1988.

Delegates to the chapter brought home the mission statement and their sense of the leadership's determination to implement it but not all members received the news with enthusiasm, just as they had been slow to respond to a similar challenge after the 1980 general chapter. Anne Kavanagh was a delegate and elected to the leadership team in 1985 but although she favoured the option for the poor she feels in retrospect that the leadership was too radical in the way it presented the mission to the congregation. Mary Jo Hand was a delegate at the 1985 chapter and superior of the community in Rathmines at the time. In her view the option for the poor came upon the congregation 'a bit suddenly'. It would have been better if there had been more preparation and if it had started with the grass roots and moved up gradually. The delegates at the chapter had high ideals and the consultants, like Elizabeth Moran, were 'steeped in the option for the poor', but, according to Mary Jo, there was a gap between the leadership and ordinary members of the congregation. Many were not ready to hear the mission statement and she is conscious that perhaps the delegates 'mistold it' when they returned to their communities. For her, 'It's a conversion more than anything else and a conversion doesn't happen at a chapter, it's more a form of grace.' On the other hand, she thinks, 'although we didn't accept it notionally well, it seeped through to individuals.'

It certainly affected the choice of ministry of the congregation, as the 1980 chapter had already done. In 1986 Mary Fallon established St Mary's Community Centre for the poor and elderly of Rathmines in Richmond Hill and moved to live near it, in Mountpleasant Avenue. She continued this apostolate until 2001. In the same year sisters opened a new community in Oakland Park, Cox's Demesne, a local authority estate in Dundalk. It was described as 'the neediest area of Dundalk' in the social analysis carried out by the Irish region. Clare Ryan still lives and works in Cox's Demesne, in a house in Cedarwood Park where she established a prayer and healing centre in the service of the local people. A new community was established in 37 Beresford Street in inner city Dublin where from 1989, Magdalena Gunn, Carmel Woods and Consilii O'Shaughnessy provided courses for the community in prayer, literacy, embroidery and art, among other things. This was as a result of an approach by Christopher Twomey OFM of Halston Street parish. (Carmel, alone by then, left the house in spring 2011.) The congregation also became stakeholders in the new parish, primary school and community school of Blakestown in west Dublin in 1987.

Betty Dalton was appointed regional superior in west Africa in 1986. She feels that the option for the poor, which she entirely supported, did set up a certain tension between people who were working hard in the schools and others who 'went off trying out different things'. The teachers 'felt neglected, under-appreciated and out of fashion'. The African sisters were 'not too hung up on' the option for the poor. 'They felt it would be a nice sideline but that it would not put bread and butter on the table. It did not become the mainstream in Nigeria but did become part of the yardstick for measuring whether to undertake an apostolate or for evaluating the success of an apostolate.'

The issue of putting bread and butter on the table applied too in Ireland. Sisters who went to work in parishes or in projects for the poor after the general chapters of 1980 and 1985 were for the most part unsalaried or received just a small stipend. They could not have made the decision to move out of education if other sisters had not kept their salaried jobs in schools. Besides, those who stayed in teaching were active in their local communities through agencies like the St Vincent de Paul Society, or women's groups such as Dóchas in Monaghan, of which Anne Jordan and Máire Cannon were founder members. Some of them organised second-chance education after school hours.

In Betty Dalton's period as west African regional 1986-89 she tried 'to get people to let people do something along the lines of the option for the poor as an attachment to their core business'. Just 'letting people' was not Dorothy McCloskey's way: 'When I reflect on the statement of mission that we have adopted for ourselves I get a sense of the enormity of the challenge of it: that we should 'become a household of disciples, a community in the service of a mission…I want to see any new community strongly reflect our preferential option for the poor. I would also see apostolic mobility as essential if we are to be of real service in today's world.' (*Newsletter*, 1985)

A more feminine, collaborative, form of leadership was beginning in the congregation but the challenging energy of the 1980 and 1985 mission statements was intellectual and masculine.

St Louis Sisters had just the year previously made the first serious and systematic study of their charism. Many of them now puzzled about the connection between the option for the poor and the vision of Louis Bautain and his followers. In *Link* magazine of Christmas 1990, Pauline McGovern, one of the institute's theologians, addresses this concern. Quoting from the St Louis constitution of 1844, she places the congregation, then and now, 'on the borderline where Church and world meet'. The renewed St Louis Institute, like the new St Louis foundation of 1844, should, in the words of the original constitution, 'harmonise with the movement of the age, respond to its needs, understand it in depth, feel with it, and thus direct it more surely…'

'If the St Louis Institute is at one with the Church, it will, like the Church of today, [discover] 'the face of evil chiefly in structures of injustice which hold millions everywhere in bondage, at local and global levels. Response to this structural injustice, the real meaning of the option for the poor, is inescapable for the Church as an agent of prophecy and healing.'

But, no doubt echoing the hope of many of her consœurs, Pauline expresses the desire that in the forthcoming general chapter (of 1991) the mission statement would contain more definition and detail: 'Which of us has not felt that ideals like "answering the cry of the poor" and "struggling to transform unjust structures" seem either too general or too global to hold a great deal of meaning?'

Dedicated as she was to the congregation and to furthering the option for the poor, much of Dorothy McCloskey's second term of office was overshadowed by the cancer that was diagnosed in 1987:

by pain, by severe treatment, both chemotherapy and radiation, and by terrible sickness, although she did have periods of remission. The leadership team of Dorothy, Miriam Thérèse O'Brien and Anne Kavanagh living in community together would have been an intense and intimate experience at the best of times but must have become almost unbearably stressful after it became clear that Dorothy's illness was terminal. Betty Foley of Rathmines community wrote in a commemorative publication after her death: 'Your sickness filled the house, Dorothy, spilled out into every room, into the hall and out the opening door. Silently and unobtrusively they revolved around your sickness...'

Dorothy's approach was to challenge rather than mandate, calling on sisters to establish new ministries with the poor and new community lives to fit these ministries, even if this meant living alone or in small groups among those they served. The sisters in Brazil, imbued with liberation theology, were certainly living the mission statement from the beginning. Dorothy visited the Brazilian novitiate in Goiânia with great joy in 1988. She went on visitation to France the summer before she died, and the new community established in Moissy-Cramayel in 1990 was a project close to her heart. Everywhere she went – to England, to Africa and California – she challenged the sisters to live the option for the poor. She spent the last months of her life in St Louis Nursing Home in Monaghan and died on 20 December 1990, a few months before the general chapter of 1991 would have brought her term as superior to a natural end.

The 1991 general chapter, acknowledging from experience the real vulnerability of a central leadership team with three members if one were to get ill, elected four sisters to leadership: Anne Kavanagh as congregational leader, with Bridget Ehlert, Anne Murray and Marion Reynolds. All were committed to continuing the option for the poor and the process of change but without Miriam Thérèse O'Brien, who returned to a liberation ministry in west Africa, it was a more moderate leadership. The delegates acknowledged the pain and struggle (and disunity) around the 1985 mission statement but upheld its basic tenet: 'In its imperfection the mission statement is an attempt to reformulate our charism in the light of contemporary understanding of poverty with its systemic causes. The chapter invites all members of the institute, in a climate of gentleness and respect, to let the mission statement and the constitution dialogue with each one's experience…'

For the first time the 1991 general chapter focused on an ecological component. Lack of care of the earth was seen as a fundamental cause of poverty worldwide and care of the earth was seen as a fundamental part of the institute mission. The chapter invited the institute to 'a renewed sense of the sacredness of creation', recommending care of the earth as 'a vital part of the way we are in mission and express who we are.' (Enactments, 6) There was a call for sisters, already a 'household of disciples' to become by extension responsible for the great household of earth, the house and home of humanity. It was proposed that the story of the universe could be represented as a single comprehensive narrative and that respect for the resources of the earth could bring a whole new understanding of religious poverty: sharing, simplicity, safeguarding the prospects of future generations.

In 1993 the Irish regional team established an ecology group that included Catherine Brennan, Mary Jo Hand, Mona Lally, Pauline McGovern, Eileen Monks and Anita Muldowney. The group's mission was to raise awareness of ecological issues, participate in intercongregational and ecumenical ecological initiatives and provide rituals and educational opportunities around ecological themes for sisters in the region. In order to develop the region's sense of the spirituality as well as the practice of care of the earth, Mona produced several issues of a magazine called *Earth Echoes*. In addition to arranging prayer services for the summer and winter solstices and the spring and autumn equinoxes the group organised an annual 'earth day': Pauline McGovern's *Words for the New Millennium* was launched on Earth Day 2000 and creation theology has proven to be one of the most fruitful areas for cooperation and growth in collegiality between sisters and associates; Mary Jo Hand and Catherine Brennan were two of the founders of the associate movement in Ireland. In 2007, Catherine Brennan was also a founding member of Eco-congregation Ireland, an ecumenical environmental movement.

The 1991 general chapter left it to the separate regions to take a corporate stance on justice rather than trying to impose a single stance for the whole congregation, something one might see as a reaction to the strong central leadership of Dorothy McCloskey. Some regions did not take a formal stance; others struggled with it. For example, the west African region in its post chapter assembly in December 1991 produced this corporate version: 'Following our founders' vision of a world healed, unified and transformed, we, Sisters of St Louis, commit ourselves to being women for justice in all aspects of our living and ministry.'

By the 1997 general chapter, as the gradualists might have predicted, the struggle around the option for the poor seems to have disappeared, perhaps because the mission was broken down into more specific and more manageable areas, including justice, women's issues and care of the earth. The link between poverty and lack of care of the earth was spelled out again in the enactments of the chapter.

The call of the 1997 chapter was for 'the promotion of justice, peace and the integrity of creation (JPIC)'. Throughout the institute sisters began campaigns to focus on environmental and justice issues. To give just a few examples: the state of Tocantins in the Amazon region in Brazil, in which Barrolandia is situated, was a particular focus of concern for environmental campaigners. On the ground, according to Katey Dougan, 'we tried to conscientise our people that burning their land has terrible consequences for the environment. Unfortunately, Tocantins has one of the highest records for burnings in the whole of Brazil.' Human trafficking was a key issue for California: the rights of migrant domestic workers in the UK for Margaret Healy; street children in Ghana. The JPIC campaign issues of the Irish region were the cancellation of Third World debt and the promotion of fair trade.

The 2003 general chapter continued this focus, part of the mission statement reading: 'Through all our ministries, we resolve to become agents of change in transforming unjust structures and in promoting peace, reconciliation and the integrity of creation.' In the Irish region the ecology group continued the active work it had begun during the previous decade, collaborating with an enthusiastic associate membership.

As well as reiterating 'solidarity with the poor and marginalised' and maintaining 'commitment to transforming unjust structures', the 2009 general chapter identified a new call for sisters everywhere to 'live in right relationship with God, with one another in the family of St Louis, with other people and with the whole community of life in a just and sustainable way'. The mission, which the leadership holds in the memory of the congregation and facilitates the congregation in achieving, is an organic thing, like the congregation itself and its leadership structures. 'Right relationship', although essentially containing all the same elements of mission as the statements of previous general chapters – justice, empowerment of women, the belief that not challenging unjust systems is in effect upholding injustice – expresses them in a softer, more feminine, more individual and more practical way. It is within the understanding and the everyday life of any individual to focus on her own relationships. It is the definition and detail for which Pauline McGovern appealed in 1990, emphasising 'gentleness and respect' more than it challenges and alarms.

14

The Charism Assembly of 1984

'A community of faith bound together by our common quest'
Gabrielle O'Connell, 1984

Mention of *Ut Sint Unum* had disappeared from the Monaghan *Constitution* by the 1920s and it wasn't until 1989 that it was restored: 'So that the desire most earnestly expressed by Our Lord Jesus Christ…may be accomplished in them: 'That they may be one, as Thou, Father, in me and I in thee, that they also may be one in us.' *God Wills It* was the title of the 1959 centenary history by Pauline McGovern and, although Columbanus commissioned a new crest for this centenary that had the motto *Ut Sint Unum* as well as the traditional *Dieu Le Veult*, it seems that concentration on the second half of the motto blinded the congregation to the first part.

Dieu Le Veult is the 'motto' on all chapter reports until Vatican II, a useful reinforcement for the vow of obedience. Several sisters mentioned to me that *Dieu Le Veult* was their comfort when they were missioned, unexpectedly, to distant or uncongenial locations. Before Vatican II, obedience was seen as unquestioning submission to the will of God, mediated through one's religious superior. Today Catherine Brennan, coordinator of associates in Ireland, calls it a 'masculine' motto: hierarchical, patriarchal, authoritarian. According to this paradigm, *Ut Sint Unum* is, in contrast, feminine, inclusive and relational.

Vatican II's *Perfectae Caritatis* (1965) directed congregations to rediscover their founders' 'spirit and aims', a process that was neither easy nor fruitful for some orders: 'It is for the good of the Church that institutes have their own proper characters and functions. Therefore the spirit and aims of each founder should be faithfully accepted and retained, as indeed should each institute's sound traditions, for all of these constitute the patrimony of an institute.' For the St Louis sisters this process may not have been straightforward, most of the patrimony of the order being in France and in French, but at least it was possible and, it turned out, fruitful. It is in Paul VI's *Evangelica Testificatio* (1971) that the word 'charism' is first used, in a paragraph reinforcing the message of *Perfectae Caritatis* that institutes should look for inspiration and renewal to the philosophy of their founders.

Despite Pauline McGovern's work on the origins of the institute and Bríd O'Doherty's thesis on Louis Bautain, the congregation was slow to see the importance of *Ut Sint Unum* and its value for the new Catholic world order. In a publication to mark the silver jubilee of the institute's arrival in California, in 1974, there is a detailed 'interpretation of the St Louis coat of arms' which claims that *Dieu le Veult* is 'inexhaustibly rich and beautiful' but in reality relates it to little more than obedience. *Ut Sint Unum* appears on the crest but is not mentioned and the word 'charism' is not used. We know that many sisters in California were quick to embrace the changes proposed by Vatican II and to attend training courses in the 'new' theology but it does not seem to have occurred to them at this point that their own institute had a neglected theology that was worth reviving.

The 1980 chapter under Dorothy McCloskey discussed a proposal to make the archives in Juilly available to the congregation. Bríd O'Doherty had already worked on the archive when she was researching her thesis on Louis Bautain but at this point Bríd Long, who had been teaching and studying in California since 1966, was missioned to Juilly to classify the archives, which she carried out according to a system adopted internationally. She began her work in 1981.

Dorothy McCloskey later asked for proposals for an open international assembly of St Louis sisters to promote collegiality and cohesion between regions. In November 1983 Canice Durkan, on behalf of the leadership team, sent a letter of invitation to the congregation to participate in a special event that was being planned to commemorate the centenary of the death of Mère Thérèse de la Croix. Bríd Long, then based in Juilly, and her colleague and friend Max Taggi, an Italian Jesuit, developed a proposal for a ten-day assembly that would be a mixture of talks and reflection. Bríd and Max Taggi also put themselves forward as facilitators. They developed a process for reflection and sharing around the presentations and asked those who attended to consider what needs were being served when the congregation was founded and how the inspiration of the charism could take flesh as religious responses to the needs of their own day. Charism is literally a gift, a gift alive in the people who hold it, a gift that is for the use of the Church and its people.

Carysfort College in Blackrock, Dublin, was the venue for the charism assembly of 17-25 July 1984 and more than a hundred and forty sisters from all the regions of the congregation attended, ninety from the Irish region. Gabrielle O'Connell gives a detailed account of the assembly in the October 1984 issue of *St Louis Newsletter*. She experienced it as 'the closing of the gap' between herself and other sisters from all over the globe whom she had never met or whom she had not met for many years: 'For we were that week a community of faith, bound together by our common quest.' At the official opening Dorothy McCloskey urged the sisters attending, 'to allow ourselves to be touched by some aspect of the week's experience, to open our hearts'.

The charism assembly was a truly international gathering, with liturgies inspired by each region in turn and in each language and the 'Our Father' said simultaneously in all the languages of the institute: Irish, English, French, Portuguese and Twi, Yoruba, Igbo, Tagora and Ewe from west Africa. Small groups of sisters shared their own response to the rediscovery of the institute's charism. Pauline McGovern spoke on the theme: 'Founder's charism or founding charism?' – coming down strongly in favour of the latter: fidelity to a founding charism is based not on stasis but on the constant desire to adapt to meet new needs and new challenges. Marie de Paul Neiers discussed 'The Spirituality of Louis Bautain' and Mairéad Hughes his educational philosophy (the subject of her master's dissertation in UCD): Mairéad said that Bautain saw education as 'enabling people to come to true freedom'. Bríd O'Doherty, the institute's leading authority on Bautain at the time, traced the common threads of *Sint Unum* through all the constitutional documents of the institute. Anne Kavanagh, who belonged to the California region, gave a seminar on Louise Humann and Máirín Barrett on Mère Thérèse de la Croix, whose work and personality she had come to know so well from the minutes of the council meetings of les Dames de St Louis in the archives in Juilly.

It was a great source of pride to the one hundred and forty sisters from the different regions present at the assembly that highly competent and erudite St Louis sisters themselves gave all the papers except for Monsignor Paul Poupard, expert in Louis Bautain and editor of his work, who gave two talks on Bautain. Monsignor Poupard was made a cardinal the following year.

At the end of the assembly, there was a panel discussion with one sister from each region outlining the challenges for the future of her region in the light of the week's discoveries and reflections.

Dorothy McCloskey concluded: 'We are taking away a spirit rather than a set of facts. We have been deeply touched not just by cold history but by allowing ourselves to be led forward towards a new life.'

The charism assembly of 1984 created a new bond among the sisters from all the regions of the institute. The history of the congregation and its charism were opened up to them in new ways and they were encouraged to imagine fresh possibilities for living their charism. Bautain was a 'strong' founder – a man of formidable intellect and refined philosophy – and there is a body of literature in the Juilly archives that has still to be mined in full. Pauline McGovern, with *Words for a New Millennium*, and Máirín Barrett, with her several publications on the ancestors and founders and her teaching and research presence in Juilly have made a valuable contribution to the sisters' continued commitment to *Ut Sint Unum*.

The charism assembly also reinforced the mandate and direction of the following year's general chapter, one act of which urged: 'Having done some work on our charism and founders, and being more aware of our spirit and founding charism, since 1980, that we try to bring a more authentic, conscious St Louis presence to mission and to continue to clarify our understanding of who we are as Sisters of St Louis.' In 1985 Dorothy McCloskey wrote: 'Through the charism assembly...we got in touch with the dream that inspired our existence...a founding dream or inspiration is never completely fulfilled. We have to ask ourselves: "What is *our* living experience of this founding dream of Louise Humann and Louis Bautain? How can we be faithful to it now?"'

15

West Africa: In and Out of School

'I wouldn't have missed a single day.'
Miriam Thérèse O'Brien, 2006

Many sisters who started out in mainstream education or nursing apostolates in Nigeria or Ghana found themselves transforming this ministry into something they believed more useful, serving the growing indigenous Church or, more radically, working for justice in west Africa. Explicitly or implicitly they were responding to the challenge of the preferential option for the poor that came from Vatican II and became part of the congregation's mission from 1980. St Louis sisters engaged in so many different non-school ministries that this chapter can do no more than describe a representative sample.

Maud Murphy's life has been full of surprises. She studied Irish in UCD and was surprised that she never taught it. She was a surprised regional leader for England and even more surprised to be chosen as congregational leader in 1997. The one thing she was not surprised about was when Michael O'Leary appeared before her in Knock airport on 12 September 2011 to generate publicity from the fact that she was Ryanair's four millionth passenger in or out of that airport – and to pay for the publicity by donating money to charities of her choice.

Maud was missioned to Nigeria and taught in Ondo and Owo for seven years. As she remembers it, in 1978 the west African regional superior Breda O'Hanrahan was 'stuck for someone' to succeed Patricia Moloney, who was retiring as principal in St Louis Secondary School in Kano, and Maud happened to appear at the right moment. At thirty-four she was the youngest person on the staff, according to herself the wrong colour, the wrong gender, the wrong religion and the wrong age to send into a patriarchal society in which the civil administration was militantly Muslim. The worst blow of all was that the experienced Ita McGuane, who was to be her vice-principal, was killed in a car accident on her way back to Kano just before the start of term, on 24 August 1978.

Maud settled in to administration and improving the plant at the school. Although it was a Catholic school, owned by the diocese, the state paid the teachers' salaries and, during Maud's time as principal, the ministry of education encroached more and more on school selection policy. When the school was established in 1951 its main clientèle had been the daughters of Catholic Igbos who had settled in the north. Then the Emir sent his daughter to St Louis and the school began to attract Muslims. Although there were plenty of other schools in Kano, the ministry, insisting that the native Hausa population of Kano state was 100 per cent Muslim, imposed a quota of Muslims that eventually rose to 80 per cent of the school population. The remaining places were for children like the Igbos whose origins were outside the state.

Despite official denials, there *were* Hausa living in rural areas outside Kano who were not Muslim and some of them had become Christians. Seán Hayes, an SMA priest and friend of Maud, was evangelising these 'Maguzawa' as they were called (the Hausa word means 'those who ran away [from Islam]') and she agreed with him that they should have the chance of education. She went out with him to the bush and hand picked seven Maguzawa girls aged between twelve and fifteen. They were Catholic and had had minimal primary education or exposure to western culture.

When the pupil lists were sent to the ministry at the start of the year, Maud was ordered to remove the seven Maguzawa girls from the school although she told the officials (many times) that they were indigenes, Hausa. Religion was not mentioned: a classic case of the elephant in the room.

When she refused there was official retaliation. The first thing Maud heard was that the fathers of the girls had been put in jail, allegedly for not sending them to the local village school. They were released but at the end of the month no salaries arrived for the teachers and the ministry told her that there would be no salaries until the school removed the seven Maguzawa. Maud appealed for support to the Archbishop of Kaduna and he negotiated with the ministry but the school was closed for a period until the impasse was resolved. An advantage on the school's side was that the daughters of the president of Nigeria and other influential public figures were among the pupils. Eventually, Maud got the funds to pay the teachers and the Maguzawa children stayed, some of them becoming lawyers, doctors and nurses. Now St Louis sisters run a hostel in Kano for about a hundred younger Maguzawa children, so that they can attend primary school. Maud sent €2000 of the Ryanair money that fell from the sky in 2011 to support this hostel.

Also during Maud's period in Kano, the ministry of education wanted to build a mosque and the school offered them a large site at the back of the school – the Catholic Church was at the front. There was another standoff between the ministry and Maud and the Archbishop of Kaduna about the location of the mosque, until eventually the ministry built a huge mosque at the back of the compound.

Maud finished in Kano in 1985, the year of the chapter that adopted the preferential option for the poor, and moved to Lagos to coordinate an apostolate for people on the street. This was part of the Samaritan Project, initiated by the Nigerian Conference of Women Religious in 1983 and launched by Miriam Thérèse O'Brien and two American sisters from another congregation. The project focused on the destitute and homeless and one of its major apostolates was the Lagos State Rehabilitation and Training Centre, Majidun, twelve miles outside the city: a compound in which anything up to twelve hundred people were kept willy nilly by the authorities. They were homeless, destitute, disabled, mentally ill, prostitutes and petty criminals, men, women and children, rounded up on the streets of Lagos and deposited in a fenced-in area. The German mission organisation Misereor gave Maud a car, a driver and some funding: later she got a taxi licence and used the plate to drive through Lagos when congestion laws would have prevented her from doing so (no wonder she got on so well with Michael O'Leary). Maud spent those years giving talks to organisations and 'getting, getting, getting': funding, materials, help of all sorts.

Hannah Boylan succeeded Maud in the Samaritan Project and worked there until 2000. She had trained as a nurse and midwife and worked for ten years in the hospital in Ado-Ekiti. Her 1992 report of the project is an extraordinary catalogue of the generosity of individuals, corporations and various expatriate communities, enabling the project to offer medical and psychiatric care, start a school for the children and open craft centres for inmates to earn a little money. Food and materials, from laterite for the roads to medicines to Christmas gifts, were donated by foundations, philanthropic organisations, businesses, airlines and embassies in extraordinary quantities. Chevron Nigeria repaired the roads; the Irish embassy donated a bus; the British embassy gave sewing machines; the Sheraton Hotel let Hannah take the lightly used guest soaps and plastic laundry bags, which were untold riches for people who had less than nothing. Just as commendable were the individuals who volunteered their time: novices from Akure, seminarians and a local psychiatrist, Professor T. Asuni, who took a personal interest in the plight of the schizophrenic and psychotic inmates. Also among the benefactors were St Louis schools in Carrickmacross and Dundalk. The Samaritan Project is ongoing.

Meanwhile, in the Kano area, Brigitte Burke, who began working in the primary school there in 1970 and served as principal for twelve years, devoted herself to outreach with the women and children of the villages from 1990. 'The children were simple and I was used to a rural life,' she says. Daily travel was essential but not easy and Brigitte, a cyclist since she borrowed Sheila McGovern's bicycle when she first came to Kano, took to using a Honda 75 that one of the priests got for her. (Later she had a four-wheel drive.) She and Christiana Kure based themselves in a small house in Refawa during the week, coming to stay with the community in Kano only at weekends. Later Brigitte concentrated her efforts on Nassarawa Kuki and Tudun Wada, teaching children and organising training courses for teachers, and she spent some years working with

Fionnuala Cole on the training and empowerment of women. She had become involved in adult literacy in Kano and was responding to the appeals of the SMA fathers who were evangelising the village children.

Martinian Bergin's project of choice was a leprosarium near Akure. She succeeded Anita Morley, the first novice mistress in Nigeria, in 1971, after spending three years teaching with Clare Ryan in Ikare. There was a huge leprosy village three miles from Akure, a village of burnt-out cases, which had been started by American missionaries and was by then government-run but neglected. Martinian joined the welfare committee and used to take the novices out on a Sunday for a service. When her six years in the novitiate were completed, she asked regional leader Breda O'Hanrahan if she could work in the leprosy settlement instead of going back into school. The commissioner for health in Akure was the wife of the local king; she arranged for Martinian to go to do a course in Benin and after that she was recognised as a health superintendent. She was employed by the ministry for health and spent six years there, working with the ministry, trying to get better facilities and medicines. They got a water supply, a little shop set up and started off candle making and weaving, producing craftwork that they could sell.

Martinian never did go back to school in Nigeria, although she taught again in Ireland. After six years at the leprosarium, she returned to Kano and her years there were spent working with women in literacy programmes, in parish work and in setting up the Rite of Christian Initiation for Adults (RCIA). Once she came back to Ireland for family reasons in 1987 – as she thought, for a limited period – she never again worked in Africa, something about which she is disappointed but philosophical.

Nobody better exemplifies the congregation's commitment to social justice and liberation theology in Africa than Miriam Thérèse O'Brien (1945-2006), who was missioned to Nigeria in 1974. Two years later she left her teaching job in Owo to set up the Samaritan project in Lagos and joined a pastoral team in Mushin, a poor suburb. There was no preferential option for the poor in the sights of the congregation at this time but liberation theology had spread in the developing world and among missionary orders after the Medellín conference in 1968 and as a result of the example of Brazil in particular. The goal of the pastoral team was to build community in the parish by running courses of different kinds and giving health education. This grew into a development programme, of which Miriam Thérèse was coordinator, for small Christian communities, thirteen in all, each involved in a number of projects, including youth development, adult literacy and primary health care. It was a far cry from rows of girls in neat uniforms in the congregation's fee-paying schools in Kano and Akure.

Miriam Thérèse was elected to central leadership at the 1985 general chapter, serving as assistant to Dorothy McCloskey until 1990-1. It was at this chapter that the order committed itself to a preferential option for the poor and there is no doubt that Miriam Thérèse led by example both before and after her term of leadership. She was one of those who most fervently wanted to break the link between formal education and the St Louis Institute and wished the sisters to look at other forms of apostolate, especially primary healthcare. Betty Dalton, who had done a degree in sociology in Maynooth in the 1970s and who served as west African regional superior 1986-9 remembers giving Miriam a copy of Paolo Freire's *Pedagogy of the Oppressed*; Miriam said it 'blew her mind'.

In 1992 the Jesuit Refugee Service (JRS) sent her to Gbarnga in war-torn Liberia, where she set up a team to work with lay people, offering services such as capacity building and a women's development programme. In September 1994 Miriam returned to Monrovia from Ireland to find that all-out war had broken out in the city and that her team had fled to Côte d'Ivoire and Guinea, suffering injuries and loss of family members along the way. She went first to Danané, the capital of Côte d'Ivoire, and the refugee service went into action both in Danané and in Guinea, with Miriam Thérèse basing herself in Guinea. When, in 1996, Fionnuala Cole was missioned to join Miriam to work with refugees in Côte d'Ivoire – after a career in education and leadership in Ireland,

Fionnuala thought of this as a short-term assignment – she found that Miriam had moved on to Guinea so she stayed in Danané, also working as part of the core team of the Jesuit Refugee Services. There they provided similar services, including teacher training and health education, as well as feeding centres for the refugees. Miriam Thérèse was coordinator in Côte d'Ivoire and Guinea, the only woman to occupy such a position, answering to the international director, Mark Raper SJ.

When they were able to go back to Liberia, Miriam Thérèse's team established a local NGO known as the Development Education Network–Liberia (DEN-L) to continue the training programme. The JRS supported the sisters in Gbarnga until 2002. Then Fionnuala Cole went to Nigeria but Miriam Thérèse continued to work with DEN-L. She died after a short illness in December 2006, aged only sixty-one. 'I am grateful,' she wrote in 2006, 'for the fourteen years which I have spent in Liberia. I wouldn't have missed a single day.' DEN-L later constructed a residential training centre in Gbarnga that is named in memory of Miriam Thérèse.

In Kano Fionnuala used the skills she had learned in Liberia, forming teams for teacher training, youth training, pastoral teams and hospital staff. The only other Irish sister based in the area at that time was Brigitte Burke, who worked in the bush. Brigitte and Fionnuala ran workshops in the villages, for teachers, for women and for pastoral workers. There was constant demand although travel was a problem because the roads were so bad. Fionnuala stayed in Nigeria doing this community work until 2006. Brigitte also came home, for family reasons, in 2006, although totally absorbed in her work with the villagers – she had spent thirty-six years in the Kano region.

As a means of implementing the option for the poor adopted by the 1985 chapter, Dorothy McCloskey asked former teacher Mary Roche to investigate the possibilities for the development of primary health care centres in the area around Zonkwa. Zambina was chosen as a centre, with forty satellite villages, and Mary took a primary health care course in Liverpool. A house was built in Zambina in 1988 with the help of funding from Misereor. Training of voluntary health workers began the following year, both from the local area and from further afield in the state. Mary worked in Zambina until 1994. She died in 2007.

Dorothy McMahon always wanted to be a missionary but her first posting in Nigeria in 1978 was short-lived as she developed malaria while teaching Science in Ikere-Ekiti. She then spent almost a decade in the temperate climate of Kiltimagh. When she went back to Nigeria in 1988 she knew she didn't want to teach and it was Miriam Thérèse who suggested primary health care to her, as Mary Roche was already making a start on this in Zambina in the north.

Dorothy and Catherine Adelegan (a nurse and midwife) were missioned to start a primary health care programme in Ijio-Meso, 80 km west of Iseyin, where the Sisters of St Louis had a hospital, near the border with the Republic of Benin. The road from Ijio to Iseyin was poor, liable to disappear altogether in the wet season, and there was no electricity. It was not: 'How far to Ijio? but 'How long to Ijio?' as it could take three hours or a day or two days to get there from Ibadan, 80 km beyond Iseyin. A Missionaries of Africa (MAfr) priest from Ireland, John Millane, ministered there when they first came and a charismatic Frenchman of the same order, Irénée Edmond, who lived and breathed liberation theology and was totally committed to his basic Christian communities, replaced him. The MAfr order also provided funding for the project.

The Bishop of Oyo, Julius B. Adelakun, paid several supportive visits to the little community and from his letters to Dorothy it is clear that he found in her a kindred spirit. The sisters built a new convent, which was officially opened in 1993, and several other Nigerian sisters worked with them for a period. Anne Kavanagh, then institute leader, did community experience with them in 1994, before an ELM. The work of the sisters included the training of primary healthcare workers, vocational training – St Teresa's Vocational Training Centre was opened in 1991 – youth work and parish work. Funding for these ministries also came from Misereor.

Ijio was a fascinating place to be because of its isolation and the two sisters were really 'inserted' in the community. It was a Yoruba area, although with its own dialect and strong traditions, including the pagan festival of Oro, which was forbidden to women: they were locked in their rooms for the duration. Ijio was a harmonious interfaith community, where there was a lot of intermarriage except for the Baptists (says Dorothy) who did not like Catholics, rivals as they saw them.

Ijio, although hell to get into, seems from Dorothy's account to have been a kind of heaven when 'Sister Black' and 'Sister White' were installed there. The people had no expectations of gender roles and Irénée involved them in all his ministry, sending them to outposts to perform liturgies and administer the sacraments. She was sad leaving Ijio after six years – although it did have its drawbacks, like being cut off entirely for more than a month after a bloodless coup and having to drive through riots and local demonstrations on the way to Ibadan. But she went on to work in primary care in Zambina, replacing Mary Roche, who already had in place a well trained staff.

Phil McGuinness, like Dorothy a science graduate, spent fifty years in west Africa, first in Ghana, in Kumasi, then in Owo. Although initially a reluctant missioner she turned out to be superb at the job: she established science departments and built laboratories in the schools and remained as principal in St Louis Grammar School, Akure, until 1991, through years of government interference in staffing policy, in enrolment and in administration and finance. When she was about to retire a chance meeting with (as she puts it) a 'young man from the Canadian High Commission' set her on another path that kept her in Nigeria until 2009. Amazed to find that she was still principal of a Nigerian school, he asked her what she would like to do when she retired. A substantial cheque arrived from the Canadian High Commission as a result of her reply that she 'wanted to do something for dropouts'. Her young man said that education for women was the buzzword in his organisation. With this cheque and the help of Tom Fitzgerald, the Kerry-born SMA brother who created so much infrastructure in Nigeria, she built twenty-one classrooms, which became the Mater Dei Skills Training Centre. There Phil's 'dropouts' learned cookery, weaving, dressmaking, dyeing, basic English and maths, so that, as she puts it, they could earn a little money for themselves and 'wouldn't be asking their husbands for ten naira'. Brother Tom also helped with building a kitchen, toilets and a chapel in the leprosarium outside Akure, in which ministry Phil succeeded Martinian Bergin.

Visitors to Akure admire the fine chapel in the St Louis compound, which is also the work of Phil McGuinness. When the government banned religious services in school and insisted that the school chapel be used for meetings, she turned it into a library and had a chapel built on the other side of the compound, to serve the Catholic pupils and the local people as well as the sisters. Her first tranche of funding for the job was 10,000 naira (€9000). Enter Brother Tom, donations from many sources, pupils who helped during the holidays and some stained glass from a Dublin company, bought during Phil's holidays and shipped to Akure. The church took five years to complete and was dedicated by Bishop Alonge of Ondo in 1983. When Phil left Africa for good she 'cried all the way from Akure to Lagos'. She keeps in touch with the school by preparing commentaries on the Sunday readings and emailing them to the pupils.

Máire Blair, like Phil, came reluctantly back to Ireland in 2009. Not having lived at home since 1954, she found readjustment difficult, even to the post-Celtic Tiger world. In Nigeria she worked in administration in schools and hospitals and did prison visiting in her spare time, and she spent her last few years in Bauchi diocese, at first working for John Moore SMA (bishop from 2004 until his death in 2010) and then with Colette Corvin in the villages, a work she loved, although, unlike Colette, she does not speak fluent Hausa. Now she helps in administration in St Louis High School, Rathmines.

Colette is the last St Louis sister from Ireland remaining in Nigeria. Based in the village of Miya in Bauchi diocese in the north-east, she has been in Nigeria, with some breaks, since 1962. She taught in Kano, Minna and Bida and worked in Kontagora, where, with Leone Keegan, she became involved in primary evangelisation and adult education. Kontagora is a remote area in Niger State where the indigenes, the Kamberi, live in huts in the bush which they disguise with crops of maize and millet. Colette developed the ability to locate these huts and she and other sisters built up a relationship with the people and offered the women some training in cooking, knitting and English.

Colette went to Bauchi in 2007 to work in catechetics at the behest of Bishop Moore. In a large diocese that is predominantly Muslim and with only a small team of priests, he ensured the training of catechists who would go into the rural areas to lead Church services and look after development projects. Colette is now involved in renewal work for groups of catechists and *masu bishara* ('people of the Gospels' – local evangelists). She conducts all her groups in Hausa. When she went back to live in Belfast she found it impossible to settle there. She has no concerns about living on her own and feels entirely at home in Miya.

It is more than sixty years since Isabel, Eymard and Augustine arrived in Kano to open a primary school: decades in which the missionary achievement of the Sisters of St Louis has been impressive and wide ranging. Now it is the Nigerian Sisters of St Louis who choose the ministries they will become involved in, as well as continuing the work of schools and hospitals, many of them established by Irish pioneers.

When Miriam Brady was a senior in Monaghan her class put on a concert with scenes from *Julius Caesar*. They raised £200 among the staff and the pupils and presented it to Ghana pioneer, Joseph Mary Connolly, who was home at the time. To Miriam's great surprise, Joseph Mary said to her: 'You'll be in Kumasi some day.' Sheela Gillespie was Miriam's superior in Kumasi when she was finally missioned there in 1964. Because the community in Kumasi was building a church, she went out with sixty pieces of luggage containing necessities for the altar and vestments for priests: on a cargo boat, slow but luxurious.

Miriam would not have much time for relaxing in Ghana. She arrived on a Friday and on Monday was teaching English and religion in the teacher training college. An outreach programme began when some sisters decided that they should supply what would now be called continuing professional development for the girls who had graduated from the training college over the previous ten years and were teaching in outlying villages. Maths and religion were the most difficult subjects for them to teach so Miriam and others would arrive in the villages on Saturdays to give refresher courses. By the late 1960s/early 1970s they realised that catechetics needed a lot of attention: 'new' catechetics were coming in after Vatican II and Miriam trained for a year in Mount Oliver in Dundalk before undertaking this work.

Miriam became a member of Bishop Sarpong's diocesan catechetical team, along with a Dutch SMA priest and a Ghanaian. Peter Kwasi Sarpong, a man of ideas who is credited with 'inculturation' in the theological sense – integrating the music and symbolism of the Akan people with Catholic liturgy – wanted a mobile catechetical unit, the first in Africa, so that the trainers would go out to the villages instead of the catechists coming to Kumasi. Miriam found the Ghanaian Church advanced, she thinks because of the influence of Dutch SMA priests who evangelised it and the leadership of the anthropologist Sarpong. The team developed a catechetics course which at first they distributed to the teachers and catechists on sheets of paper. They needed catechetics textbooks, and it was Sarpong who proposed that they should include all the main religions in one textbook so that the government would print and supply the books to the schools. A committee was formed with Miriam, an OLA sister, a Presbyterian, an Anglican, a Methodist and two Muslims, which produced five textbooks for primary school and three for junior secondary school: as an interfaith project it was challenging but successful.

When John Paul II came to Ghana in 1982 it was not Bishop Sarpong who made the greatest impact on him but Bishop Sarpong's mother. She came to meet the pope, dressed in her finest *kente* cloth and laden with gold jewellery, but, embraced by the papal arms, she left the marks of the charcoal with which she had dressed her hair all over his pristine white coat. Miriam heard him quickly say to his aide, Bishop John Magee, 'Get me another coat.'

With funding from Rome, a Ghanaian priest was sent to Mount

Oliver for training on catechetics. Miriam, believing that the service should be entirely indigenised, left Ghana in 1984.

Mary O'Donovan was missioned to Kumasi in 1967 to teach in the training college. After a spell in Zonkwa she returned to Ghana to teach in the secondary school in Takoradi. This was the 1980s, the time of famine, and the sisters, like the population in general, often went hungry, or had to survive on bananas. After she finished teaching in Takoradi and had a much needed sabbatical, Bishop Sarpong asked Mary to run the pastoral centre in Kumasi. It was the outcome of one of several Africa synods which gave voice to the laity and which Mary feels put the African Church so far in advance of the contemporary Church in Ireland. The people of Kumasi said they wanted adult education, training, Sunday school and bible studies and these were what Sarpong set out to supply. Mary trained past pupils of the St Louis schools for the biblical apostolate and also worked in leprosy ministry and in her own parish, preparing the liturgy every Wednesday night for many years.

Mary knew that there was need for marriage formation and over time she set up a programme of formators – married couples themselves who were trained one day a month for two periods of ten months – for the diocese of Kumasi, the first of its kind in Africa. She resolved to hold her training programme on Saturdays but Bishop Sarpong, well versed in his native Akan culture, warned her that she could not do it on Saturday as this was traditionally the day for funerals in Ghana. Funerals or no funerals, Mary persisted, the trainee formators appeared on Saturday and Sarpong had to admit that she was right. The programme was held in St Louis middle school in Kumasi: everything about it was voluntary and there was no cost for participants. This diocesan marriage formation programme is still going strong. Mary O'Donovan left Ghana in 2000, the last Irish sister to do so, but found it was years before she properly 'left Africa' or perhaps before Africa left her.

16

The Evolution
of the Education Ministry in Ireland

'Only stay if you love them.'

Conception Hynes

In 1947 the St Louis Institute was continuing the tradition of an education ministry established by Geneviève Beale in its foundations in Ireland and England. Its secondary schools in Ireland were known for the quality of education they provided for girls and for their achievements in music and performance. Monaghan and Carrickmacross, Kiltimagh and Balla, were at that time 'A' schools in which all subjects were taught exclusively through Irish, something that appealed to nationally minded parents, and the superior general, Columbanus Greene, a nationalist from north of the border, had the reputation of being a fervent *Gaeilgeoir*. Vocations were plentiful and increasing in numbers, so that the boarding schools – all the schools except Rathmines – were able to draw on the necessary personnel to care for and supervise the pupils. Most of the teaching staff in these schools were sisters.

After thirty five years of radical change, from the late 1960s, four St Louis secondary schools in the Republic – Monaghan, Carrickmacross, Rathmines, and Dundalk – now bear the name of St Louis as part of the Le Chéile trust. They are still recognisably St Louis schools and the teachers, many of whom who were themselves educated by the congregation, are eager to preserve its traditions. There are two maintained grammar schools in Northern Ireland, St Louis, Ballymena, and St Louis, Kilkeel. The congregation is also a trustee of St Louis Community School in Kiltimagh, Ramsgrange Community School, County Wexford, and

Blakestown Community School in County Dublin. St Genevieve's High School in Belfast passed into the trusteeship of the diocese of Down and Connor in 1995.

Although all the congregation's schools shared the St Louis ethos and many sisters had the experience of teaching or being principal in more than one school, as staffing requirements dictated, each had a unique atmosphere and flavour. In the years before free education when Marie Céline O'Byrne was principal, Carrickmacross was a small learning community with a hundred and twenty boarders and a sprinkling of day pupils. The school had such a good name, academically, that it drew students from the whole country. Examination results were very important. This led to (benign) rivalry between St Louis schools when scholarships granted to the top forty students in the Intermediate Certificate were announced. Girls competed for twenty first class scholarships of £40 and twenty second class scholarships of £30. (Incidentally, boys' results were assessed separately: they were awarded thirty six first and thirty six second class scholarships. It was not just the Church that was patriarchal in the middle of the twentieth century.) Anne Jordan, who taught both in Carrickmacross and Monaghan, notes that in the 1980s, after the option for the poor had replaced results and scholarships as the priority for sisters who remained in education, competition instead centred on who was doing most for the deprived pupils, the troubled and the underachievers.

If you asked past pupils of Carrickmacross for their memories of school, 'Music would be sure to loom large,' according to Marie Céline. Every student sang in a choir, those with instrumental skills formed the orchestra, and piano lessons ran right through the school day. Sisters and past pupils recall school musicals, mainly light opera – Schubert, Gilbert and Sullivan - and variety concerts with song, dance and drama.

For some, the attraction of Carrickmacross over Monaghan was the smaller numbers which, it was thought, created a more friendly atmosphere and allowed for more individual attention. But for most there were personal links – a girl's mother was a past pupil or older relatives or a girl from her own area had achieved excellent examination results. So pupils felt confident of a place in the civil service, in the training colleges or at university, and social and cultural activities, while valued, were the icing on the cake in earlier years.

Not so when art became a subject recognised for matriculation. In the early 1970s, to the delight of the pupils, the school management put resources into the art department for the first time, something that encouraged a schoolwide surge of creativity. Under the leadership of Enda McMullan and later on lay teacher Siobhan Finnegan, a past pupil, art achieved a high profile throughout the school, with students being awarded top grades in public examinations year after year. Carrickmacross alumnae reached the highest professional levels in art, architecture and fashion design, both nationally and internationally. Enda is part of the team, along with art department colleagues Siobhán Finnegan and Patricia O'Reilly, that provides props and stage sets for the musicals that now form part of the programme of transition year. Marie Byrne acts as commercial manager for the musicals. The St Louis tradition is alive and well, although the show of choice is more likely to be *Hairspray* or *Les Misérables* than *Lilac Time* or *The Pirates of Penzance*.

Carrickmacross is known for its lace as well as its artists and musicians and this delicate, superfine confection still has periods of popularity among haute couture designers. Lacemaking was begun as a cottage industry in the 1820s and revived by St Louis sisters at the end of the nineteenth century. The lace became popular in the 1960s and several sisters taught lacemaking for the Vocational Education Committee (VEC) and in the convent. After the retirement of Cronan McNicholas, who had presided over the classes, the St Louis Lace Centre was transferred to the town's Lace Cooperative. Carrickmacross lace, stitched in Windsor, was used in the wedding gown of royal bride Kate Middleton in 2011. St Louis sisters also revived lacemaking in Clones from the time of their arrival in the town in the early twentieth century.

The boarding school of St Louis, Monaghan, was renowned for its academic excellence and its own quality musical productions, and supplied a seemingly never ending flow of high calibre entrants for the order's novitiate. Monaghan took in sixty boarders every year and had plenty of personnel to teach and supervise them ('a novice around every corner,' as one sister, a past pupil herself, remarked). The school had a number of outstanding mistresses of schools: Raphael Nugent, Laurentia Stuart 1914-36; Columbanus Greene 1936-44.

Donogh O'Malley, Minister for Education, announced free secondary education unexpectedly in 1967. It was possible for schools to opt out of the free scheme and some religious orders chose to do this. But the St Louis Institute decided that all its schools should participate in the scheme, although nowhere in the archives is there a record of the council's discussions that led to this decision – so perhaps it seemed an entirely natural one.

The numbers of local day pupils pouring into schools like Monaghan and Carrickmacross from September 1967 meant that principals were scrambling to turn dormitories into classrooms and erect pre-fabricated structures and in the longer term planning extensions and new classroom blocks. There were no other Catholic girls' schools in these towns so there was no question of turning pupils away, no matter how inadequate the government's preparation for free education had been.

Dorothea Canty (an tSiúr Doireann) had presided in Monaghan since 1946. But she must have known that the deluge had arrived when she handed over to Thérèse Ryan in 1970. Increased numbers meant recruiting extra teachers, who were in short supply countrywide at this time. The first male teachers appeared. In the early 1970s Monaghan innocently appointed a teacher with extreme left wing (and, it turned out, Republican) views who systematically recruited pupils, creating cells of disaffection and serious discipline and morale problems. His contract was not renewed.

Soon it became clear that teaching all pupils exclusively through the medium of Irish had become unrealistic. As secondary education was no longer for the privileged few it would have required resources that were simply not available to bring so many pupils up to the required standard. Management and staff also struggled with the question of whether to stream or not to stream: with a large intake of pupils who had a very varied level of ability, opinion was divided on the psychological and practical consequences of such a decision, not to mention the morality.

The 1975 general chapter described both the curtailment that had already taken place in the education apostolate and what was planned to take place over the next decade. From around this time, boarding schools began to be phased out: they had become unnecessary as well as untenable, as children in rural areas now had access to secondary schools through the school transport scheme.

In *Reflections*, published in 1977 to mark the closure of the boarding school and the end of an era, the editor, Kitty Fitzsimons, herself a past pupil, captured the contradiction that was Monaghan: 'It could be…both liberating and stifling, snobbish and homely, magnanimous and mean. It set your sights on the stars and kept your feet on the ground.' But St Louis Secondary School is not in the past: it celebrated its hundredth anniversary in 1998 and is a thriving school with six hundred pupils.

The foundation in Bundoran was Monaghan's first branch house. The town had no secondary school but the sisters operated a 'secondary top' (which prepared pupils for the Intermediate Certificate only) until Ard Lughaidh secondary school opened in 1965. Ard Lughaidh was the first St Louis Secondary School to take boys, as there was no boys' secondary school in Bundoran, and it later took over the premises of Stella Maris Domestic Science College, which had also been run by St Louis sisters.

Bundoran had a limited catchment area (as laid down by the Department of Education in the years after free education was introduced) and there seemed to be little scope to increase the enrolment of Ard Lughaidh so in 1984 it was decided to withdraw from the trusteeship of the school once that year's intake had completed its five years of education. Although it seemed at first as if the diocese of Clogher would become trustees, the school finally closed in 1994 and the property, which was part of the Crudden Trust, reverted to the diocese. The boarding school in Bundoran remained open longer than any other St Louis boarding school. Bundoran now has a community college, Magh Ene, with three hundred and fifty pupils and a handsome new campus. The congregation has maintained a presence in the town with four sisters and two associate groups facilitated by Marie du Rosaire Diver, Marion McGreal and Adrienne Byrne.

St Louis sisters gave eighty years of service in secondary education in Kiltimagh. The sisters' first venture in the town, in 1897, was a technical school for girls. Kiltimagh thrived as a boarding school, drawing pupils from all over the country, with a good proportion of Irish speakers from the western seaboard. Its proud tradition of excellence meant that it was many times the winner of the national *Sciath* (shield) for drama and music in Irish, competing with sister St Louis schools. In the years following the introduction of free education, boys were enrolled, at the behest of the local community. In becoming coeducational the school had to adapt the former boarders' accommodation to provide extra classrooms, sports fields and changing rooms. New subjects like woodwork, technology and technical graphics were introduced to cater for the new cohort of students. All these facilities were provided at considerable financial cost to the congregation.

Kiltimagh also had a VEC school, Coláiste Raifteirí, and it soon became clear that this small town, with a restricted catchment area and in a region with high emigration, would be severely challenged to support two post-primary schools. It was clear that the optimum solution would be a single school serving the whole community and providing quality education and a broad range of subjects.

In the mid 1970s negotiations began between the stakeholders: St Louis, the Department of Education, the VEC and the local community. It was not easy to reach agreement as St Louis had cherished traditions which some feared would be under threat in the event of a merger. The Department of Education supported the amalgamation of the two schools, which would result in either a community school or a community college. The negotiations continued over a long period and were affected by the political instability of the early 1980s, local and national elections and changes of government and personnel. St Louis also suffered the tragic death in a road accident of one of its negotiating team,

Marie Jeanne Stanley, something that stymied progress for some time. Eventually the Department of Education agreed to the establishment of a community school and the deed of trust was signed by the joint patrons, St Louis and Mayo VEC.

St Louis Community School, located on the site of the former St Louis convent and secondary school, opened in September 1993. The Department of Education remodelled and refurbished the buildings and the school currently enjoys beautiful modern facilities with some lovely old architecture. The convent chapel is used as a place of worship by the school community. The last St Louis principal, Mary O'Connor, did not apply for the principalship of the new community school and its first principal (1993-7) was Hugh McTigue. 'Louisville', a new community in a new home, was formed to replace the convent community.

St Louis Secondary School, Balla, was only six miles from the earlier foundation of Kiltimagh, from which it had sprung. Gabrielle Mary O'Connell, who was later principal, first went there in 1944 and this is her account of the unique atmosphere of Balla:

'Balla was of all things a homely place. I first saw it in the war years when it took a seven hours' train journey to reach on the old turf trains. It was just a large country lodge. It was a fairytale place, a tiny version of my own school in Monaghan where everything was huge, well ordered and formal with two hundred and fifty boarders. Here was a *meitheal* of men [a group assembled to do a particular farming job] having giant breakfasts in the kitchen on their way to bring in the harvest and the head nun polishing the hall door. The boarders arrived next day, all sixty-five of them. As there was no rural bus service there were very few day pupils and of course there were no private cars.

'For many years the school's intake was never more than seventy girls and as we were in a truly rural area, my first feel of the place was its intimacy. Everyone was known to everyone else and all the girls had sisters either above or below them in the school. Music was a dominant note: the annual school concert involved every child, even those who could not sing, something that would never happen in Monaghan. The curriculum was the same in all our schools but it was the extracurricular that counted in the day to day life of Balla. There were choirs, orchestra, individual singing lessons and somehow a feeling of lightness and warmth.

'Balla was not a competitive school and some parents liked it for its easy pace but there was the same level of dedication and involvement of sisters and staff as in Monaghan. It went more by its own norms and there was a healthy drive to do as well as everyone else.

'So school went on tranquilly until the bombshell of February 1975, when, after consultation and reflection, St Louis decided that Balla would close in 1978. The buzzword of 'curtailment' had affected us all. Immediately a committee of local people went to meet Colmcille Stephens, the superior general in Dublin, hoping to reverse the plan. But Colmcille did not see any chance of survival for a school of no more than two hundred day girls.

'To complicate matters at this stage, the SMA college at nearby Ballinafad announced that it would be closing and that it would take no new pupils after 1976. There was panic in the area at the possibility of losing all second level education. A second meeting with Colmcille proposed that the school in Balla would be retained as a day school for boys and girls. The institute made it clear that it would negotiate with local parents only if a proper board of management were formally appointed with a manager. John Horgan SMA was appointed manager, an inspired choice as he had taught in both schools.

'The new structure planned for the first intake of boys in September 1976 and Father Horgan oversaw the conversion of dormitories into classrooms for woodwork and other practical subjects for the boys. St Louis sisters saw the importance of keeping the existing school running in the St Louis tradition until the community withdrew in the summer of 1978. Then the school premises and sports grounds were transferred to the new entity, to be called Balla Secondary School, a company limited by guarantee and the only school in the country of this model. Pat Sheridan, who had been a highly regarded deputy principal for many years, was appointed principal. Lucina Cunnane kept the St Louis spirit alive in the school, commuting from Kiltimagh to work as a career guidance teacher. St Louis Balla, which had first opened its doors sixty years earlier, closed them on a mission truly fulfilled.'

Dún Lughaidh in Dundalk was a late St Louis foundation (1950) and when it became a boarding school in 1955 attracted pupils who wanted a St Louis education but did not feel that their standard of Irish was good enough for the demands of an 'A' school. Dún Lughaidh, which had the distinction of being partly accommodated in a tower house called Bellew's Castle, also became well known for prowess in debating, for its success in the Young Scientists' Competition and, like all St Louis schools, for excellence in music, with its own orchestra. The link with Juilly provided an annual exchange of Dundalk students to France or Cours Bautain students to Dundalk. Dún Lughaidh, like the other St Louis/Le Chéile schools, now has an enrolment of about six hundred pupils and a strong identity as part of the trust.

For Méabh Ní Uallacháin moving from Dún Lughaidh with its orderly ambitious pupils to Pobalscoil Éanna, as Blakestown Community School was officially known, was certainly eye-opening. As part of the option for the poor, sisters were 'inserted' in the parish and the developing primary school as well as the community school, sharing trusteeship with Servite fathers. Very few pupils continued to third-level education, certainly until Blanchardstown Institute of Technology opened locally. On the other hand 'there was great freedom' in not having any mention of points (for university entrance). In Dundalk sisters did everything from cleaning to making tea for visitors to locking up and it was a burden lifted not to have to do any of this in Blakestown: if there was a problem with the plant someone was paid to look after it. Teaching Irish in Blakestown was challenging, as was school life in general, but Méabh worked there for many years. Dolores Maguire, who lived in the Blakestown community, taught travellers in Corduff, west Dublin.

Ramsgrange College of Rural Home Economics (or 'Practical School', as it was known for generations) was founded in 1906, replacing the boarding school or 'school for farmers' daughters' that the founding sisters had established in 1871. The teenage students of the college studied laundry, husbandry, dairy, poultry-keeping and cooking, with a view to jobs in the rural economy, housekeeping or running efficient households of their own. Immaculata Dempsey's connection with the college dates back almost to the year of its founding, as her mother's name appears on the register in 1907. She became a student in the college in 1939 and entered the novitiate there the following year. A native of County Wexford, she is the last surviving sister to have spent her whole religious life in Ramsgrange.

The sisters in Ramsgrange were also in charge of the four small primary schools: Duncannon, Shielbaggan, Ballyhack and Ramsgrange itself. Every morning until the first van arrived in the community, three ponies would be tackled and three groups of sisters, complete with lunch boxes, would set off in their trap for the three-mile journey to their outlying schools. In this rural community they knew all the families and their sorrows and joys and performed a myriad social and pastoral services. Immaculata, perhaps a little idealistically, says that the community inside and outside the convent was so harmonious that, 'We knew friction only by name.' Gradually the principalship of the primary schools passed into lay hands.

The College of Rural Home Economics closed in 1984 when the Department of Agriculture stopped funding institutions of this kind in the light of changing rural life, a closure felt keenly by sisters like Immaculata, who had given her whole life to teaching and administration in the college. The old primary school and the lodge that used to serve as a holiday home for sisters were given to the local community and now function as St Louis Day Care Centre, which serves elderly people within a radius of twenty miles.

The small secondary school in Ramsgrange was a late addition, opening in 1967, not long before curtailment began in other boarding schools. Although, according to the council minutes, there was 'a shortage of graduate sisters' at the time (Africa and California made heavy demands on personnel and this was the year of the introduction of free education) the congregation decided to go ahead with this school because of 'the earnest entreaties of the people of Ramsgrange and the generosity of the Ramsgrange Friends of St Louis to the missions'. One of the solutions to the shortage of graduates was that sisters who were teaching in the primary and junior schools in Rathmines were sent to UCD to do a BA degree by night, by special dispensation of Archbishop John Charles McQuaid. Paschalina O'Shea was in the first group of five sisters to undertake a night degree and recalls the restrictive conditions imposed by the archbishop.

Columbanus and her council gave permission for the foundation in Ramsgrange in May 1967 and the first intake of more than forty girls arrived on 1 September the same year, thanks in large measure to the energy of de Lourdes Duffy, the local superior. To make the school viable, the sisters took in a limited number of boarders from throughout County Wexford and further afield. Du Saint Esprit O'Leary was a forward looking although disorganised administrator, according to her second in command, Paschalina, and welcomed the establishment of Ramsgrange Community School from the amalgamation of St Louis and Shielbaggan Vocational School in 1977. A good number of sisters taught there, including Annuncia Murphy, Jane Vereker and Noreen Hurley – who arrived hot-foot from Nigeria for her interview for the vice-principalship – and Finola Cunnane worked there as chaplain. The community in Ramsgrange left the big convent in 1991. As in all such cases it was a time of heartbreak and loss: Immaculata was the last to lock the door and 'cried the path over'. Wexford VEC later bought the old college for use as an outdoor education centre.

The St Louis foundation in Ballymena dates from 1924, when Canon McDonnell bought a substantial house for the sisters. A new grammar school was opened in 1954, under the terms of the 1947 Education Act, which set up a two-tier secondary education system with a qualifying examination for children at the age of eleven. During the 1960s there was a thriving community of twenty-four sisters who played an active role in the parish as well as running the school and boarding school. In 1970 the management introduced coeducation and the school continued to expand, needing a new extension. At the time of writing St Louis, Ballymena, is a coeducational grammar school with almost a thousand pupils. St Louis Grammar School, Kilkeel, is now a coeducational 'specialist school in technology' and has almost six hundred pupils.

St Joseph's Training School in Middletown, County Armagh, served a different need from mainstream education. Carina Muldoon, a primary teacher, remembers that Columbanus 'offered her the option' of Middletown in 1966 and, after doing a diploma in social work in Leicester University, she and Mary O'Driscoll came to work there in 1967. Carina spent the rest of her working life in St Joseph's. For her Middletown had a special charism and she was impressed by the kindness of the sisters on the staff, among them Conception Hynes, who said to her, 'Only stay if you love them' [the children]. The team found the Northern authorities were willing to provide funding running to several million pounds annually if they 'laid out a good business case and convinced them' and were able to show good outcomes for the expenditure. It was exceptional for a small residential centre to have a swimming pool and gym as St Joseph's had. Provision was much better in the North than in the South for most of Carina's time in Middletown.

Carina and her colleagues set out to deinstitutionalise the centre, perhaps inspired by the way the congregation itself was being de-institutionalised in the 1970s, and received funding to build units that were more like a home, with en suite bedrooms, kitchens and open fires 'to comfort the children'. They recruited resident staff, for whom they built twelve apartments – there were forty staff in all between teachers, care workers and various kinds of instructors, for about thirty girls – and for a period Canice Durkan ran a small hostel in Belfast to provide a home for girls after their release from Middletown. Carina and Mary Healy became agile legal workers, advocates for the children, challenging law and creating precedent in court.

On 24 July 1990 Catherine Dunne, who worked in St Joseph's, was killed by an IRA bomb on the Killylea Road, a short distance from Middletown, as she gave a lift home to a colleague, Cathy McCann. The target of the attack was a car in which three RUC constables – Constable William Hansen, Reserve Constable Joshua

Willis and Reserve Constable David Sterrit – were travelling. All three were killed. Catherine's passenger, a young mother, recovered from the injuries she received in the blast. Catherine was, in the current phrase, a collateral victim of terrorist violence, not the target of the attack, and the sheer randomness of her death was part of its horror.

Catherine, a Dubliner, was educated in Balla and entered St Louis in 1971. She was assistant deputy director in Middletown, where her athletic talents found a great outlet. One of the youngest sisters in the congregation in Ireland, she glowingly described her life in an *Irish Times* article by Christina Murphy on 9 May 1980: 'It's just knowing that I'm in the right place...feeling the contentment.'

At the time of Catherine's death, her close friend Uainín Clarke recollected her gentleness: 'Sunday night was a warm night. There were a lot of moths getting in. Catherine couldn't bear to have them killed. She collected each one and put it safely outside.'

The congregation made a great effort not to lose sight of the loss suffered by the families of the murdered RUC constables, some of whom attended Catherine's funeral. It was a challenging time for many Northern sisters and for those based in Middletown, who had run the gauntlet of RUC and British army checkpoints for years, many of these discourteous and obstructive. Fiona Fullam, regional leader at the time, wrote to the sisters on 30 July 1990 with a plea 'to move out from behind our own barriers and make peace'. Catherine's death was 'a moment of truth for us but also a moment of grace. It is a prophetic moment for us as sisters of St Louis but especially as sisters of St Louis faced with this northern situation.'

In 1996 a new children's order, imported from Britain, passed into law and the school became a voluntary organisation, called St Joseph's Adolescent Centre. It was stipulated that each child had to stay in the centre on a voluntary basis and could not be impeded even from running away in the middle of the night, something for which the sisters felt they could not take responsibility. The model changed from block funding to a system based on occupancy and the community in Middletown 'saw the writing on the wall,' as Carina puts it. The centre officially closed on 1 July 2000, after almost a hundred and twenty years of caring for children, but before long the North-South Ministerial Conference (Education) had acquired the buildings for use as a centre of excellence for children with autism spectrum disorders. Michael Woods, Minister for Education in the Republic and Martin McGuinness, his northern counterpart, announced this innovative cross-border development in April 2002.

The sisters sadly vacated the convent in Middletown in 2010, forming a small community nearby. For Carina, leaving the convent was even worse than closing the school, as she felt a 'sacramental history' about the building. Every convent that had to be closed, every community that was broken up caused intense grief and loss, especially for sisters who had spent many years in a particular house. Etheldreda Ryan, who spent thirty-three years in Ballymena and was in her nineties when the convent there closed, insisted on being the person to take the host from the tabernacle for the last time as she had been the one to put it into the tabernacle in the first place. Stories like this are woven into every community and house of the institute.

The first St Louis foundation in Belfast was at the invitation of Bishop Philbin of Down and Connor. A girls' secondary school for the new and growing parish of St Agnes in Andersonstown, west Belfast, was first mooted in 1965 and when the convent in Cushendall closed that summer Mona Lally and Clare Maguire went to Belfast to establish the school. On 6 September 1966 St Genevieve's Girls' Secondary School opened, with an intake of five hundred and fifty pupils, neatly dressed in a variation of the Fraser Hunting Tartan chosen by Mona. Alas, no desks – the shipment was delayed for a month by a strike on Liverpool docks. For the duration, the girls had to make do with books on their knees.

There were initially nine sisters on the staff of St Genevieve's, including the principal Mona and vice principal Clare. Alone among St Louis establishments the new school was not named St Louis, to avoid confusion with St Louise's, a comprehensive college for girls on Falls Road.

When St Genevieve's opened its doors it was a secondary

intermediate school, for girls who had failed to get places in Belfast's grammar schools, like St Dominic's and Rathmore, but Mona and Clare and their colleagues determined to prepare their pupils for public examinations, then junior certificate and senior certificate, later GCE O-Levels and CSE – something not normally open to secondary school pupils. From 1971 a 'consortium' of nearby De La Salle school for boys and St Genevieve's began to offer A-Level classes and in January 1979 the name of the school was changed to St Genevieve's High School. Thanks to the sisters' vision the first Irish girl ever to get a coveted place in Balliol College, Oxford, was a St Genevieve's pupil, Kathleen Leonard, who went to study jurisprudence there in 1982.

The Northern Troubles had its first direct impact on St Genevieve's when families on the Lower Falls Road were burned out of their houses in August 1969. For the rest of that summer, tension between Catholics and Protestants remained high. The school hall became home to refugees and De La Salle was a coordinating centre and clothes and bedding distribution depot, while welfare authorities and voluntary workers helped the catering staff to feed three hundred people. After a short honeymoon when Catholics saw the British army as protectors and especially after internment was introduced in 1971, west Belfast effectively became a war zone with riots, disturbances, shoot outs, bombs and burnings of buses and cars.

As part of Operation Motorman, which began on 31 July, soldiers of the Royal Fusiliers and Royal Green Jackets occupied the school on 3 August 1972. Luca Henry, who spent almost all her teaching career in St Genevieve's, and was principal 1985-95, describes it: 'They came up to Louisville on Glen Road and demanded the keys from Mona [principal at that time] and there was nothing she could do. The school was a vantage point and they wanted to occupy it.' A week later a Russian rocket and a bomb demolished the De La Salle gym and badly damaged St Genevieve's assembly hall, shredding the curtains and splitting the piano in two. Fortunately there was no loss of life. The soldiers moved into a three-storey classroom block when school reopened in September, and the seven hundred and fifty pupils had to be accommodated in twenty mobile classrooms, sandwiched between the army and La Salle, with limited access to other areas of the campus. The situation was described by the authorities as an 'educational disaster' but school life went on, the staff determined to maintain some normality for the pupils. Bishop Philbin intervened with the British army, which moved out at the end of November, and the school facilities were reinstated in May 1973.

There are now a thousand pupils in La Salle and nine hundred in St Genevieve's, which has a new school building. The latter has seventy teachers but no sisters on the staff since Mary Connell retired, although Anne McCourt is still chaplain and looks after pastoral care. In this way she stays in touch with the young people of the area and their needs, which is important for the maintenance of the youth ministry which she runs with Luca in the community house in Hillhead Crescent. There they 'nurture' young people, trying to develop citizenship, justice, decency and honesty, as well as some aspect of faith. They recruit the young people from the school, from families, often families with problems, that they have known for two or three generations. For Luca and Anne it is a way of giving to the community outside the education system and giving something to young people whom the education system has failed.

A new convent, Louisville, was built on the Glen Road in 1967 and over the years the original community of teachers from St Genevieve's was augmented by sisters studying in various colleges and hospitals and others working in a variety of ministries: primary schools, parish work, retreats and chaplaincy. Barbara McArdle left school to work with Eurochildren, an organisation founded by Robert Matthieu, a Belgian priest who was director of Caritas in Antwerp. It offered the children of the Troubles in Belfast and Derry the chance to live for a month or more with a family in Belgium and the possibility of returning each year to the same family. Later the organisation was extended to France, Germany, Switzerland and Austria. Barbara's full time involvement meant that Eurochildren could take advantage of a new government-funded employment scheme to acquire a premises and give employment to some eighteen people to help with organisation and secretarial work.

Louisville closed in 1999; now some sisters live in smaller communities throughout Belfast, while others live alone.

The schools established by St Louis sisters thrived as day schools and, as time went on, under lay principals. After the introduction of free education St Louis High School in Rathmines expanded greatly. It had eight hundred pupils when Eilis Ní Thiarnaigh was principal there from 1976. A new block of classrooms was added in 1978. St Louis Primary School in Williams' Park, Rathmines, became coeducational in 1984 after the closure of the boys' school in Richmond Hill, and Anne Murray, principal of the High School from 1980, and her staff researched the feasibility of a coeducational secondary school, an idea that the primary school staff and local parents strongly supported. The decision to remain a girls' school was, according to Anne, not philosophical but practical: because the school had recently completed a big building programme there was no money for further development although it was still over capacity; nor was there enough space to develop sports facilities for boys or for subjects that boys might want to study.

One of the jewels in the crown of St Louis Rathmines is the choral group Cantairí Óga Átha Cliath (Young Dublin Singers), which was founded by Proinsias Ó Ceallaigh, a music inspector, in November 1960. Since the premature death of Ó Ceallaigh in 1976 it has been directed by the indefatigable Brian Ó Dubhghaill, also a former music inspector. The choir, which has a junior and a senior component and a repertoire of classical and contemporary choral music, is based in the primary and high schools in Rathmines, and has performed and competed successfully all over Europe. The principals of the primary school, Madeleine Healy and her successor, Hermann Devlin, provided essential support in the development of Cantairí Óga, as did subsequent principals of the primary and secondary schools in the maintenance of what must surely be the outstanding school-based choir in Ireland – as well as the most long standing.

In June 2005 Pauline Johnson invited all the St Louis schools to come together in Dublin for a performance of Handel's *Messiah*, which took place the following January in the Church of the Three Patrons, Rathgar. This extraordinary logistical feat was coordinated by pupils past and present, teachers past and present and parents and relatives of pupils and sisters. The combined choir was jointly directed by Eileen English and Sinéad Fay from Carrickmacross, Pauline herself and music teacher Clíona McDonough from Rathmines. The choral experience that audience members described as 'moving' and 'uplifting' was a tribute to the institute's great musical tradition, which is alive in all the St Louis/Le Chéile schools and to the spirit of collegiality that links the staff and pupils of the different schools, a true reflection of *Sint Unum.*

In 1975 the congregation agreed in principle to set up boards of management in all its secondary schools but this took some time to implement. Traditionally, although this was probably not articulated by the leadership or the sisters themselves, religious orders in the person of the principal carried out all the functions of a board: ownership, caretaking, maintenance of the school plant and accountability. A lay principal could not be appointed in any school without having a board of management in place. Essentially what was required and what was finally arrived at was a system that would allow the congregation to license its premises to a board of management (with a lay principal) to run a school, while observing the relevant statutory provisions.

As Anne Murray describes it, religious schools under the old system were like a family business, which was fine when the family was working well but could become dysfunctional and was, in time, sure to present succession issues. Among the advantages were the hidden subsidy of active retired sisters giving voluntary service, like Madeleine Healy, former principal of the primary school, who gave extra maths classes to first years in Rathmines in Anne's time.

Anne became regional leader in 1986 after her term as principal in Rathmines. The congregation had to appoint a lay principal in Ballymena when Síle Canty retired in 1987 and there was no sister available to replace her. After this everyone realised, although some with reluctance, that lay principals were the future and that management structures were needed in all the St Louis schools.

Religious orders, as proprietors of the vast majority of Catholic schools in Ireland, north and south, were faced with the question of how best to license their schools to the boards of management that would run them, with lay principals, once religious were no longer available to play this role. St Louis became part of a combined trust body called Le Chéile ('Together'). The order's representatives worked for several years with eleven (later twelve) other congregations, including De La Salle brothers, Dominican sisters and Holy Faith sisters, all with between four and eight schools. Le Chéile took years of collaboration before coming to fruition and the composition of its charter was a long, long process of 'folding in', the heritage and identity of all the congregations. In Anne's words the trust 'has been practising collaboration for ten years'.

From now on Le Chéile will appoint the boards of management, hold induction and training, supervise the formation of chaplains and sit on interview boards for principals and deputy principals. The boards of management are accountable to the trustees and are required to provide budgets, end of year reports and building plans.

In the community schools, Ramsgrange, Kiltimagh and Blakestown, the St Louis Institute is a joint trustee with the local VEC. Community schools are governed by deeds of trusts, so the institute could not hand over their trusteeship of these schools to Le Chéile: at the time of writing, they are under review. However the community schools are associated with Le Chéile: they attend meetings and the annual conference, and Le Chéile staff are available to the schools in an advisory capacity.

In September 2009 St Louis commissioned and licensed its schools to Le Chéile for three years so that the trust could in turn commission and license the schools to the boards of management. The schools pay €1 per student to license the plant. The trust and charter were officially launched on 6 March 2009, when the relevant congregational leader presented the chairperson of the board of management of each of the fifty participating schools with a lighted Le Chéile candle.

St Louis sisters were as much involved in primary as in secondary education in the Republic and Northern Ireland. Except for Balla, everywhere St Louis sisters had a secondary school they had a primary school: often the primary followed the secondary within a few years, such as in Dundalk, in 1953. In some towns, like Clogher and Clones, sisters worked only in the primary school, thereby becoming thoroughly inserted in the community. Because of its situation so close to the border with Northern Ireland, the primary school in Monaghan was itself an interface during the Northern Troubles: as Maura Dempsey, who was principal there, remembers, the school had to integrate children from families of all shades of political opinion and children of the security forces who were based in the area, as well as a good number of Northern families who fled sectarian violence to settle in the South. Máire Cannon, the last St Louis sister to work full-time in education, retired in 2012 from her position in this primary school, which was established, in its original location, by the pioneers from Juilly in 1859.

With the exception of Rathmines infant and primary schools, which belong to the congregation and are jointly managed with the parish, all the schools in which the sisters taught were parish schools. When St Louis, Rathmines was established, in 1939, the parish, like the country, had few financial resources and the sisters put a great deal of effort, time and their own money into the development and maintenance of the school. Rathmines differed from schools in small towns, drawing its pupils from up to thirty-five parishes all over the south inner city and southern suburbs, and it has always been considerably larger than the sisters' other schools. For these reasons the sisters who taught there did not have the same connection with a specific parish community but they made up for this by the relationship they built with pupils and their parents.

Madeleine Healy and Scholastica Gibbons were two of the most influential principals in the history of Rathmines, Scholastica of the infant school from the foundation in 1939 until 1973 and Madeleine of the primary school 1941-69. Until the new curriculum was introduced in primary schools in 1971 classes were very large, even after the lifting of the marriage ban allowed married women teachers back into the classroom. (Loreto Hickey had a class of seventy-three in Rathmines in 1974.) Overcrowding was common; long-suffering teachers had to teach four separate classes in the hall until an extension was built in 1956. There was a great deal of rote learning by pupils, who sat in compliant rows facing the teachers. The curriculum was extremely structured in Rathmines, as in all the primary schools, geared towards the primary certificate – which pupils sat at the end of sixth class until it was abolished in 1967 (and many less able pupils failed) – and exams for scholarships to secondary schools, which pupils traditionally took at the end of seventh class. Madeleine Healy had a great eye for the bright girl who would win a scholarship to a St Louis boarding school in Balla, Kiltimagh, Monaghan or Carrickmacross and had such a good knowledge of her charges that she matched pupil and school very neatly.

'Madeleine gave us great training,' says Mairéad Conole, another Rathmines graduate. 'She kept us on our toes.' It may have been hard going, with group work and inspectors dropping by unannounced, but, says Mairéad, there was a great *esprit de corps* both in the school and in the big convent community and someone would always cover books or mark copies with you in the evening.

Rathmines was a pilot school for the new child-centred curriculum which was unveiled in 1971 and for various other developments in the teaching of religion and secular subjects. Scholastica and Madeleine embraced the changes with enthusiasm: the former was doing group work with her infants from the mid-1960s and Madeleine pioneered new maths and group teaching from the late 1960s. For a 1969 article in *The Irish Times*, Michael Heney visited Rathmines, describing it as 'a large convent school in a fashionable part of south Dublin city'. The article belongs to an age of discretion before celebrity culture was invented: among headmistress, teachers and pupils, no one is named. The picture is rosy, even Utopian; classes are about forty (only); children are self-motivated; there is achievement both for the able and the less able; and it is difficult to get the children to go home in the evening, such is their enjoyment of school.

The dissenting voice of an older teacher who is alleged to have muttered, 'We used to have chalk and talk, now we have walk and gawk,' is not represented in the article but is recalled by Maura Dempsey, who was on the staff in Rathmines at the time. Rathmines became well known as an innovative school and attracted visitors and experts from all over the country.

Rathmines was described as 'fashionable' in the *Irish Times* article but in reality it has a very mixed catchment area. For Marion Reynolds, who succeeded Scholastica as principal of the infant school in 1974, it was one of the school's finest attributes that the poorest children got to know the sons and daughters of privilege. The school was one of those chosen to participate in the Rutland Street Project, funded by the Van Leer foundation: this involved setting up a pre-school and assessing the outcomes for the children. The resulting body of work was incorporated in the revised curriculum introduced in 1999. Madeleine, along with Mary Fallon and Helena Moss, also began a social/educational ministry in Mountpleasant Buildings, an area of deprivation known as 'the Hill', in an effort to improve the morale of the people who lived there. As part of this, children could avail of classes in music and cookery. When Williams Park absorbed Tranquilla, a primary school on Upper Rathmines Road, and the boys' school on Richmond Hill, the social mix became even more pronounced.

Rathmines, according to Maura Dempsey, was a 'breeding ground for the missions and the training colleges in Africa'. It certainly made a contribution to pedagogy and education policy in Ireland. It is still a varied and lively school, having become more and more cosmopolitan as the community in which it is located absorbed people from many lands during the years of the Celtic Tiger.

17

Ghana Today

'A chance to grow'

Martha Appiah-Kubi, 2011

Martha Appiah-Kubi is new to the Ghanaian team that began its leadership term in spring 2011. She has spent much of her career in formation: after training in Jos and working in Akure for two years, she came home in 1995 when Ghana became a region and established the formation house in Kumasi. For several decades Ghanaian novices had been receiving two years of formation in Akure. As Martha puts it: 'When I came of age I realised we were left alone and had to do leadership ourselves. On our own we were just Ghanaians.' Nigeria has a greater number of older sisters (in their sixties) than Ghana and for the Ghanaian sisters it was as if they prematurely lost a generation, not just of grandmothers but of mothers, and had to make their own way without the benefit of the wisdom and experience of others (a particularly grave loss in a matrilinear society).

When Ghana became a region in 1995 a few Irish sisters remained, but not as long as sisters did in Nigeria. Consilii O'Shaughnessy, who had been working in the National Catholic Health Secretariat in Accra since 1991, served on the first leadership team, with Georgina Edwine (regional) and Helena Owusu Fosua. Mary O'Donovan was back in Kumasi, working in catechetics and marriage formation for Bishop Sarpong. When she left it was 'just Ghanaians' on their own.

Josephine Apiagyei became head of the regional leadership team in 2011, her second term as regional leader. Three of the team members in Ghana maintain full-time jobs and Lucy Mary Afful is a full-time student. With thirty sisters in the region and a greater concentration of communities in one geographical area, Ashanti, or its neighbouring Akan area, Brong-Ahafo, the team's task is much less challenging than that of the provincial leadership in Nigeria. Apart from Accra, which is four to five hours' drive away, the other seven houses are clustered around Kumasi in the southern half of the country. There are two communities in the interior, in the diocese of Konongo-Mampong: Mampong, a teaching apostolate (public school) is only thirty minutes from Kumasi but Oku, which has a health apostolate as well as a nursery, primary and junior secondary school, is quite a distance away.

Ghana is a notably homogeneous region and team: most of the sisters are Ashanti, as are three of the team, with one, Martha, a Fanti, another Akan tribe. All the leadership team members are teachers and three of the four team members worked for a long time in formation, itself a collaborative ministry, which developed their knowledge of the sisters in the region and the issues the region now faces.

Ashanti's matrilinear culture, which means that inheritance and responsibilities follow in the female line, means that getting married and having children is seen as very important, especially for girls. Ghanaian people often comment on women who are unmarried as somehow lacking something (a husband and family) and the sisters of the region are conscious of supporting one another as unmarried religious women. It was certainly not part of Josephine's parents' plan for her to enter religious life, as she did in 1983. She went to school in St Louis in Takoradi when Irish sisters taught there before it was taken over by the government. At the time of hardship and hunger in the country when she was finishing school she had particular reason to admire the dedication of St Louis sisters like Máirín Barrett, Ann Concannon and Betty Dalton. Not only did they stay and teach in Takoradi and Kumasi; they mastered and taught subject areas in which they were not qualified because so many Ghanaian teachers had left the country. She also remembers with affection and respect Marie du Rosaire Diver, who was principal of St Louis Secondary School, Kumasi, Marcia Foley and Finola Cunnane, who before her final profession worked in the Drug Distribution Centre in Accra.

Josephine used to be a teacher in Kumasi but now works for the Catholic Education Unit as an inspector, a job for which she is paid by the government. She lives with Lucy Mary Afful and others, in community in the regional house in Parakou, Accra. Her day job, as part of a team of four, is to inspect the sixty eight Catholic schools that are spread across the archdiocese of Accra: the work involves counselling and helping the teachers with the curriculum in a spirit of collegiality rather than inspection per se. The charismatic Gabriel Charles Palmer Buckle is now archbishop of Accra and, Josephine says, 'a very welcoming colleague'.

The number of vocations in the region is stable and there is little attrition. The leadership is confident that St Louis sisters will continue to have vocations in Ghana as they seem consistently to get one, two or three postulants – and sometimes even more – every year. This is not a big number but, as leaders in the order always say, it is more important to have quality than quantity when it comes to vocations.

Ghanaians gained a great deal by going for formation in Akure, despite the loneliness these mostly teenage girls felt in the new culture of Nigeria – several sisters mentioned differences in food as one of the main reasons for adjustment. Sisters from the two countries formed lasting bonds. Georgina Edwine, a senior sister in Ghana, was in the novitiate at the same time as Winifred Ojo and it is evident when one sees them together that they are real sisters. Georgina initially trained as a primary school teacher and also worked in formation, first in Akure as assistant to the novice mistress in the 1980s and then for many years with temporary professed sisters in Kumasi. Now she is responsible for formation on the leadership team, working as administrator in the primary section of St Louis Jubilee School in Kumasi. Mercy Boateng is principal and Evelyn Serwa Adjei, Patricia Sarpomaa Mensah and Mary Takyiwaa Mensah are the other sisters on the teaching staff.

The Ghanaians try to maintain links with Nigeria, celebrating with the communities there and over the past few years grieving with them the deaths of sisters. Benedicta Boakye-Yiadom has volunteered to join two Nigerian sisters on the new mission to Ethiopia. But the sisters in Ghana would wish for greater contact with their Nigerian consœurs, perhaps to share again some element of formation or renewal or simply to share in the energy of being Sisters of St Louis.

It is clear from talking to the Ghanaian leaders that they have a deep desire that sisters should be well equipped for the changing world, to play their role as best they can. If Josephine were not taken up more than full time with leadership and her job in the inspectorate she would have liked to participate in movements to influence change in her country, like Friends of the Earth, but she is glad that her work in education allows her to bring ecology to the training of teachers.

Georgina Edwine came from Kumasi but went to school in Accra to the Holy Spirit sisters, who had no Ghanaian members, and it was when she met Bernice Broohm that she became attracted to the St Louis Institute. Bernice, she says, was 'very dynamic, forceful and wise'. At that time Georgina didn't know the difference between an international order and an indigenous order. This was in the very early days of the native sisterhood, as she is one of the older sisters of the region, and her grandmother, who reared her after the death of her parents, was afraid that she would not persevere and would come back home to Ghana in disgrace. She also felt keenly her responsibility to Georgina's late parents to put their daughter on the 'right' path in life (marriage).

She got to know Irish sisters in Kumasi when she attended the order's teacher training college. Still a novice when amalgamation took place in 1976, she was fully in favour of it, as she did not want to break the link with Nigeria. 'We are all Africans. Nigeria is important to us because we trained together and formed relationships. Some people were less keen on the amalgamation. Ireland is very far but for some decisions we have to refer to Ireland and the link is always there. It is always in our minds that we belong to a group.' The Irish sisters in Ghana told Georgina and her contemporaries about Ireland and they in turn convey a sense of the Irish missioners and the congregation's roots in Juilly to younger sisters.

The Jubilee School in Kumasi was established in 1998, the fiftieth anniversary of the first foundation. It began as a nursery/primary school but has grown, in response to demand from parents, to include a junior high school. This school is private – the sisters built it and they want it to continue to be a St Louis school – whereas all secondary schools are now government schools. The Jubilee School receives no public funding but the fees are reasonable, although the sisters have to pay teachers according to the government salary structure in order to get good staff. They offer bursaries and the fees they charge are not as high as other schools. In Georgina's words, this school 'is not for the very poor or the very rich'.

The decision to operate a private school was not without controversy, in view of the institute's option for the poor, which has prevailed since the 1980s, but the Ghanaian sisters see the necessity for private education because religious instruction is not permitted at all in government schools. As Georgina puts it, 'To train the young we have a private primary school.' The sisters' aim is to inculcate Christian values in their pupils and in this way make a difference that will filter through society, as their pupils will be mothers, professionals and formers of opinion in years to come – Ghana is about 10 per cent Catholic. So they have given up feeling guilty about running a private school, which is successful and over-subscribed.

Like the St Louis schools in Nigeria, the Jubilee School attracts Muslims and pupils of other Christian religions. Parents of all faiths feel that in Catholic schools, run by religious, their children will be looked after and well taught and disciplined. All the pupils attend classes of Christian teaching: Catholics have classes in Catholic worship and everyone who is not a Catholic goes to a more general worship class.

About half the St Louis sisters in Ghana work in education: as well as teaching in the Jubilee School, sisters work in public primary and secondary schools and in St Louis College of Education,

Mbrom, Kumasi, which celebrated its golden jubilee in 2010. Joyce Eyiaah was the last sister to teach in Roman Girls Junior Secondary School, as St Bernadette's Catholic Girls' School, where the 1947 pioneers went to teach, is now called. The other half of the region's employed members are nurses, working in Catholic hospitals, in the clinic in Goasa and in the clinic in Oku which was established by Ancilla Fox, Esther Adzah and Helena Owusu Fosua in 1993.

Sisters of St Louis began their ministry in St Michael's Hospital, Pramso, in 1989, at the request of the then archbishop of Kumasi, Peter Sarpong, as nursing personnel was needed in the hospital. Elizabeth Osei, the pioneer, commuted from Mbrom community in Kumasi and Veronica Buah joined her a year later. In January 1997, Mary Owusu Frimpong, an ophthalmic nurse, went to work in Pramso, where her services were badly needed. She is also executive secretary for health in the diocese of Obuasi. Kumasi was divided into five dioceses in 1995 and Pramso became part of Obuasi diocese. The sisters' convent was built by the diocese and they took up residence in August 1997. It is now called Thérèse Brek community.

Genevieve Sekgpeb joined the community in 2005 and worked as a pharmacy technician in the hospital; she is currently on study leave at the Catholic University, Sunyani, studying public health. Dorothy Abuah joined the community in December 2011, working as a formator with the two postulants who live there.

Sisters also worked in St Martin de Porres Hospital, Eikwe, from 1989 to 1994.

St Peter's School is a public Catholic school located in Wioso, in the diocese of Goasa, which was established in September 2000. In August 2008 the Bishop of Goaso, Peter Atuahehe, invited the Sisters of St Louis to come to the school in the hope that they would help make a more holistic education available to the students. He was aware that the existing low educational levels resulted in a strong rural to urban drift because poorly educated people were obliged to leave for the cities in search of menial jobs. Attendance at school was very poor, as mothers took the children with them to the farms, where they frequently suffered snake and insect bites or even got lost in the forests. In November 2010 two sisters, Joyce Eyiah and Naomi Nkrumah, began to work in this deprived apostolate. Currently the school has an enrolment of six hundred and twenty boys and girls, of whom one hundred and thirty four are in the junior secondary school. In 2011 Esther Adzah, a nurse, joined the Goaso community and has responsibility for running the clinic at Domeabra – this eloquent word means 'prove your love by coming over'.

All the Ghanaian sisters who are working are drawing government salaries as teachers or nurses and only one sister is retired as yet. Some temporary professed sisters are completing their initial training in teaching or nursing and other sisters are qualifying for a higher degree in a particular discipline or studying abroad. The region left the St Kizito Parish, Nima-Accra, after more than twenty years of involvement in a very deprived community, 'for lack of personnel,' according to Josephine: 'We were too few and spread too thinly.' Ghanaian sisters no longer work full time in catechetics or parish ministry, although many are involved in this kind of work in their own communities after working hours. The sisters, as in all regions of the institute committed to the empowerment of women, have been involved in the Women's Council of Ghana for many years.

Although she became seriously ill during her novitiate in Akure, Martha Appiah-Kubi, who comes from the Kumasi region, had a strong sense of belonging 'to the St Louis family'. There were seven Nigerians in her set and she had Davnet McGreal and Ann Concannon as novice mistresses. In Kumasi she lived in community with some of the Irish sisters, a different kind of family, and an experience that she appreciated: pioneer, Joannes Hayes, Juilly's Clare Ryan and Breda O'Hanrahan, who was the superior and in charge of junior temporary professed. Martha is qualified not alone in formation but in education. Having studied in Nottingham for a master's degree in educational administration she now teaches in St Louis College of Education in Kumasi.

During her term of leadership Martha will carry on her full-time lecturing job as well as fulfilling other responsibilities in the college.

In her first term she handled finance on her own; this time there are two bursars, Martha and Lucy Mary. Josephine deals with education and is the public face of the Ghanaian region, while Georgina is responsible for formation.

It is Martha who expresses most clearly her sense of the role the Irish sisters played in her development and that of her consœurs. She thinks she was too young and untried to be in charge of formation, although she was trained and had had experience in Akure, when she was asked to come back to Kumasi 'quite suddenly' once the Nigerian province and the Ghanaian region were formed in 1995: 'This was forced on us when the Irish left as we did not have an older generation of Ghanaian sisters. On the other hand not having the Irish around gave us a chance to grow.'

Lucy Mary Afful, who comes from the central region of Ghana, encountered the St Louis sisters in her boarding school in Takoradi. She spent a year in Dublin, studying formation, in 2001-2. When she came back from Ireland she was put in charge of the novices in the formation house, a job she did until 2009. She found formation work 'sometimes a bit difficult and lonely' and found there was no escaping having to make tough decisions at times. Although there was a formation team the members were not in Kumasi with her on a day to day basis. Somebody was in charge of postulants, someone in charge of junior professed, someone from the regional team had responsibility for formation, someone else was in charge of aspirants and the whole team met no more than a few times a year.

Lucy Mary is currently doing a postgraduate course in business and finance. It will take about six years to finish as it is a distance course. A reluctant team member, she agreed to take on leadership because she felt her course of study allowed her the flexibility to be on the team and gave her some financial skills.

The vision of the Ghanaian leadership is to keep and improve the existing apostolates in education and health. Good formation and good education for the members are a priority, as is helping sisters to grow in confidence. Education is part of the financial husbandry of the region, an investment in security. The better educated the sisters are the better the salaries they will be able to contribute. The strategic plan formulated at the region's chapter includes planning for the future and how to care for the sick and the elderly when the need arises.

What emerges clearly from talking to the Ghanaian leadership team is the hunger of these women for continuing development. For instance, Georgina would like to train to be a spiritual director but doubts that she would be able to follow such a course of study in Ghana (and she would be reluctant to move abroad to study).

Project writing is part of the responsibility of the leadership team but formal applications for funding to international mission organisations can be counter cultural in Ghana. A local chief might give the sisters a piece of land to start a school or clinic. This would be an oral contract, a tradition that has worked perfectly well in Ghana for centuries. But the region cannot seek funding for a school built on such a piece of land because the paperwork would not be considered legally in order. Lucy Mary, who finds that project writing is often a frustrating business, would prefer the region to be self-sufficient but knows this is not a realistic aspiration.

Dorothy Abuah studied communications in Leeds 2010-11 and is now the link person for communications in her region. Aware that teaching and nursing are very much the apostolates of the order, she was surprised but gratified when the region offered her the chance of doing the communications course 'out of the blue'. She, along with Theresa Peter from Nigeria, had done the formation course in Loreto House in Dublin the previous year, something that pleased her because she was able to live in community in the mission house with a companion on her course. As well as doing communications work, she is currently involved in formation with postulants and temporary professed sisters who are based in Pramso and Kumasi.

In October 2007 the region celebrated the diamond jubilee of the Sisters of St Louis in Ghana in St Louis Secondary School, Kumasi, an occasion of great joy and *sint unum*, with Nigerian sisters as honoured guests. 'At the end of it all, the sisters and the guests could not help but to lift up their hands and shake their bodies in praise and gratitude to God who has made all things possible.' (*St Louis Online*, January 2008).

The Ghana region is still a work in progress. Josephine Apiagyei says, 'We came up as Ghanaian sisters in a time of transition. Now we are trying to suit a new model of leadership to our own culture.'

18

Nigeria Today

'When your ovation is loudest'
Rita Akin-Otiko, 2011

Rita Akin-Otiko became Nigerian provincial on 25 August 2011, one of a team of five. She is the fourth provincial since the province was inaugurated in 1995: her predecessors were Isabel Mann, Patricia Ebegbulem and Patricia Ojo, the last two of whom were provincials for eight years. As befits a part of the institute where most sisters are in their thirties and forties and the oldest (Patricia Ebegbulem and Dorothy Yayock) are only in their late sixties, the leadership team is youthful and dynamic. None of the five has ever served in leadership before and it is the first time that there has been a team of five. But they will have plenty to do over the next four years in a country as vast, populous and diverse as Nigeria, with one hundred and fifty six sisters in twenty communities, including two foundations outside Nigeria, and a troubled politico-religious situation at home.

Life in Nigeria is stressful because the political situation is uncertain. Even aside from the recent murderous Muslim-Christian conflict, the sisters all comment on the sense of instability in the country as a whole. Whereas previously elections were held every four years in each of the thirty-six states simultaneously, now there are elections and changes of leadership at different times because of electoral irregularities. There is unemployment and unrest, violence and kidnappings.

Although the country is rich and food and oil are plentiful, ordinary people have had no sustained experience of government working for the common good. The sisters see their education apostolate as playing a role in educating responsible citizens and future leaders.

Before she became provincial Rita was principal of Louisville Girls High School, Ijebu-Itele, Ogun State, for eleven years. It was the first private secondary school owned by the St Louis sisters and opened its doors on 11 September 1998. She is clearly proud of the school and regrets having to leave her job of administration and teaching English and drama to take up leadership but, as this actor manquée neatly says, "It's good to leave the stage when your ovation is loudest.' For the province it was essential that the school be private (receive no government support) and that the sisters rather than the diocese should own it, as all the other St Louis schools had been taken over by the government. It began as what Rita calls 'a simple normal school' but in comparison to government schools it was so well run and had such good outcomes that it attracted the children of the rich. Rita justifies private schools as the only way the sisters can provide the kind of holistic well resourced education they aspire to – public education in Nigeria is habitually under resourced and overcrowded. Once the government took over the St Louis schools the order no longer had any control over the enrolment. For example, there were formerly three hundred plus students in the secondary school in Ikere-Ekiti; now the school has three thousand. When the government allowed sisters to set up private schools again and bishops invited them to their dioceses the province decided to follow this course of action.

The sisters can also use their private schools as a means of redistribution of income. Louisville Ijebu-Itele has a 'bridge of care' project: the girls donate money to feed and clothe the pupils in the three local primary schools and provide materials and training for the teachers. Rita describes it as 'rich children caring for poor children'. The site of sixty acres on which the school in Itele was built was given as a gift by a friend of the congregation and the school is profitable.

Rita says that the parents of the fee-paying pupils are pleased that the school asks for this social contribution from their daughters. The intake includes Muslims but the parents of these girls are equally favourable to the bridge of care and in her view the school is a 'model community'. It has five hundred and forty pupils aged between ten and sixteen, with forty on scholarship, full or partial. The schools operates a trust fund to provide for scholarships but some wealthy parents undertake to sponsor the education of a poorer child. According to Rita, 'We try to run it as a family school with a simple uniform and a good atmosphere.' After taking the West African Senior School Certificate (WASSC) some of the girls study in Nigeria, others abroad.

The province is now a good mix of Igbo, Yoruba and members of various minor ethnic groups from the north and non-Igbo parts of eastern Nigeria, such as Christiana Kure's ethnic group, Kagoma, from southern Kaduna. For Nigerians tribal identity is still strong but as the institute wishes to be counter cultural it de-emphasises, downplays the differences. From talking to the leadership team it seemed to me that tribal differences genuinely hold little importance for the province.

In Nigeria there has been an average of seven new postulants a year for the past ten years but the province is not blasé about vocations: it maintains an active profile, giving talks and visiting schools. Many of the entrants have already been to college but the congregation does not lightly turn anyone away. Winifred Ojo, a Nigerian on the central leadership team, attributes the high level of entrants to the congregation in Nigeria to the fact that: 'At the moment the only available avenue of service is religious life. There are not many single ladies: you are either married or a religious. Young women feel that the best way to free themselves for the service of God is by entering the convent.'

Itele has not yet produced any vocations and Rita attributes this to the fact that the well to do parents are 'too ambitious' for their daughters to have successful careers. But it is a source of pleasure and pride to her that she so often encounters St Louis alumnae doing well in all walks of life. Women in Nigeria are now taking their places in the cabinet, in the judiciary and in the professions.

About one third of the Nigerian congregation is involved in education (fifty six in all), most sisters teaching in government schools and in the order's nursery-primary schools. As well as Ijebu-Itele the province has a private school in Gwagwalada, 50 km from Abuja, the capital. It was established in 2006 and Carmel Mary Fagbemi was principal until shortly before her death in 2010, succeeded by Josephine Tiav. Because the Federal Capital Region around Abuja is a prosperous area, the school is self supporting, although it is new and 'not yet rich'. In appreciation of Carmel Mary's efforts to develop the school the parents of Louisville pupils wished to contribute financially towards her medical expenses but she died before this was realised. Faithful to their initial intention, the parents decided to use the funds they had collected to bring to fruition one of Carmel Mary's dreams: to provide quarters for the lay staff so that they could complement the work of the sisters in supervising the students. These staff quarters are now being built and a dining room is being provided by the province.

The province hopes to open a third private high school in Kaduna state before the end of the term of the current leadership.

The province's strategic plan for the next ten years is to concentrate on four apostolates in Nigeria: social work, pastoral work, health and education. This represents not so much a change or a rationalisation as the recognition of its core apostolates and a resolve to consolidate rather than to branch into other areas. For example, in order to be able to mission two sisters to the new foundation in Ethiopia the province had to let an apostolate in Ikare-Akoko 'fizzle out' by withdrawing a sister who was teaching in a government school. Among the social apostolates are a home for the sick in Ibadan; the Samaritan project for destitute and abandoned people in Lagos; the leprosarium in Akure, which also involves pastoral service, as sisters bring Communion to the residents; and Ondo, where sisters look after abandoned children.

Founding new schools is an expensive process and the province as a whole has to be financially stable and self-sufficient, while needing to subsidise some of the really poor apostolates, like Ijio, the community founded by Dorothy McMahon and Catherine Adelegan, and Ewulu (Louis Bautain farm) which is in the care of team member Janet Makinde and which the congregation is trying to revive on a more limited basis than before. The area of Ogwashi-Uku, near the farm, where the sisters have a hospital, is also poor.

From the provincial chapter of 2011 the team carries a number of mandates. Primary among them, as in all the regions of the congregation, is 'right relationship' – to be in consonance with self, with God, with other sisters, with people in the wider society and with the planet – which is of particular significance in Nigeria as the sisters bear witness to *Ut Sint Unum* in a divided country.

Quality of life and health also became a serious issue for the Nigerian province with the premature deaths from cancer of three sisters – Carmel Mary Fagbemi, Lucy Akindiose and Juliana Nwabuzo – over a seven-month period in 2010-2011. The team aims to provide a simple but healthy standard of living for its members and not spread itself too thinly, as perhaps it tended to do in the past. Bishops from all over Nigeria, as well as the Republic of Benin, constantly appeal to the order to establish new education, health or pastoral apostolates in their dioceses but these empowered women have learned how essential it is to be able to say no.

The new leadership team has divided the province into five administrative areas, one for each team member. Étampes, Itele, Akpassi and Lagos are Rita's responsibilities. The team member lives at least for part of the time in community in her own administrative area and attends monthly meetings in the provincial house in Ibadan. Each team member also takes responsibility for a particular aspect of the work of the team: Christiana Kure is bursar, Rita looks after education, Stella Akinwotu formation, Janet Makinde health and Catherine Ologunagba project writing.

Before she joined the provincial team Catherine, a science teacher, was principal in St Louis Secondary school in Kano, the first secondary school founded by the congregation in Nigeria for Kaduna diocese, now a voluntary agency school with six hundred pupils. Christiana Arokoyo succeeded Catherine as principal. In 2011 the school celebrated its sixtieth anniversary of unbroken St Louis administration. Like Ijebu-Itele and all the other schools where St Louis sisters in Nigeria work, it is an example of inter-faith collaboration in the interests of the girls' education. Many past pupils of Kano now have influential positions in Nigeria and abroad and the wife of the vice-president of Nigeria went to school there. By the time the next provincial team is chosen, a past pupil may actually be vice-president – or even president.

Catherine has responsibility for the scattered communities in the northern part of the country, where the sisters are less numerous than in the west: one community each in Kano, Bida in Niger State and Gwagwalada and two in Zonkwa, reflecting the extent of the sisters' apostolate there in education and health. This foundation, which the early missionary sisters carved out of the bush, has a primary school, hospital and a school of basic midwifery, and Dorothy Yayock has a pastoral ministry. There is also a postulant community. Bida, the foundation in Niger State in which Mary Murray served, had a secondary school but this was closed: the congregation returned to Bida on the invitation of the new bishop and runs a primary school there now. The school in Jos that was founded by St Louis sisters is in the hands of Our Lady of Fatima sisters, an indigenous order. Catherine lives in community in Gwagwalada in the southern part of her region, as it is nearer to the provincial house in Ibadan.

For Catherine, being in leadership in an international order means that the province's approach is more global and more enlightened, even though the work is local. She helped with secretarial work at the 2009 general chapter in Ireland and strongly supports mobility for mission. She believes education is a priority for sisters – not just the necessary qualification for an apostolate like teaching or nursing but training in administration and finance, and she would like to see more sisters working in the pastoral area, in Church ministry, spirituality and chaplaincy.

Janet Makinde is one of the two nurses on the Nigerian leadership team. There are twenty trained nurses in the province, sixteen of them involved in active ministry. She first encountered the St Louis sisters in Kano, near her home. As she came from a fervent Anglican family she had to struggle to become a Catholic, and, like Winifred Ojo, says she was attracted by the 'simplicity' of the sisters and their habit. After training in Zonkwa she worked in several hospitals, including a year on loan in Oku in Ghana, a place of great need. She also worked in Ewulu, in primary health care and on Louis Bautain farm, and now she is responsible for Ogwashi-Uku in Delta state which has two houses: one in Ogwashi, where there is a hospital, the second in Ewulu. The farm in Ewulu has not been a success and Janet says that from now on the leadership will look for volunteers who will be enthusiastic about rural life rather than simply appointing people to work there. One of her ambitions is to have a bigger community in Ogwashi and revive the farm, which was started by Juliana Nwabuzo, along with the primary healthcare service in Ewulu. The area is remote and the road to the farm poor, although there is some hope that the discovery of crude oil nearby may bring a tarred road. The people of Ewulu also want education so, as Janet sees it, the main work in Ewulu will no longer be the farm itself. The farm has a piggery but this demands a lot of attention so the plan is to sell it and to concentrate on plant produce, especially on the more than two thousand palm trees that produce a valuable crop of oil. It is another example of the congregation's determination to concentrate its efforts where they will have the best results. Janet lives in community in Ikere-Ekiti, which is home to St Louis Grammar School and a nursery-primary school that the province founded in September 1997: this community is among her responsibilities.

Christiana Kure, at forty, is the youngest on the leadership team. She looks after the communities in Iseyin and Ijio as well as those in Ibadan. She has no previous experience in finance but was principal of the school of midwifery in Zonkwa. After first profession she worked in primary evangelisation and basic education in Refawa with Brigitte Burke. This community, a satellite of Kano, was the best she ever lived in 'because of the simple faith of the people' (and no doubt Brigitte's generous zeal) and she was sad when a decision was made to close it down. She trained as a nurse in Zaria and served in several of the community's hospitals in the province as well as spending two years in St Louis Clinic, Akpassi, in the Republic of Benin, 2003-5. She never wanted to teach but was posted to Zonkwa, 'sharing the nursing experience with the student midwives,' and enjoyed it despite having to combine administration with far too much classroom teaching because of a shortage of tutors. In Zonkwa basic amenities like water and electricity are poor so it was difficult to get people to come to work there and she was not able to pay the tutors as much as they would have earned in a government training school. But it was a quiet, peaceful place until the post-election violence of Easter 2011 in which more than five hundred people are thought to have been killed there. Like many sisters working in administration, both in education and in healthcare, Christiana's wish after her term of leadership would be to return to bedside nursing.

In Christie's view, Hausa Muslims who came from Kano and Zaria in the northern part of Kaduna and settled in southern Kaduna for business were the originators of the conflict that began as political unrest after the presidential election of April 2011 and soon became a crisis. The Muslims, who, she says, 'want to lead by all means', were outraged when a Christian from the south, Goodluck Jonathan, was elected president, rather than a Hausa, and some of them were encouraged to violence by politicians. It has festered and broken out in various locations throughout the north, spreading even to Abuja at Christmas 2011. There are hardly ever any arrests or prosecutions and Christiana believes that some politicians pay the security forces to turn a blind eye.

At Easter 2011 casualties of the violence were brought to the St Louis Hospital in Zonkwa and the communities were confined to their convents for a week. They could not buy food and the electricity supply was so poor that they could not preserve food. Christie was then community leader in the postulants' house in Zonkwa, where there were three sisters as well as twenty postulants. After four days she drove the two hours' journey to Jos to get food for the postulants, ten of whom had arrived in Zonkwa only the previous month and were frightened for their lives. This group of ten postulants was later moved to Gwagwalada with their director, Theresa Peter. The other ten finished their postulancy in July and seven went on to the novitiate in Akure.

Stella Akinwotu, the oldest member of the provincial team,

is a secondary teacher with training in guidance, counselling and teaching religious knowledge. She is responsible for communities in the west of Nigeria: Ondo, Akure and Owo. Akure has a nursery and primary school for pupils aged three to ten, while St Louis Secondary School was taken over by the government. Ondo has a developing nursery-primary school employing three sisters, while one sister works in the secondary school, which was also taken over by the government. Stella was always interested in pastoral work and, after two years of teaching, she worked at this in Ikare until the house closed down, then in formation in Akure, then looked after the pastoral care of the girls in Louisville Girls' High School in Ijebu-Itele. For her, as for the rest of the Nigerian team, the central challenge is 'right relationship', which includes the resolution of any difficulties in community life. As each of the team is responsible for no more than four communities she hopes they will be able to visit each community in the country once every two months.

Stella believes that if the province is strategic in its thinking and careful with its resources there will not be a problem with personnel as long as vocations are steady: some of the houses will even be too small as many of the communities are currently no bigger than three or four sisters. She too is concerned about the health of the sisters. All three sisters who died recently were active until illness struck them down: 'They kept working and did not realise they were ill.' The leadership now calls on all sisters to be vigilant and to take good care of their health. 'The problem,' Stella says ruefully, 'is that we are workaholic.'

When Cáit Gibbons went to teach in Kano on mobility for mission, she was impressed by the fervour of the Nigerian sisters and their capacity for work (*Seo agus Siúd*, May 2010): 'Many of the sisters I talked to have at least three jobs on hand. As well as their main ministry [teaching or nursing in most cases] many are involved in work with aspirants, formation, Friends of St Louis Missions, associates, membership of the Conference of Religious Women in Nigeria… parish work, helping the priests with liturgies, sacrament preparation, RCIA.' When she commended them on their output they would reply, 'This is how we were trained.'

This is what Stella means by 'workaholic' – a noble institute tradition established by the pioneers in Kano in 1948.

In keeping with another noble institute focus on social justice and solidarity with victims, Patricia Ebegbulem has been involved since 1999 in working against the trafficking of women and girls from the developing countries into Europe and America. It is a serious problem for Nigeria: it is estimated that in Italy alone there are 15,000 Nigerian women involved in forced prostitution. As coordinator of the African Network against Human Trafficking, Patricia, who is based in Lagos, compiled in 2011 a handbook for schools, *Stop Trafficking in Women and Girls*.

The Republic of Benin, a former French colony, is Nigeria's neighbour to the west and only one-eighth of its size. In August 2011 St Louis sisters celebrated the tenth anniversary of their foundation in the country. Like Nigeria itself, Benin has had a turbulent and violent history since it gained independence from France in 1960. For almost twenty years the country suffered economic hardship under a Marxist dictatorship but since 1990, when it was renamed the Republic of Benin, democracy has taken root there.

In 1999 Bishop Antoine Ganye invited the sisters to his diocese, Dassa-Zoumé, to provide health and education services, and two years later, on 25 August 2001, three Nigerian sisters – Josephine Tiav, Maria Ilo and Mary Ogunjobi – established a St Louis community in Akpassi, a rural area a long distance from the capital. Now three other Nigerian sisters live and work there. Anthonia Titi Abe, who was licensed as a doctor in the University of Ilorin in March 2008 (the only practising doctor in the congregation) and Martina Ariyo, a nurse, work in a health clinic. Constance Dibie is able to draw a salary for teaching in a private school that helps to maintain the community. Most of the people of Akpassi are so terribly poor that they cannot even afford to pay for essential drugs and most often rely on traditional medicines. Antoine Ganye, now Archbishop of Cotonou, spoke of the continuing needs of his country in the hope that other St Louis sisters might be missioned there for education and medical care. But the needs in Nigeria are also great, although Rita, the provincial leader, would like to establish a bilingual French-English school in Benin: French is the *lingua franca* as there are so many local languages, even varieties of Yoruba.

The twentieth and final community of the Nigerian province is not in Nigeria itself but in France. The community based in the presbytery of Saint Baptiste de Guinette in Étampes, *a sous-préfecture* situated south of Paris (part of the *grande banlieu* or extended suburbs of the city) in the diocese of Évry, comprises Gladys Ekhareafo, Veronica (Chinyere) Okpara, who were missioned to France in Akure in November 2010, and Cécilia Uzodike.

Cécilia has lived in France since 1990, when an international community, attached to the French region, was established in Moissy Cramayel in the diocese of Meaux. For various personal and administrative reasons this community lasted only one year but Cécilia has worked in France ever since, first in Évry 1990-2005, where she had a job with the diocese, and lately in Étampes in the same diocese. Not alone was Évry a *ville nouvelle,* the diocese of Évry-Corbeil-Essonnes, as it came to be called, was a new diocese, from 1966. The second bishop of Évry, Guy Herbulot, she describes as 'a man of vision'. He worked to bring the Church to the people in the *cités populaires* (working class neighbourhoods), encouraging priests and sisters to share the lives of their parishioners by taking ordinary jobs.

In September 2005 Cécilia was appointed coordinator of parish life and a representative of the Catholic Church in civil society. She, Gladys and Chinyere work in collegiality with the pastoral team of five priests and a permanent deacon in the *secteur pastoral* (deanery) of Étampes and have responsibility for the day-to-day organisation of the parish of St Jean Baptiste de Guinette, where there is no resident priest. Guinette church was built in 1962 to cater for immigrant and migrant workers who came to make aircraft parts or work on farms in the surrounding area of Beauce.

Cécilia Uzodike is a force to be reckoned with. When I visited Étampes I met her in the local hospital where she had had a knee operation. A steady stream of parishioners came to visit her;

The central leadership team in Kilkeel, July 1975.
Standing, from left: Mary Jo Hand, Madeleine Healy and Dorothy McCloskey,
newly elected assistant superior general.
Seated, from left: Eustace O'Gorman and Colmcille Stephens, re-elected superior general.

Catherine Dunne, who was killed by an IRA bomb
near Middletown, County Armagh, in July 1990.

*Maura Byron (left) hands over the principalship of Louisville High School
to Frances Leonard, Woodland Hills, September 1969.*

Teresa Brett, pioneer in Maase-Offinso, Ghana, in 1951, in her role as tutor.

Bury St Edmunds, 1970. Standing, from left: Gabrielle Durcan, Emma Foy, Una McGuinness, Madeleine O'Callaghan, Theodore Lysaght, Aloysius Cawley. Seated, from left: Pancratius Givens, Zita Quinn, Helen O'Neill, Catherina Kenny, Patricia Rogers.

Maud Murphy with children in Lagos, 1985.

Eileen Nolan teaches guitar in Ikere.

Silver jubilarians, Akure, August 2002.
From left: Carmel Mary Fagbemi, Bridget Agum, Brigid Andoh,
Stella Akinwotu and Margaret Yusufu.

Deirdre O'Hanlon on the occasion of her 2007 award of Chevalier dans l'Ordre des Palmes Académiques. *From left: Daniel Haquin, Maire de Juilly, Cardinal Paul Poupard and Jean Luc Walker, Directeur du Cours Bautain.*

Irish associates with Marion Reynolds (far left) and Catherine Brennan (second from right) at the international associate conference in Loyola Marymount University, California, in 2008. From left: Angela McCrossan, Maura Costello and Malachy Marron.

Miriam Thérèse O'Brien with Franklin Siakor in Liberia or Côte d'Ivoire, about 1996. Franklin wears a JSR (Jesuit Refugee Service) T-shirt.

St Louis Jubilee School, Kumasi.

The inauguration of the Ghana region, 1995.
Anne Kavanagh is congregational leader and the bishop is Peter Sarpong of Kumasi.

Vera Cruz, Brazil, 1997/8. Standing, from left: Margaret Hosty, Suely Marinho de Sousa, Antonia (novice), Katey Dougan, Carmel Mary McCarthy, Bernice Broohm. Seated from left: Dorothy Yayock, Helen Regan, Elenice Natal de Lima, Fatima (associate).

Celebration of a hundred and fifty years of St Louis in Ireland, April 2009. Standing, from left: Eithne Woulfe, Ann Concannon, Isabel Mann, Maeve O'Reilly, Uainín Clarke, Martin McAleese, Mary O'Donovan. Seated, from left: Anne Kavanagh, President Mary McAleese.

in fact, she was working from her hospital room. It is clear that Cécilia, Gladys and Chinyere have a community as well as pastoral and religious function in Guinette that their parishioners greatly appreciate. Olga, one parishioner, eloquently dismissed the old-fashioned Church that she experienced all her life as stuffy, boring, moribund. Not so the ceremonies in Guinette today: lively, life-giving, colourful, musical were the terms she used.

Informality rules here. Everyone calls Cécilia 'tu', whereas *vou-voiement* prevails in the convent in Juilly. The French, so punctilious and rule-bound, have taken Cécilia to their heart and she is now a French citizen. When she was a student in Benin University, Jean de Grandsaigne, head of the French department and author of the *France-Afrique* textbooks, encouraged her to major in French: 'They will need you some day in France,' he said. Why am I not surprised to hear Cécilia say that when she was in primary school she wanted to be 'a female priest'. She had never met a sister; nor did she know that such people existed. Now Cécilia knows that dreams do come true.

In March 2012 the Nigerian province agreed a *convention* (contract) with Bishop Michel Duost, of Évry-Corbeil-Essonnes. Gladys and Chinyere have their *lettres de mission* as pastoral agents for the deanery of Étampes. The contract is for three years for the whole community. Through Rosita Brady, through Angela Woods who came from California to work for two years in Courcouronnes and especially now through the community of three who *are* the Church in St Jean Baptiste de Guinette, Étampes, the congregation is fulfilling its aim, articulated at the 1985 general chapter: 'to give life to our presence in France'.

19

California, North America and Brazil Today

'I believe I live the charism of unity in the work I do.'

Terry Dodge, 2011

In the years after Vatican II, many of the sisters in California left the teaching apostolate and trained for paid or voluntary work in counselling, spiritual direction, bereavement counselling, parish work, inter-faith dialogue, chaplaincy, in retreat work, like Laura Gormley, in facilitation of general chapters and assemblies like Bridget Ehlert. Rita Carroll ran a family centre in Dominguez School in a poor area of Long Beach. Judith Dieterle worked for many years as Associate Director of the Office for Catechesis in the Archdiocese of Chicago. Terry Dodge is executive director of Crossroads, in Pomona, California. Karen Collier is parish life director in St Agatha's in Los Angeles. The exploration of different models of community life led to smaller communities and, as in Ireland and England, to sisters living alone.

The big St Louis enterprise in California is Louisville High School, Woodland Hills: the plant and site are entirely owned by the Sisters of St Louis and work is in hand to ensure appropriate governance into the future as a Catholic school. The president is Myra McPartland, a former principal, and four sisters sit on the board of governance. Louisville has five hundred students and a good number of them are on some kind of financial aid so the school depends a lot on fundraising.

Of the nine American-born sisters in California, four are in regional leadership as of 2011 – Karen Collier, Judith Dieterle, Terry Dodge and Bridget Ehlert – as well as Donna Hansen in central leadership. This is the first time California has had an all-American leadership team, a reflection of the ageing of the Irish sisters who were missioned there from 1949. Elizabeth Gildea, the oldest sister anywhere in the congregation (born 1911) lives in the community of El Monte with the youngest member of the community outside west Africa, Stacy Reinemann (born 1961). Elizabeth, who was missioned to California in 1952, trained in Mount St Mary's and had a long teaching career in various schools in Los Angeles, still takes some classes in Nativity School, El Monte, which was the very first foundation in California in 1949. Although as a Catholic school Nativity charges fees, Stacy, the principal and one of the last sisters in full time education in California, does everything in her power never to refuse a place in the school to a child from the low income largely Hispanic neighbourhood. Stacy and private education are uneasy bedfellows but she is committed to making her kind of private education work.

Judy Dieterle became regional leader in California in 2011. She entered the novitiate in Woodland Hills in 1967 – a transitional phase: short habits and short veil – with congregational leader Donna Hansen and eight others. Only one of these remains: Margaret Hosty, who came to Woodland Hills from the juniorate in Clogher (after it moved from Cushendall) and has been on the region's mission to Brazil for many years.

Judy qualified as a teacher and taught in several Los Angeles schools before she, like Maura Clerkin and Margie Buttita a few years earlier, felt that more was being asked of her than a comfortable west coast teaching life. She arrived in Brazil in 1979, having had to wait a year for a permanent visa, and after the usual CENFI formation, helped the group of sisters to empower local people in Barrolandia and Colméia before beginning a formation programme on the outskirts of Goiânia. In all she spent fifteen years in Brazil and has just completed eighteen years in Chicago as associate director of the office for catechesis and youth ministry. This was not something she planned: the job was offered to her after she studied to be a spiritual director in Loyola University in Chicago while on a sabbatical. Initially Judy kept her hard-won Brazilian visa open by going back there every two years but when it became clear to her over time that she would stay in Chicago she transferred back to the California region.

For Judy it was difficult to leave her post with the Chicago archdiocese in 2011 but, a woman who is simultaneously adventurous and prudent, she felt the call of a new position, the regional leadership. She is a full-time leader, at least for the moment, as the other team members have full-time day jobs. The team has divided the work of leadership into four broad areas: Terry is the treasurer and works with the two main fundraising groups, Sisters of St Louis League and Les Dames de St Louis; Karen has responsibility for social justice issues and links with social justice organisations; Bridget is the link with Louisville High School planning committee; and Judy herself looks after healthcare and development issues and liaises with associates, something new for her as the California associates began after she left for Brazil.

At the last regional chapter the sisters decided to commission an actuarial study of the properties belonging to the Californian region. Another mandate was to prioritise the health and wellness of the sisters, a good number of whom are now elderly. From the 2009 general chapter came the call to look at the meaning of religious life and the development of a deeper spirituality. For many sisters, who worked so hard and achieved so much during a long lifetime as religious, it can be difficult, as Judy puts it, to 'find their value in being rather than doing…[as] doing has been their whole life.'

Sisters who taught in California were not paid by the state and were not allowed to contribute to social security until the 1970s. Social welfare provision for the elderly is nothing like as good as it is in Ireland, the UK or France so the region depends a good deal on the generosity of donors. These individuals can also specify if they would like the money they donate to be used to support one of the missions outside California.

The sisters prudently established a retirement fund and will soon need to draw on this for living expenses. In fact prudence has been a characteristic of the financial management of the region, according to Terry, the current treasurer. This careful stewardship of the region's limited resources was established and maintained by earlier superiors and treasurers, such as Catherine Foley, Eugenia McInerney, Cabrini Dolan, Monica Quigley, Terry herself, Margaret Fitzer and Michèle Harnett.

Terry, the second youngest sister in the US (born 1952), who is beginning a second term in leadership, is executive director of Crossroads, an organisation for women who have been released from prison and woman who are incarcerated. She finds it convenient to be 'Sister Terry' as, in the work of advocacy for the forgotten and despised, it 'gets her into places [she] might not otherwise get into.'

The St Louis charism of unity attracted her, the sense of family, beginning with individual sisters who taught her in grade school in St Cyprian's. She was, she says, 'not a likely candidate for religious life: always in trouble'. For her, religious life means a real commitment to bringing about change. She 'fully embraced' the controversial 1985 mission statement: 'I loved it from the beginning. I believe that I live the charism of unity in the work I do.'

Terry taught grade school and then worked in Louisville for five years; it was Maura Byron, regional in 1988, who released her from school to prison ministry, a decision very much in keeping with the withdrawal from education and the option for the poor of that decade. For a year Terry worked as a volunteer in prison ministry, until hired by Crossroads, an organisation founded in 1972 by a group of prison visitors. She has no formal qualifications in social work but she says that her MA in feminist spirituality from Immaculate Heart College gave her a 'backdrop' for the work she is doing. Crossroads has three residential houses: twelve beds that are available for six months to women who have been released from incarceration. Then there are nine beds for people who graduate from the programme and need a little further help.

Terry does speaking engagements to educate the public, improve awareness and raise funds. Crossroads is not a popular charity by any means, getting by on grants from foundations, donations from Churches and federal money. There were two years when Terry couldn't afford to pay herself the modest salary she normally earns: the community supported her during this period.

In recent decades, unity was not always evident in the communities in California although it was 'a deep longing within the sisters', according to Donna Hansen: 'The region went through a period when the sisters found it very difficult to talk to one another about their differences. Perhaps it was a cultural gap, a generational gap, an experiential gap. Some of the sisters felt they had made an enormous sacrifice being missioned to California without being consulted, thinking they might never see their homes in Ireland again. Others struggled with cultural differences in the formation process, with divergent opinions about community lifestyle and varied expectations of planning for the future.'

Judy Dieterle recalls: 'It was a painful time but the region made a commitment to a communication skills programme that facilitated healing. It took an investment of time and money with expert facilitators for two groups over a six-month period to give the region the communication skills to work through [these] issues.'

There are now three sisters from the region in Goiânia, Brazil: one Irish (Margaret Hosty); one American (Margie Buttita); and one Brazilian (Elenice Natal de Lima). The community is based in two apartments in the city of Goiânia, two hours by car from Brasilia, still in the interior but further south than the original foundation in Barrolandia, Tocantins.

Margie has spent more than thirty-five years in Brazil. Attempting always to respond to the needs of the people, she has now moved away from pastoral ministry in response to an appeal by the episcopal conference for volunteers to work in new housing settlements which are growing up in many places as a result of the rural exodus. This work is funded by the German charity Adveniat. In Goiânia there is one such settlement that has four thousand families with little infrastructure and no schools. Margie works here with an intercongregational team of seven or eight people, which has helped to provide Bible classes, basic healthcare, pastoral care for children, Church leadership and formation and activities for adolescents. After thirty-five years in Brazil, she can see how crucial education is and that it goes hand in hand with the empowerment of women. The team encourages women to go back to school, even primary school, then high school. Margaret Hosty is also dedicated to working with AIDS carriers and their families. Elenice, who recently retired from teaching, has just returned to Goíania from a year spent learning English in California.

The Church in Brazil has become much more conservative since the heady days of *la linea* in the 1970s and 1980s. Margie says that the Archbishop of Goiânia, Washington Cruz, is 'a good man but lukewarm' as regards the empowerment of the poor and conscientisation. As in Africa, a lot of fundamental and Pentecostal churches have sprung up and the Catholic hierarchy, under pressure from Rome, thinks that the way to counter this trend is to go back to more conservative roots.

Although Margie has worked for so long at the cutting edge of liberation theology, for her the question of whether or not it was a successful experiment in Latin America is open to debate. She thinks that the Church was so associated with social action in the minds of the people that they became confused. For them Catholicism was less theological than political, and fundamentally they regard all politics as party politics and untrustworthy.

The California region also has a mission in Ahoskie, North Carolina. The preferential option for the poor was uppermost in the sisters' minds after the 1985 chapter, and when Dorothy McCloskey visited California after the chapter she encouraged them to research the possibility of a 'home mission' in some disadvantaged area of the United States. They chose Ahoskie, a community with a large African-American population, where a quarter of the people lived below the poverty line.

In 1992 Teresa Marry and Brigid Dunne were missioned to start the foundation. Stacy Reinemann joined them after two years and stayed until 2001. Teresa and Brigid still minister there. In Ahoskie Catholicism is the minority religion and most of the local people are Baptists. Religious women were a totally foreign concept to the people there when the sisters arrived.

As with most ministries, the beginnings were slow. As they did in Brazil, the sisters gradually realised that one of the most pressing needs was education, so they taught in a community college as well as becoming involved in catechetics, instruction for the sacraments, adult education and the empowerment of women. They have now retired from teaching work. In the absence of a priest they provide liturgies and administer some sacraments and their ministry also includes Hispanic migrant workers. In order to be able to work with these migrants more effectively, Teresa and Brigid went to Mexico to learn Spanish. In 2000 seven Mexican children made their First Communion in St Anne's mission church, the first such ceremony for thirty years.

In September 2011, after a long process of discernment about the where and how of a new mission in the US, Bríd Long and Michèle Harnett drove from California to New York to take up residence in Washington Heights in the northernmost reaches of Manhattan, an area with a largely immigrant population, much of it from the Dominican Republic. Alice Keenan, an Irish-born sister of the California region, is also part of the Washington Heights community. Members of the new community will engage in diverse ministries in the area of social justice, working on behalf of victims of human trafficking and with the immigrant community.

20

Cours Bautain
and Catholic Education in France and Belgium

'Discipline, soutien et épanouissement'
('Discipline, support and development')
Le Figaro, 5 October 2011

When the last French principal of Cours Bautain, Marie Joseph Deville, died in 1971, Deirdre O'Hanlon (for ease of pronunciation known in Juilly by her name in religion, Thérèse-Marie) who succeeded her, presided over a period of change and consolidation. In 1979 the pensionnat closed, like the St Louis boarding schools in Ireland in the same period. In the 1980s Cours Bautain was separated into a primary school and collège (unviable numbers meant that the school had stopped being a lycée, a senior college, in 1971). The collège now has its second lay principal, Eric Gohier, in succession to Jean Luc Walker, who held the position 1996-2010.

Since 1991 Cours Bautain has had a board of management, established with the help of a congregational lawyer, which includes Deirdre and Clare Ryan. Deirdre, who retired from teaching in 1996 is the representative of the trustees, the St Louis Institute. Daniel Haquin, the Mayor of Juilly, has been the chairman of the board for many years. The four Haquin daughters attended the school, like generations of the Haquin family in the past. The school pays the sisters a small sum that is set aside for maintenance and development and continues to improve its facilities, with an impressive new *gymnase* and the acquisition of a garden beside the school that is intended for use as a sports ground.

In 2007 Cardinal Poupard, a hero of the St Louis sisters for his PhD thesis that officially rehabilitated Louis Bautain, invested

Deirdre O'Hanlon with the insignia of *Chevalier dans l'Ordre des Palmes Académiques*, on behalf of the prime minister. The first superior general, Mère Thérèse de la Croix, received the same honour, her certificate signed by none other than Jules Ferry, the minister for education and later prime minister who is credited with firmly establishing *laïcisme* in the French education system.

Clare Ryan replaced Mercedes as superior in 1960 and after two spells in Ghana, came back to live in Juilly for good in 1986. She took over the catechetics programme and still teaches a small group, although she celebrated her ninetieth birthday in August 2011. Many of the pupils of Cours Bautain are not Catholic but no one is exempted from participating in a catechetics class for an hour a week, as the principal explains to the pupils when they are enrolled.

Like Clare, Deirdre O'Hanlon wishes passionately for Cours Bautain to remain a Catholic school in the service of the local area. It is as yet not quite clear how this will be achieved but the sisters are investigating various avenues, such as a trust in combination with other religious orders on the lines of Le Chéile in Ireland. Nothing is simple for Catholic educators in France. Cours Bautain is a different kind of school from the *pensionnat* Collège, focused as it is on catering for the educational needs of Catholics and others in and around Juilly. Although Catholic schools in France have to charge fees – the government now pays salaries for teaching hours only, nothing for the administrative work of the principal, for ancillary staff or the upkeep of buildings – those in Cours Bautain are modest, about one-third of what is charged in Collège de Juilly at the time of writing. Discussions with Collège de Juilly have resulted in Cours Bautain making place in its classes for the primary and nursery pupils of the Collège.

From 1981 to 1985 Margaret Flynn of the Juilly community, a teacher in Cours Bautain at the time, represented this area of the institute and on Pentecost Sunday 1990 the Franco-Belgian region was officially inaugurated, with Belgian sister, Thérèse-Marie Mutsers, as the first regional superior. It was her unexpected death that precipitated the closure of the Sclessin house. Now there are only six sisters in all in Juilly, five Irish and one French, governed by a system of co-responsibility, and all the Irish sisters are officially attached to an Irish community. Marie Pierre, the only French sister and the last of the native Dames de St Louis, was taken under the wing of the central leadership team in the generalate in Dublin. As long as there is even one French sister, Irish sisters will stay in Juilly. Marie Pierre, in her early eighties at the time of writing, still makes the journey to central Paris three days a week, to do voluntary work in Secours Catholique.

Elizabeth Beirne and Anne Killeen, who now live in Juilly, spent many years in the Dames de St Louis community in Sclessin. They learned French (and Flemish) and trained as primary teachers after being missioned to Sclessin together in 1953, not long after reunification. Except for Thérèse Marie Mutsers, most of the sisters were much older than them, sixty and upwards. When they got their teaching diplomas after four years of study, they couldn't teach immediately as they had to be Belgian citizens and it was necessary to have ten years' residence to apply to become a citizen. In the end they got a *dérogation* (waiver) signed by King Baudouin as there was a shortage of teachers at that time (only three of the Belgian sisters in the community at Sclessin were trained as primary teachers).

Sclessin is an industrial suburb of Liège and most of the pupils were the children of second-generation Italians (many of them Sicilian) whose parents had come to work in the coal mines. Although not well educated themselves, they were anxious for their children to have a good education and religious instruction. As well as teaching in the school Elizabeth and Anne were active in the parish and when they left Sclessin for Juilly in 1995 they had no worries about the school's continuing ethos as both school and convent belonged to the parish. But after so many years, they did leave a large part of their hearts in Belgium. Marie Henry, who gave many years of devoted service as district nurse, was the last Sclessin sister in healthcare, in keeping with the tradition established by the Dames de St Louis at their foundation and which continued in Sclessin without interruption. She was greatly missed when she was missioned to Juilly in 1993 to care for the elderly sisters there.

Elizabeth tells the story of Marie Bernard Cazaunau, a French sister who had come to Sclessin from Juilly in 1955 and lived until the age of ninety. She helped in the kitchen and looked after the garden. On the day before she was to leave Sclessin to go back to Juilly, the parish priest announced that she was leaving and everyone came to say goodbye to her as she came out of church. She died at midnight that night and never did go back to Juilly.

Rosita Brady acquired French in the seven years she spent in Juilly (1954-61) and she was the only Irish sister in Thier-à-Liège for the last eight years of the house's existence. Her wish to return to Ireland for family reasons in 1969 was one of the factors that precipitated the closure of the community. Marie du Sacré Coeur, the principal of the girls' primary school there, retired and it was decided to combine the community with Sclessin. Two French-born sisters moved back to Juilly at this stage. Thier-à-Liège is a suburb of Liège of which the main economic activity is market gardening, and Rosita was active with the 'Patronage' (youth club) outside school time and the group of 'Crusaders' that she organised during school recreation. So much so that she returned to Sclessin in 1987 after the death of her parents and spent ten years in France.

Belgium felt the influence of liberalisation earlier than Ireland as the primate, Cardinal Leo Suenens, was a strong believer in *aggiornamento* (the modernisation of the Church) and influential in Vatican II. In Belgium there were no vocations even in the early 1950s: that is why Irish sisters were sent there. While the Irish sisters accepted this reality – with the single exception of Annie Ferson in 1963 – it must have been hard for them to imagine that Ireland would follow the same trend.

It was a dear wish of Dorothy McCloskey, superior general 1980-90, that the St Louis Institute should give back to France some of the grace it had received from the mother region, by establishing a new community that would respond to current-day needs. Thérèse Marie Mutsers, Rosita, Barbara McArdle and Marie de Paul Neiers researched different options and decided that the new community should not be in Juilly but somewhere there was a need more in keeping with the option for the poor, one of the *villes nouvelles* (new towns) that had been built in different locations to house immigrants and migrants from different areas of France. The location chosen was Moissy-Cramayel, thirty kilometres south east of Paris but, like Juilly, in the diocese of Meaux. It was an international community comprising three Irish sisters – Anne Murray, Davnet McGreal and Rosita Brady – and Nigerian Cécilia Uzodike – and Dorothy herself was present for the official opening of the house at Pentecost 1990. But the parish could afford only one salary and before too long Anne and Davnet returned to Ireland. Rosita spent ten years working in catechetics in Moissy, while Cécilia moved to Courcouronnes in the diocese of Évry and then to Étampes. The community in Étampes is now part of the Nigerian province.

On 5 October 2011 the front page of *Le Figaro* announced: *'L'enseignement catholique n'a pas connu pareille hausse depuis vingt ans.'* The new academic year had seen the greatest increase in enrolment in Catholic schools for twenty years: 12,053 pupils more than the previous year, with 30,000-40,000 aspiring pupils unable to get places. Catholic schools represent 95 per cent of private education in France and are strongly in demand even in areas that are predominantly Muslim. (Muslim families, the newspaper suggested, value the 'respect for the spiritual dimension of the individual' that is present in Catholic schools and see private education as a form of *ascension sociale*. Furthermore, the government ban on wearing 'conspicuous religious symbols' such as khimars in school does not apply in private schools.)

The newspaper's editorial expressed fears for the future of the *école publique*, *'creuset* [crucible] *de l'intégration à la française'* since the time of Jules Ferry, in favour of *'établissements qui garantissent discipline, soutien et espèrent-ils, résultats a leurs enfants'* ('establishments that guarantee discipline, support and, they hope, results for children'). There are more than two million children in Catholic education in France.

In the meantime Cours Bautain continues to thrive, almost sixty years after the amalgamation of Juilly and Monaghan and the arrival of the first young Irish sisters to work in France. Its fees are modest, its ethos is local and, as four of the sisters, Marie-Pierre, Deirdre,

Clare and Anne, live in the convent that is attached to the school, the sisters still have a strong everyday presence there. This is what the local parents like to see. Although the sisters accept that the time may not be too far away when they will have to leave Juilly, their fervent wish is that Cours Bautain should continue as a relaxed and open Catholic collège in the service of the local area.

21

The English Mission

'Holding the egg not too tightly, not too loosely'
Philomena Morris, 2011

The first St Louis foundation in England was established by de Sales O'Byrne in Redditch, Worcestershire, 24 km south of Birmingham, in December 1912, and a private secondary school opened in January 1913. It was short-lived: the intake included a relatively small proportion of Catholic pupils and the sisters were disappointed in their hope of being given jobs in the primary school in Redditch. In 1919 the congregation was offered charge of the elementary and secondary schools in Great Yarmouth, a fishing port on the Norfolk coast, and it was decided that the community in Redditch would transfer to Yarmouth. The sisters from Redditch formed the new foundation in Yarmouth, replacing members of a German order who had been moved from the area, and the school in Redditch closed in April 1920. In Yarmouth the sisters took over St Mary's parish school and established St Louis High School, initially in the same premises.

Teresa Walsh, who comes from Ballylongford, County Kerry, and now lives in Newmarket, spent more than seventy years in Yarmouth, where she was missioned in 1936. Laurentia Stuart was sent as superior to Great Yarmouth just before the war broke out on 1 September 1939 and Teresa remembers making a trip back to Ireland with Laurentia, during which she made her final vows. The war had begun by the time they came back and they travelled on a blacked-out boat from Larne to Stranraer. Yarmouth would have been particularly at risk if Germany's planned Operation Sea Lion, the invasion of England by sea, were implemented, so it was decided to evacuate the children of the town according to a blueprint that had been drawn up many years previously. In the summer of 1940 the sisters prepared for the evacuation, storing some of their furniture in Bury St Edmunds, but for reasons of security they were not told until the night before the move, on 2 June 1940, that they were going to Retford in Nottinghamshire, about seven hours' train journey from Yarmouth.

In Retford, the sisters and the nine hundred plus children who had been evacuated from various schools in Yarmouth were billeted with private families and the sisters taught classes on the priest's lawn for a few weeks in September before finding a disused primary school and then a church hall. Eventually they settled the community and the school in a large empty house, West Retford Hall, where they had a good enrolment until, later in the war, the evacuated children began to return home once the threat of German invasion had passed. Some of the sisters returned with them to Yarmouth so the community was divided between the two distant locations. Sisters spent five years in all in Retford. The bishop and parish priest were keen that they should remain in charge of the school there, and superior general, Columbanus Greene, came over to investigate the possibility but nothing came of it. The Retford sisters went back to Yarmouth and some of the furniture from Bury was taken instead to Aylesbury, where a new foundation opened in September 1945. Yarmouth was badly bombed and there was a lot of destruction of property but not one of the St Louis pupils was harmed.

Looking back at the war years now, more than sixty years later, Teresa says, 'You can laugh at it.' Even in the blackout, life was (at least) not monotonous because there were air raid warnings. There were RAF airfields in East Anglia and the sisters would sometimes see dogfights as the German bombers tried to get back to their bases in the north of France after a mission.

Many foods were unavailable for the duration of the war and everything else was rationed. Ration books were issued, colour coded for individuals, pregnant women or families: the books contained pages of small stamps, called 'coupons', which shoppers had to use when buying their allocation of particular foodstuffs and which the shopkeeper would have to cancel by stamping or signing.

Meat was very scarce in Britain as much of it was imported, but plentiful in Ireland, a big producer. Teresa remembers a fair bit of illegal traffic: 'We used to get a turkey from home. They would put rashers in between the pages of a newspaper. I got a copy of *An tOileánach* with all the pages cut out to make a box and filled with rashers.' Bacon cost a lot of coupons and butter and sugar were scarce in England; the convent community had its own internal system of rationing.

When American GIs arrived in England in early 1942 (the US had declared war on Japan on 8 December 1941), they brought more plentiful food with them, some of it exotic for the English. This was when the sisters discovered the delights of spam (tinned processed pork meat, the name coming from 'spiced ham') which they bought in army shops and which required fewer coupons than ordinary meat. Not alone did the GIs open up the food supply; they provided a big psychological boost, although the war was 'not over in a week', as war weary English people hoped when they first saw the Americans.

The congregation officially withdrew from Yarmouth in 2008 although the St Louis private secondary school closed in 1973. Some sisters went back to Ireland, others, like Teresa, moved to Newmarket. All the properties in Yarmouth had gone: 'everything levelled to the ground,' as Teresa laments – the private secondary school that the sisters had established, the convent and the elementary school that had predated the sisters' arrival in East Anglia. There is no Catholic secondary school in Yarmouth now: the nearest is in Norwich, twenty miles away.

Jesuit priests brought the sisters to Bury St Edmunds, Suffolk, in 1924. There the congregation had a Catholic primary school, St Edmund's, and a private school where the intake was both Catholic and non-Catholic. The experience of Catholic education was a broadening one for children from other religions and was valued as such by their parents, a practical example of ecumenism, *avant la lettre*. The sisters soon opened St Louis High School, which became

a 'middle school' when the school system changed. In 1986 the
school was redeveloped and a secular principal was appointed. The
mission owns the school property so it granted a lease for ninety
nine years to the diocese of East Anglia. The community left the
convent in 1989 and it was leased to a business firm. The first
English novitiate was opened in Bury in 1980; this later transferred
to Newmarket. Two St Louis sisters, Marie O'Reilly and Ann Bolton,
live in Bury now.

Four St Louis sisters arrived in Newmarket in 1936 and opened
a private primary school. In 1970 it became a voluntary aided
school: the sisters were employed by the education authorities and
the children no longer paid fees. Since 1998 it has been run by the
diocese of East Anglia and although the sisters are not involved it
retains the name of St Louis Primary School. Since the post-war
era the sisters in Newmarket were involved in catechesis, going out
on Saturdays to the American air base at Lakenheath to teach the
children of Catholic servicemen. Newmarket is a big premises, with
the convent, two apartments created from the conversion of the
stable buildings, Colmar cottage in the grounds, the archives of the
English region/mission and a retreat centre.

The Old Stable House opened in 1980 as a centre for spirituality, renewal and development for people of all faiths and denominations. Madeleine O'Callaghan was appointed directress and
the centre provided a variety of retreats in a peaceful, therapeutic
and holistic environment. It was always the intention that the Old
Stables would be financially viable through the contributions
of retreatants, rather than a profit making venture. It is still run
as a retreat centre and also used for meetings, conferences and
celebrations. Marcia Foley is the current director.

Colmar Cottage was made available in 1990 as a dwelling for Lua
Ennis and Mary Murray, who had moved out of the convent. At that
time selling the convent was under consideration because of the
small size of the community there. However, the sale fell through
and the leadership team at the time had the building refurbished.
Sisters who need a supportive environment but do not need nursing
care live there now.

Theodore Lysaght, a science graduate, was missioned to New-market in 1952 to set up the laboratory in the new school. School, convent, science laboratory – everything was in the one big house in which a small community of sisters now lives. There was very little money at this time, especially in Newmarket and Aylesbury, as, unlike Yarmouth and Bury, the sisters there did not have paid teaching jobs in the primary school. Theodore says of her time in Newmarket: 'We lived on bazaars and the goodwill of people.' But for her there was challenge aplenty and the joy of achievement as well as a 'great social feel and nice environment' and 'a sense of vitality and good humour in the schools network'. Because of the reality of the Catholic Church in England (under financed, inadequate personnel, a minority religion) sisters always did work 'on the side' as well as teaching in school – catechetics, visiting the sick – which must have contributed to their bonding with the communities in which they were located.

It was a question of providence. 'We just went along and we had a strict training in obedience.' This was the era of *Dieu le Veult* rather than *Ut Sint Unum*. The need of the time was education. Theodore spent twelve years in Newmarket and was then moved to Bury, which had been built up and was better equipped than Newmarket, with good sports facilities. The community was bigger also and the sisters were involved in three schools: a primary school with five sisters; a secondary school with four sisters as well as lay teachers; and a private junior school to generate fee income. When education was reorganised the secondary school became a Catholic comprehensive school. Theodore was offered a job but felt 'that there was something lost in these schools as the numbers were so big.' Like many sisters in England, she found her way into a different ministry, in her case a chaplaincy team, then worked in catechetics in the parish of South Harrow and Northolt in the diocese of Westminster. Theodore now brings her experience of chaplaincy and catechesis to an associate group in Dundalk.

The associate movement never quite got off the ground in England, perhaps because there were too few sisters and they were too scattered. Nor did England prove a fertile ground for vocations:

most of those who entered did not stay. Religious vocations and the associate movement alike were probably too counter cultural for post-Christian England in recent decades. All the more to admire in the courage of Osyth Gomersall, an English convert, and Alban Messenger, from an Anglican background, who entered at fifty and twenty eight respectively and shared the novitiate in Monaghan with a large number of Irish teenagers. Alban, a qualified art teacher, braved the hardships of wartime travel to join the 1940 group of postulants.

In the early 1990s a number of young women wished to enter the congregation, having spent time with Teresa Duffy in Nottingham and Mary Jo McKeefry in Dukinfield, near Manchester. It was felt that it would be better if they could do their novitiate in England rather than in Ireland and Bláthnaid McCauley, Madeleine O'Callaghan and Marie O'Reilly were asked to form a team to accompany and train them. Out of that group one sister made final vows but she has since left the congregation: the novitiate lasted no more than a few years.

Maeve McDevitt was missioned to Aylesbury, Buckinghamshire, in 1953, when this post-war foundation was eight years old. The sisters had a proper primary school but classes for the senior school were held in the convent. There was no central heating. It was not luxurious, in fact the sisters were very poor, but as Maeve says, 'We didn't even think about complaining as that was simply the way things were.' At this stage there was no public funding at all for Catholic schools. As well as teaching, the sisters did all the administration, cleaning and maintenance work for the school. But, says Maeve, 'There were lots of young sisters and we had great fun.'

Aylesbury had a real sense of 'mission' about it and the sisters made do and built things up gradually, much as they did in Kano and Kumasi. On Saturday mornings they went out to the local churches to teach catechism to children who didn't go to Catholic schools. Some sisters also became involved in what was then called 'instructing' adults for reception into the Catholic Church, including inmates of what was originally a women's prison in Aylesbury. They received no payment for this: the Catholic diocese was as poor as themselves. It was, says Maeve, 'a minority community and downtrodden' (only 8 per cent of the current population of England and Wales is Catholic). Later on the schools became voluntary aided and government paid most of the costs. The school and convent buildings in Aylesbury still belong to the region but are leased to the diocese.

There was a 'big cry' for someone to move into catechetics as a result of Vatican II and, after taking a diploma in Liverpool, Maeve worked in the diocese of East Anglia from 1973, organising youth days and training adults as team leaders. She transferred to Westminster diocese after studying for a master's degree in catechetics in Toronto, and started a centre for training catechists that was funded by the Conference of Religious in England and Wales. Maeve was very happy teaching catechetics and catechists, which for her has always been a moving experience of spirituality – 'heart speaking to heart' – rather than an intellectual activity.

Bláthnaid McCauley began her ministry in England in the big community in Yarmouth, where she found Pancratius Givens an enlightened and cultured superior. She was principal in the primary school in Newmarket at the age of twenty four. In the 1980s, the sisters there, under the challenging leadership of superior Paul Mary Conneely, 'revisited the call of [our] founders', as Bláthnaid puts it. St Louis sisters were among the first religious to opt entirely out of private education and for the maintained model. The community in Newmarket, which up to then had lived in a cocoon, 'totally oblivious of what was on our doorstep', did a social analysis of the town as part of the option for the poor and found a serious drug problem and, in the racing business for which the town is famous, grave exploitation of apprentices and stable workers, some of them from Ireland. There was one priest serving a radius of thirty miles, who was delighted to accept the help the sisters offered in parish ministry. Paul Mary Conneely built a parish community of two hundred people in Newmarket. The sisters began to host an evening Mass in the convent and a shared meal to which people in the local community were invited.

Bláthnaid took early retirement 'after my fourth Offsted' (a major inspection that takes place every six years). She knew she couldn't survive another year of teaching but felt deskilled after leaving, although she had 'run a great school'. It was Phil Morris who suggested university chaplaincy and in opportune fashion two jobs were advertised. In a search for fresh pastures she opted for the more distant (from Newmarket) Brighton rather than Cambridge. Now she works as part of an interfaith team with staff and the 40,000 strong student body of both Brighton and Sussex universities. Brighton has the biggest gay population in Europe so sexual orientation is a particular issue. Bláthnaid is on duty 24/7 and involved in every kind of crisis: death, bereavement, suicide. She says she 'couldn't believe she found a ministry so fulfilling straight away' and has a very good working relationship with her colleague on the chaplaincy team, a Church of England clergyman.

The pattern for sisters in England has been to become involved in parish work, spiritual direction or counselling. Rosalie Corish, who joined the English region after leaving Accra, became a catechist and parish assistant in South Harrow. As someone who lived most of her working life in Ireland she believes that there are: 'More opportunities to do things in England. Lay people were always involved as there were never so many priests as in Ireland.'

In the early 1970s the sisters were invited to Shrewsbury Diocese to promote the work of the Children's Society in Shropshire. In 1972 two sisters went to live in Much Wenlock and in 1978 they established a community house in Wellington, ten miles from Shrewsbury. They undertook health visiting, working with prospective mothers and advising on fostering and adoption under the auspices of the Children's Society. Mary Jo McKeefry taught religious education in a Catholic college in Wellington.

Much Wenlock was Margaret Healy's first ministry in England but when she took a degree in Applied Social Studies in Hatfield University 1976-80 she chose a community development option as she did not want to be a social worker. Since she graduated she has been an activist on behalf of migrant domestic workers in England. She was converted to activism by social analysis in the early 1980s, under the influence of two priests, Maurice Keane SJ and Columban

Aodh O'Halpin. She had two brothers, both former Columbans, who were radicalised in the Philippines and in turn radicalised her. In 1980, while Ferdinand Marcos was in power, her brother Vincent established a Philippines Solidarity Network in London to support the movement for change in the Philippines. Through this, Margaret became involved with migrant workers from the Philippines.

Margaret and Aodh O'Halpin set up a centre in London in 1980 to facilitate migrant domestic workers to organise to fight for their rights. These domestic workers had no legal right to work permits in the UK, although they were brought in by employers specifically to work in the private households of these employers. They were effectively tied to their employers. Often exploited and mistreated, they would come for help to the centre in Notting Hill, sometimes as many as two to three hundred in a single Sunday. They were undocumented, had no rights whatsoever and could be detained by the police and deported without reference to anyone. In fact at the beginning Margaret was afraid the centre might be closed for harbouring undocumented workers but after they got publicity and a lot of public support they established an organisation called Kalayaan ('freedom' in Tagalog) which embarked on a ten-year campaign to change the law on migrant domestic workers, rather than just offering help to individuals. The root cause of the problem was the legislation so the law had to be changed.

The Conservatives were returned to power in four successive elections from 1979. With the help of Unite, the former Transport and General Workers' Union, which the undocumented workers were able to join, Kalayaan concentrated on lobbying the Labour party in the lead-up to the 1997 election. Finally Labour gave a commitment at the party conference in 1997 that the party in government would meet the organisation's demands, a promise that they implemented in 1998. From then on migrant domestic workers entering the UK were given permits to work as domestic workers with the right to change employer. They also became entitled to the same rights as other workers in the UK.

However, the victory was short-lived enough: before Labour lost power they moved to reduce the number of immigrants by applying a quota system and after the general election of 2010 the Conservative-Liberal Democrat coalition set out to reverse the legal changes introduced by Labour in 1998. Margaret was instrumental in establishing a new organisation, Justice for Domestic Workers in 2009, to enable these workers to campaign for their own rights and against the proposed changes in legislation.

For many years Margaret worked without pay, supported by the congregation, although she received a salary as coordinator of Kalayaan from 1991 until she left the organisation in 1997. Now she is on the boards of management of Kalayaan and Justice for Domestic Workers.

Philomena Morris, team leader in the English mission from 2011, has had several interesting careers. As a history teacher in Kumasi in the 1970s she was radicalised by involvement with the Young Christian Students movement and came to know the dynamic and controversial Jerry Rawlings, dictator 1979 and 1981-82, then elected president of a democratic Ghana 1993-2001. YCS, which adopted the 'See, Judge, Act' methodology developed by the Belgian cardinal Joseph Leo Cardijns for his Young Christian Workers movement in the 1920s, was established in Ghana by Consilii O'Shaughnessy and a priest from Benin and continued by Philomena. A movement along the lines of liberation theology and the option for the poor, YCS helped to train young Ghanaian people as leaders and many of these are still involved. Over the years YCS congresses were held in St Louis Secondary School, Kumasi, including one for students and chaplains from English-speaking west African countries.

After Phil left Ghana she worked from Rome on the international team of the Better World Movement. Influenced by Latin America, by liberation theology and by Oscar Romero, the archbishop of San Salvador who was murdered in 1980, she considers herself to be better suited to education, analysis and advocacy than to 'working on the ground'. In 2011 her paid part-time job was as a parish team leader, coordinating the activities of Our Lady of Muswell, in the deanery of Harringay.

Róisín Hannaway recently moved south from Bradford in West

Yorkshire to East Anglia. A science teacher, she spent most of her life in the Irish region, where she taught for twenty-five years. She was appointed principal in Monaghan in 1979, a position that did not suit her and from which she requested a transfer. Róisín was always interested in Church unity and interchurch/interfaith relations: for her a way of living *Ut Sint Unum*. In 1988 she applied for membership of the Columbanus Community of Reconciliation in Belfast and spent eleven years there. Columbanus was a residential community, founded in 1983 by Michael Hurley SJ (1923-2011), co-founder of the Irish School of Ecumenics, in which men and women, lay and religious, of different religious traditions, lived for a period. Michael Hurley conceived the idea during the bitter and divisive period of the 1981 hunger strikes as a means of bearing witness to peace.

After the Good Friday Agreement, Róisín left Belfast and did an M.Phil in Religious Relations in Birmingham. She was taken with the idea of an interfaith life and began to look for somewhere she could use what she had learned, transferring to the English region and settling in Bradford in 2003. Bradford has a high percentage of Muslims, mainly Pakistanis, as well as people of other faiths, and Róisín became part of the interfaith Columba community, one that was dispersed, not residential. She loved teaching Pakistani women English. The men are often taxi drivers and learn some English in the course of their work but Urdu is still the language of the home. The Muslim world *is* patriarchal but, Róisín says, Christianity is patriarchal too. About the institutional Church, at times she feels, 'I am on the fringes...Of course I want women priests and of course I want changes but now that I'm older and wiser I don't get angry any more.' Róisín spent eight and a half joyous years in Bradford before moving to Newmarket.

There are currently twenty sisters in the English mission (too few for it to be a region) and two live away: Maud Murphy in Ireland and Mary Jo McKeefry in Antigua, in the West Indies, where she runs a retreat centre. But leader Phil Morris believes it 'still has energy'. As well as the sisters who are engaged in paid work in parish ministry, chaplaincy and counselling, Louisa Poole works with the bishops' conference and is interested in ecology and climate change. Mary Murray is involved in justice and peace issues. Phil would favour a loose community on the lines of the Béguines, medieval women who were affiliated in community and apostolic mission. As it stands, there are two clusters of sisters in the south of England, one around Newmarket, the second around London. Phil wishes to 'hold the egg' of leadership – the Ghanaian symbol – not too tightly, not too loosely. The sisters in England know their own minds and most of them have had years of experience living an independent life that they consider useful to Church and society.

22

The Irish Region in Changing Times

'I feel I opened the door a bit for other women.'
Eilís Ní Thiarnaigh

It is beyond the scope of this book to describe the multitude of apostolates in which the St Louis sisters have engaged over the past thirty years: this chapter includes a small sample of sisters who have made their mark, whether the work they undertook was in the area of social justice, in education, spirituality or in theology – often as a second career, after they had served for many years in a teaching apostolate.

The renewal of religious life meant that sisters were able to respond to calls to ministry or follow their own dreams, working with lay people or other religious in NGOs or in the academic world, losing their visibility as a monolithic congregation but gaining flexibility and freedom, both personal and professional. Many of these women were pioneers, no less so than the sisters who set out for the far continent of Africa in 1947, and they will be remembered as activists, as scholars and as feminists.

After a career in teaching, in Monaghan, in Kiltimagh (where she presided over the closure of the boarding school) and Rathmines, Eilís Ní Thiarnaigh turned her mind to religious education. She took a theology degree from Heythrop College, a Jesuit-run constituent college of the University of London and a masters degree in the Irish School of Ecumenics and dared to look for a job at third level although at this time no woman had ever lectured in theology in Ireland. It was a bridge too far for Maynooth, whose lecturers, she was told, had 'pontifical' qualifications – but she got one part-time position in All Hallows Seminary, where at first all her students were clerical, and a second in Milltown Institute, which at that time was a 'Pontifical Athenaeum' (a university directly under the authority of the Holy See). It was 1983.

Over the thirteen years during which she lectured in Milltown, both institutions opened their doors to women, but until 1989 only men could receive (pontifical) degrees in Milltown. In that year it became a constituent college of the National University of Ireland and its degrees were recognised by the NCEA.

'Measaim féin gur oscail mé an doras beagán do mhná eile' ('I feel I opened the door a bit for other women'), Eilís says.

She also opened the door at least a chink to the academic study of theology through Irish. She found in the faculty in Milltown *'dearcadh Gallda'* (an anti-Irish attitude): 'Well, you have to admit there's really no theology written in Irish,' was the root of this response. For historical reasons, little theology had been written in Irish since the seventeenth century so Eilís resolved to repair that omission by writing some herself. But writing was one thing: finding a publisher was another. Not even religious publishers were interested in dipping their toe into the Irish language.

In order to have her first theological book, *Briathar Beo Dé (The Living Word of God)* (2000) published, Eilís revived a moribund publishing company, Foilseacháin Ábhair Spioradálta, which had been established under the aegis of the Jesuits in 1956. She ran FÁS until her retirement from this, her third distinct career, in 2008.

Eiís was also one of a group of sisters who produced an Irish hymnal, *An Duanra*, in 1974. Fearing for the preservation of the words and music of hymns in Irish that had been part of their schooldays and life in religion, the group, calling itself *Coiste Gaeilge Siúracha San Lughaidh* (St Louis sisters Irish committee) and comprising Fionnuala O'Hanlon, Dorothy McCloskey and Méabh Ní Uallacháin, collected words and music with the help of Tomás Ó Fiaich, Pádraig Ó Fiannachta and Liam Ó Caithnia. In the 1970s the group arranged Gaeltacht trips and other activities to promote the study and use of Irish.

What Eilís Ní Thiarnaigh did for women in theology and theology in Irish, Úna Agnew did for the systematic study of spirituality in Ireland. Úna studied for a master's degree in Duquesne University in Pittsburgh with the Dutch Spiritan Adrian van Kaam 1970-74. In her essay in *Theology in the Making* (2005) she describes van Kaam as '...working tirelessly to explicate a suitable interdisciplinary methodology for spirituality...He painstakingly distinguished the discipline of spirituality from theology and explained how the rupture between these two distinct (not separate) sciences had occurred.' His classes were always grounded in experience and he placed emphasis on 'reflective journalling as a means of integrating course material'. Úna Agnew's view is that van Kaam was 'working towards the eventual formulation of a theology of applied formation'.

Over the next decade Úna Agnew found that, although she got work in spiritual direction and in theology in Milltown Institute, there seemed little future in the academic study, or teaching, of spirituality. The one year spiritual studies programme that she directed in Milltown Institute in 1985 consisted almost entirely of theology. Van Kaam's course had opened her mind to the interconnectedness of spirituality and literature and she completed a doctoral dissertation on Patrick Kavanagh (1904-67), whose poetry contains a deep strain of mysticism: 'Reading Kavanagh, researching his background, reclaimed for me my inheritance as an Irish woman, harvesting the nourishment that native landscape offers and penetrating with Kavanagh the hidden mysteries of the Irish soul.' Her successful book, *The Mystical Imagination of Patrick Kavanagh: A Buttonhole in Heaven?* (1998) was one result of her research; a revival of her faith in spirituality as an academic discipline was another. In 2001 she took her place in a spirituality department in Milltown Institute, where she and others devised and taught a master's course in applied spirituality, the word 'applied' chosen to distinguish the course from one in conventional theology. When Úna participated in a conference, 'Mysticism without Bounds' in Bangalore in January 2011, the title of her address was 'God in Creation: "The God-intoxicated Celt"'.

Like Eilís and Úna a pioneer in what was formerly a man's world, Mairéad Hughes was the first woman chaplain in an Irish school when she took the job in Jobstown Community School in 1986. In following the option for the poor she chose to focus on those who, even in the bleak social landscape of 1980s Jobstown, were called 'the bottom of the heap', and she has worked in the area ever since. Inspired by activist teacher parents who were at the very least *engagés* – her mother was strongly involved with the INTO and her father, Charlie Hughes, set up the first classes for traveller children in Dublin in the 1940s and drew Victor Bewley into involvement with traveller welfare – she established a second-chance centre called Youth Horizons in 1988. Mairéad Hughes, with plenty of academic credentials, is quick to dismiss any attempt to label her – even being recognised as 'Tallaght Person of the Year' in 2007 causes her to blush. 'I wouldn't call myself radical,' she says, and she has the grace of simplicity.

Mairéad has seen the fruits of her labour in the young people who undertake a two-year Leaving Certificate course in Youth Horizons and most satisfyingly in past pupils who have returned to teach in the centre or serve on its board. Since 1986 she has lived in a local authority house in the community. Although she is retired from teaching, all her energies go into the centre, of which she remains CEO. It is instructive to hear her talking of buying from the builder the twin show houses in which her centre is housed for nothing more than the proceeds of two golf classic fundraisers. 'That nun robbed me,' the builder said around Dublin. Public funding contributes only a small proportion of what is needed to run the centre but Mairéad knows the benefactors who can be approached in the case of any shortfall, including the J.P. McManus and the Iris [Denis] O'Brien trust funds. The Community Support Programme run by Dublin Bus has also helped Youth Horizons.

The order receives and the order gives. The month after St Louis Institute celebrated the one hundred and fiftieth anniversary of its arrival in Monaghan from France in April 2009, members of religious orders became downright unpopular with large sections of Irish society when *The Ryan Report* on institutional abuse was published. There followed *The Murphy Report* on clerical sexual abuse in the archdiocese of Dublin in November 2009, the Cloyne diocesan report in July 2011 and the publication of child protection audits on a further six dioceses in November 2011. Truly these were *anni horribiles* for the Catholic Church in Ireland.

The St Louis Institute was not spared in the prevailing climate of disclosure, claims and compensation in relation to institutional or clerical abuse. St Martha's Industrial School, established in 1870, was part of the campus in Monaghan until, in 1957, it moved to Bundoran, when St Joseph's Orphanage, established by the Crudden Trust at the beginning of the 20th century, closed and the orphanage buildings were leased to the congregation. The building in Monaghan, which was renamed Our Lady's, was then used for the expanding novitiate.

Because of a significant drop in the number of children in care, it was decided to close the industrial school in May 1965 and by the end of August that year all the children had been placed, either back with family members or in the orphanage in Cavan.

In later years, de Lourdes Duffy, who in the course of a varied career spent a year (1980-81) working with the resettlement committee to integrate the Vietnamese refugees from communism – known at the time as 'boat people' – into Irish life, worked tirelessly to help past pupils of St Martha's who made contact with her to locate their birth certificates and any available details of their background. She and other staff of the heritage centre organised a reunion for past pupils on 14 June 1992. They were able to locate about sixty of them and some came for the occasion from the UK and the US. For de Lourdes it was the fulfilment of a long-cherished dream and her efforts left a permanent record of the eleven hundred plus children who went through St Martha's since it opened.

Mona Lally continued her work with the past pupils of St Martha's, in the end having a mailing list of ninety women to whom she sent Christmas greetings and an annual newsletter. When past pupils visited Monaghan, she helped to locate information for them, in some cases reuniting siblings who had not met for years.

There was only a small number of complaints against the sisters when the time arrived. Noreen Shankey had just become regional leader when the first solicitors' letters came in 1999-2000, something she found 'deeply upsetting', feeling sympathy both for the survivors of what was at the very least 'a harsh regime', typical of the times, and any surviving sisters who had been involved in the running of the orphanage, all of them elderly by then.

As Noreen had not entered the community until 1966, after St Martha's closed, she knew little about the orphanage and her first task was to inform herself by talking to the sisters who had worked there or had lived in the attached community. She went before the redress tribunal to represent the institute, along with representatives of other orders that had been in charge of orphanages. In common with the other congregations, the St Louis Institute made the decision to contribute funds to the Redress Board that the government established in 2002, on a basis related to the number of complaints received by that point. None of the complaints against the St Louis Institute was examined in the Ryan enquiry itself.

In the words of Noreen Shankey, reproduced in *The Ryan Report*: 'Central to our participation in the redress scheme was a desire to prevent the ordeal of past residents and ourselves having to go through the courts. As I mentioned, we had no cases against us until after the Taoiseach's apology and the redress had been announced. We also felt that the way of redress was a more humane way and that it would lead in the direction of healing and reconciliation, and I welcome this emphasis with the present commission [the redress commission] and the approach you are taking.'

It is ironic that religious congregations in Ireland have suffered so much opprobrium as a result of the publicity around clerical and institutional abuse: many sisters, as well as associates, have become disenchanted with the institutional Church. More than thirty years ago sisters from California complained at the 1975 general chapter that priests considered educated and enlightened religious women a threat and that clerics were slow to implement the precepts of Vatican II on collegiality. Feminists think the 'Roman' Church worldwide and especially the Church in Ireland has remained unrepentantly patriarchal. For some sisters the latest proof of this was the new missal that the bishops introduced in the autumn of

2011 despite the opposition of the Association of Catholic Priests, and the lack of any kind of forum for religious or lay Catholics to express their views.

For religious women reinvigorated, reinvented by Vatican II, it took a long time to realise, or perhaps to accept, how deep-seated the patriarchy of the Catholic Church is. In Anne Murray's words, the Church is 'abandoned to patriarchy', with no critical analysis countenanced – the culprits, in her view, being the interpretation of the doctrine of infallibility and the system of hierarchy. Looking at the history of the Church and the St Louis Institute since 1969 in tandem, all one can think is how much the congregation has moved and how little the Church.

Sisters did wish to preserve and celebrate something of an earlier era: the sacred music that had been part of their school and religious life. Kitty Fitzsimons was the driving force and Barbara McHugh the musical director when a group of sisters came together to revive some of this music. Twenty-nine choristers performed on the final CD of hymns and motets, along with organist Gerard Gillen, when *Sacred Memories* was recorded and the choristers launched the CD throughout Ireland in December 1997. Past pupil Mary Black did the honours in Rathmines and former government minister Dr Rory O'Hanlon was the guest of honour in Monaghan: his sister Fionnuala was among the songbirds.

In Kitty's words: 'Twenty-nine sisters came…to breathe life into the dry bones of the music. None of them in the first flush of youth, mind you. One or two were in their mid forties or fifties, the doyenne (Gertie) was eighty two and in between all those swinging sixties and seventies.'

Broadcaster Ray Lynott wrote in response to the CD: 'What a sweet, secure and committed sound you make…' As well as being sweet and secure, the music soars, above all in the solos by Canice Durkan and Kitty herself, who gets her vocal chords into the song especially written for the institute by Seoirse Bodley.

Who said songbirds could not be good businesswomen? Sales of the CD and cassette brought in €9000 after all expenses were paid, which was gifted to Nigeria and Ghana.

Noreen Shankey makes a second appearance in this chapter on the Irish region: she was institute formation directress from 1982 to 1991, having studied for a Masters in Clinical Psychology in the Gregorian University in Rome. Almost from the beginning of her life in religion she was conscious of the declining numbers of vocations: twenty-two young women entered with her in 1966 but only four are still in the congregation. So when she became formation directress she had no unrealistic expectations.

Finola Cunnane, who was a novice during Noreen's time working in formation, and Cecily O'Flynn are the only two women who entered the congregation from the mid-1970s onwards to remain sisters. Noreen has had many years to formulate her view on this: 'Why do we want to see people coming after us. Is it to perpetuate our way of life and our system? Or is it to spread the Kingdom? Although we've renewed and modified our structures to a large extent, I think religious life as we have lived it belongs to another era.' She knows that it has been difficult for the Nigerian members of the institute, who have seen a steadier flow of vocations in their country, and to a lesser extent the Ghanaians, to understand why the Irish region has not been more proactive about attracting vocations in recent years. But for her this was not an option, because of the big change in culture in Ireland and the reaction of Irish society to the excessive power the Church had wielded in the past.

Columbanus Greene had a point when she remarked, back in 1977, on the modern tendency towards 'uniqueness'. For it is as individuals that most members of the region are now working, or with lay people: Noreen herself is a member of the chaplaincy team in Royal College of Surgeons in Ireland. Sisters are not visible as they used to be because they no longer work en masse in large institutions such as schools or hospitals. They no longer wear a distinguishing habit or walk in pairs everywhere.

No one could doubt the good work sisters currently do in education; in counselling; in the ecological movement; in youth ministry; in ecumenism, in parochial work; in supporting refugees and asylum seekers – to mention just a few apostolates.

Others bear witness in the quietness of their lives: 'But sanctify the Lord God in your hearts: and be ready always to give an answer to every person that asketh you a reason of the hope that is in you with meekness and fear.' *1 Peter* 3:15.

It has not always been easy to face the loss of communities, of convents long established and inserted in local communities, north and south, and of teaching ministries (despite the competing pull of the option for the poor). Nor is it just the long established institutions that are missed when they go. A small museum was officially opened in Monaghan in February 1978, the hundredth anniversary of the death of Geneviève Beale. In December 1984, partly as a recognition of the changing times and the need to preserve a record of the sisters' history in Monaghan, and partly inspired by the renewed interest in the heritage of the congregation that resulted from the charism assembly of July 1984, the Irish region formed a museum development committee. The concert hall in St Martha's Industrial School, which had become the novitiate when St Martha's moved to Bundoran in 1956, was allocated to the project, St Louis Heritage Centre.

De Lourdes Duffy, appointed curator in 1985, energetically coordinated the jobs of collection, organisation and display of practical objects and artifacts, with the assistance of many sisters. As the refurbishment of the concert hall and the creation of the displays required a significant financial outlay, de Lourdes and Mona Lally carried out a fundraising and sponsorship campaign among local businesses and public agencies. Bishop Duffy of Clogher officially opened the centre on 10 April 1988.

Superior general Dorothy McCloskey said at the opening: 'Our memories and our stories are interwoven with the fabric of society in post-Revolution France and post-Famine Ireland and we owe it to those who will come after us to leave an account of how it was.' Mona Lally and then Maura Dempsey and Frances Faul continued the work begun by de Lourdes until the heritage centre closed in 2010.

In the same year the community suffered a more grievous loss: St Louis Nursing Home closed in March 2010, unable, as a listed building, to satisfy ever more stringent fire regulations. This was a heartbreaking occasion, a kind of death, for the sixteen elderly and ill sisters who were living there and who had to be moved to other facilities. The finality of this closure and the rupture with the past brought home to sisters more than any other event the inevitability of the congregation's demise in Ireland.

23

The Wider St Louis family

'Christians together, exploring our faith'
Ann Concannon, 2011

The Friends of St Louis Missions were established specifically to support the mission effort that began in 1947. Joseph O'Doherty, father of Bríd, witnessed in Rathmines the departure of the first group of sisters for California in 1949. O'Doherty, a civil servant and former Fianna Fáil public representative, was moved to take action to support the missionary activity and addressed the parents of the boarders in Monaghan after a performance of *The Gondoliers* and the customary rendition of 'The Hallelujah Chorus' by the school choir and orchestra. He challenged the men in the audience to support the sisters of the institute tangibly, financially, rather than merely applauding their musical achievements. In the convent parlour that night a group of fathers of sisters and pupils, all Dubliners, gathered and arranged to meet again in the O'Doherty home. Out of this the Friends of St Louis Missions, a support group entirely male at its inception – it was, after all, a business as well as a charitable venture – was founded in 1950.

Members of the Friends individually pledged to donate one guinea per year for life to support the St Louis missions, no small amount at the time, and the group was legally constituted as a charitable association with Joseph O'Doherty as chairman and Edward Monks (father of Eileen) as secretary. Jack McCloskey, father of Dorothy, was also active in the Friends. A slight inconvenience was the group's difficulty in getting the approval of then archbishop of Dublin, John Charles McQuaid, because he did not want independent organisations fundraising in his diocese. In 1951 the Friends moved their headquarters to Monaghan, where the Bishop of Clogher, Dr O'Callaghan, fully supported the group and became its patron. The move proved advantageous as it led to increased involvement of men from the north and the west of the country and soon there was a branch of Friends in every town where there was a St Louis school. The AGM, always held in the concert hall in Monaghan and concluding with Benediction and high tea, was a celebratory occasion and enabled the congregation's leadership (council as it was then) and sisters to meet their benefactors.

By 1959 there were a thousand active members, bringing a considerable flow of revenue to the sisters and anticipating the call of Vatican II for greater involvement of the laity in Church business. Joseph O'Doherty was elected life president at an early stage. Mary Clerkin, who was involved with the Friends in Monaghan after she returned from missionary work in Nigeria, admired the enthusiasm with which members participated in public collections as Garda permits allowed: 'No matter what the weather, they stood out with their buckets.' Sheila Finnegan, who worked for many years as a nurse and nurse tutor in Ghana and Nigeria, was coordinator of the Friends of St Louis Missions for almost a quarter of a century.

Among the projects the Friends of St Louis Missions supported over the past decades were schools, primary healthcare and drug distribution in Nigeria and Ghana, reconstruction projects in Liberia and AIDS clinics in São Paulo and Goiânia, Brazil. They also helped to fund the formation of west African sisters. In 2006-7 the Friends adopted a specific project, the provision of clean, fresh water for the town of Akpassi in the Republic of Benin, where sisters from Nigeria have a health clinic: the government paid to sink the well and the money raised in Ireland was used to 'construct and install overhead tanks and pipes to all points of discharge' in the village. The Friends harnessed the goodwill of St Louis schools and several responded generously, including Carrickmacross and Kiltimagh, where the transition year students jigged and reeled their way to raising €2900 by holding a *céilí mór*. The well was bored and the people of Akpassi got their clean water supply in March 2008.

In recent years the age profile of Friends in Ireland increased and with the decline in the number of sisters and their involvement in education, it became difficult to recruit younger members. The institute was, however, anxious 'to give support to the present members and to help them continue their service in whatever way they can' and from 2010, the sixtieth anniversary of the foundation of the group, it was decided that while no further AGMs would be held, each group – now comprising women and men – could forward its own donations to the institute's central leadership team. Any money received will continue to be used for schools, hospitals, community projects and to develop indigenous personnel in Africa and Brazil. Separate groups of Friends in ten locations have raised substantial funding over recent years.

A Friends of St Louis association was also launched in Nigeria: the works of the congregation there are so extensive and pioneering that there is still a great need for financial support. Since 1991 a special open day has been held in May each year for thanksgiving and fundraising. The St Louis associates, as well as friends and families of sisters and pupils, help the work of the Friends in Nigeria.

Article 1 of the original rule of les Dames de St Louis made provision for 'pious persons (female gender) living in the world...who wish to take part in the prayers and works of the congregation to be affiliated to it.' Married women were included.

The associates are no longer all women, any more than the Friends are all men but the idea of affiliation remains the same. The current associate movement has its roots in the 1980 general chapter when superior general Dorothy McCloskey was eager, given the decline in vocations, that the institute should share its charism with lay people, as other congregations had already begun to do. By 1984 committees had been established throughout the institute to explore how best to inaugurate and run an associate movement. The first region to embrace the idea with enthusiasm was California. When Dorothy went on visitation there she suggested that the sisters who were involved in researching the project should delay no longer but should each invite one person to consider becoming an associate. Laura Gormley, the coordinator, Margaret McHugh and Myra McPartland worked as a team to bring the idea to fruition, adopting the RCIA (Rite of Christian Initiation for Adults) model for formation. In the words of Maura Byron, regional leader in California at the time: 'Associates incarnate our charism in new ways – in family life, in secular environments – as laity who are builders of justice and peace, at home, at work, in all creation.' Associate life in California has as its focus praying the Sunday readings (*lectio divina*), performing a ministry in keeping with the St Louis charism and building community.

In May 1984, thirteen women were invited to participate in the formation programme and numbers soon began to grow. The first two groups completed their formation and made their commitment in 1988. A new focus, care of the earth, was introduced to the programme after the chapter of 1991 and associates began to sponsor other associates from 1993. In California one associate is Episcopalian and the congregation welcomes members from other Christian churches. The group celebrated its twenty-fifth anniversary in 2009.

Michèle Harnett attributes the success of the associate movement in California to the enthusiasm of the sisters who were involved and the fact that parish and Church life are strong in California: many of the associates are in leadership positions in their parishes. The congregation's intention is that membership of the associate movement should provide a spiritual grounding for parish and other ministries.

The associates in California usually assemble in Woodland Hills; unlike Ireland they meet in plenary session rather than small groups. Building community by participating in meetings and rituals together is very important. Once the two-year formation period is over the new group makes a commitment and is then integrated with the general group over the course of the following year. There is an annual weekend retreat and the annual renewal of associates takes place in December. The region more recently added the concept of prayer partners, a lesser commitment, for those who cannot come to meetings, because of advanced age, ill health or family commitments. Like regular associates, they commit to praying the Sunday scriptures and engage in a ministry that reflects the St Louis charism.

The associates in California were involved with activities like planning for the community's sixtieth anniversary in 2009 and discernment around the new mission in New York. Currently there are more than fifty associates in the region – a greater number than there are sisters – as well as twenty prayer partners. The emblem on the associates' pin includes the St Louis cross and the passage from the prophet Micah (6:8) that was adopted as a definition of 'right relationship' at the 2009 general chapter: 'To act justly, love tenderly and walk humbly with your God.' Irish associates have a cross and chain or pin based on the institute's emblem but with an embedded turquoise stone, in honour of Turquestein.

The first programme director of the associates in Nigeria was Isabel Mann and the first associate group was formed in Akure in 1988, to mark the silver jubilee of the opening of the novitiate there. Associates were formed in Jos in 1994 and the first group formally inaugurated in 1996. Kano followed in 1995 and Zonkwa in 2001. In Nigeria the key elements of the associate programme are clear: 'Each associate commits her life to the progress of the environment in which she lives. This goes with her prayer life. The commitment is based on the three principles of simplicity of life, dedication and the need to heal and transform our broken world.' The fourteenth national conference of Nigerian associates was held in Zonkwa in March 2008. An account in *St Louis Online* describes visits to places of beauty around Zonkwa: 'Both sisters and associates could not hold their appreciation of creation by the Supreme Being and rent the air with songs of praise.'

The communiqué at the end of the conference stated: 'As associates we are also a discipleship in our relationship with the sisters of St Louis...We have also resolved to take up zonal projects to respond to the cry of the poor in line with the institute mission statement.' Associates are involved in fundraising: they hold an open day with a liturgy, then sales and donations. As in California, associates in Nigeria outnumber the one hundred and fifty six St Louis sisters in the province. They are all women, all Catholic, and meet in eight centres (but anyone can be a Friend and contribute financially or in other ways). According to the current Nigerian provincial, Rita Akin-Otiko: 'Some are mothers of the sisters and relatives who like to have a connection with the religious life. We want them to live happy family lives and support us with their prayer lives.'

In Ghana the associate movement is not so strong, perhaps, the Ghanaian leadership suggests, because there are many competing organisations for women. There are three groups in Kumasi, of which one has seven members. As in Nigeria, the associates support the sisters with their prayer lives and by sharing ceremonies and rituals.

When Mary Jo Hand was on the Irish regional team in 1995, she was asked to try again to begin an associate movement as it had not got off the ground in the 1980s. A group including Mary Jo, Miriam Brady, Catherine Brennan, Clare McManus and Clare Ryan prepared intensively over a period of two years. Finally they had an information evening in Monaghan, out of which the founding group came: nine people did the two-year formation, seven made commitment and five remain. As well as Monaghan there are now three groups of associates in Dundalk, one group in Carrickmacross, two groups in Dublin, a group in Belfast, two groups in Bundoran and two groups in Kiltimagh. There are currently four male associates in Ireland and all the Irish associates are Catholics, although individuals from other Christian churches would be welcome.

The associates meet in small groups on a monthly basis about ten times a year. One component of the meeting is prayer and/or meditation, which uses nature, the universe and daily activities in an experiential way to touch the spirituality of those who are attending. Associates are updated about matters of interest in the institute or about forthcoming events in which they may be involved. Another part of the meeting focuses on a book that the group is reading and discussing, chapter by chapter: perhaps a theological title, or a book on creation spirituality or ecotheology, books such as *The Quest for the Living God* by feminist theologian Elizabeth Johnson and Michael Morwood's controversial *Tomorrow's Catholic: Understanding God and Jesus in a New Millennium*. The associate movement does not shy away from discussing theologians at the leading edge of Catholicism. One group of associates has assembled a small library, financed by the members.

Associates renew their commitment annually in their local group with a service of prayer and there is an annual national day when all the groups come together. The associate leadership team now includes two sisters – Catherine Brennan, the coordinator, and Pauline Haughian – and three associates – Claire Buckley, Bríd Dowling and Angela McCrossan. The leadership meets annually to plan the year ahead.

As the groups have all had the same membership since the associates began their journey, they have built up a deep level of trust. Associates are conscious of the considerable investment of time and energy of the sisters who are involved. They feel it is a privilege to have access to this kind of group work: 'sharing a faith journey that encompasses spirituality, ecology and personal development,' as associate leader, Bríd Dowling, puts it. Part of the formation of Bríd's group was the universe story, based on the work of American ecotheologian, Thomas Berry.

One of the most rewarding aspects of being an associate is having the opportunity to hear leading national and international speakers on theology, spirituality and ecology, as well as learning about the charism and theology of the institute itself. Associates worldwide also participated in a St Louis heritage pilgrimage in July 2005. Sisters, associates and Friends of St Louis made the trip first to Juilly, where the then principal of Cours Bautain, Jean-Luc Walker, welcomed them, thence to Strasbourg and Turquestein. Kathy Vercillo, principal of Louisville High School, Woodland Hills, was part of the group, keen to maintain the Louis Bautain and Juilly heritage in her school, as was the superior general of the Sisters of Our Lady of Sion, Mechthild Vahle.

For the associates, membership of the group meets a spiritual need that the Church has simply ignored. This is doubly true for the (mostly) women members. In the words of Dolores McGill: 'We are way ahead of the Church in thinking and development.' Freda Carville is one of the founding group and is now co-facilitator, with Mary O'Connor, of a new group in Dundalk. In her experience: 'I've been finding it more and more frustrating that there is no spiritual nourishment in the Church…I don't think the clergy realise that we are so lacking in it. The nuns are more adventurous and push the boundaries more.' Clare Ryan is in touch with Dundalk priest, Tom Hamill, who, in Freda's words, is 'a prophet, telling people what they don't want to hear'. For Freda some of the things parish clergy say in Church are an insult to intelligent adults, for example their feeble justification of the new missal of 2011.

Some sisters share the frustration of associates with the institutional Church. Ann Concannon who is an associate director in the Religious Formation Ministry Programme in Loreto House in Dublin, says, 'I like to work with our associates, where we can be Christians together exploring our faith.'

Part of the commitment of the associates is a ministry that the members carry out as part of their ordinary lives. Malachy Marron, who belongs to the Dundalk group facilitated by Triona McGinty and Mary Jo Hand, lives his associate ministry in his day job, running a centre for the handicapped (as well as having a horse in his stable called Bautain).

An international meeting of worldwide associates was held in Loyola Marymount University, California, in the summer of 2008, highlighting the fact that although all the associate groups throughout the world grew from the same impulse they have evolved in different ways in different countries, a good example of unity in diversity. In Nigeria the associates support the prayer life of the sisters, while in California they might play a part in some aspects of the planning or decision-making of the region. In Nigeria the culture would not allow men to attend associate meetings with women, whereas there are male associates in Ireland and California. In California, the basis of the associates is a large group; in Ireland groups comprise no more than five to seven people.

For Malachy, the international meeting of associates gave a whole new dimension to his involvement. He felt part of 'something much wider than eight meetings a year in Dundalk' and thereafter could have no doubt that the congregation wanted the associates 'to be an integral part' of its future. He observed that for all the associates, no matter where they were living, 'being part of the group had greatly strengthened their faith'. For him it's a great boon to be linked with the Sisters of St Louis, 'the whole ethos and history and achievement'.

As associate Mary Coleman puts it, associates are 'woven into the fabric of the sisters and their charism'. Mary echoes the opinion of other associates, that 'the laity lost out' in the Church and that 'the new missal has gone a step backward'. She says with feeling, 'If all the women who were at Mass got up and walked out there would be few left...Are they ever going to move? I don't think I'll see it. There's nothing happening, no life in the Church.' Margot Carthy regards the associates as 'a very important milestone in [her] spiritual journey'. For her there was a 'feminist revolution in the whole of society except the Church'.

The associates share with the sisters some of the activities of the congregation's ecology group. Beginning in 1994, the group organised an 'earth day', an annual gathering of sisters and associates with a guest speaker on theological, spiritual or ecological issues. Earth Day 2007 had as its keynote speaker Seán McDonagh, a Columban priest and committed climate activist, author of *Climate Change: the Challenge to All of Us.*

From within the congregation comes the gift of meditation. For twenty years Patricia Moloney, who is based in Dundalk, has been facilitating groups in John Main meditation. Main (1926-82) was a Benedictine priest who combined the traditions of Buddhist and Christian meditation. Patricia shares the meditation with other sisters, with associates on occasion and with a weekly group that comes together in the convent parlour in Dundalk.

The Sisters of Our Lady of Sion (Notre Dame de Sion) are also part of the extended family of the Sisters of St Louis: in this case, cousins. They too owe their existence to the Turquestein Pact and the spiritual motherhood of Louise Humann but trace their lineage through Théodore Ratisbonne, born Jewish in Strasbourg in 1802, who was one of Louis Bautain's group of followers. Ratisbonne chose not to take vows in the Society of Priests of St Louis in 1842, instead setting up a centre for the Christian education of Jewish children in Paris. This developed into the congregation called, in French, *Sœurs de Notre Dame de Sion,* which was recognised by the Papacy in 1847.

The horror of the Shoa and the establishment of the state of Israel, coupled with the *aggiornamento* of Vatican II, encouraged the Sisters of Our Lady of Sion to go back to their roots and changed their mission from educating and converting Jews to a more open and ecumenical one. According to their 1984 *Constitution,* their mission is: 'to promote understanding and justice for the Jewish community and to keep alive in the Church the consciousness that, in some mysterious way, Christianity is linked to Judaism from its origin to its final destiny.' Sisters of Sion no longer have a foundation in the Republic of Ireland but are numerous in England, Europe and North, South and Central America.

In 1995 the two congregations published a joint overview of their history and mission, written by Pauline McGovern for the Sisters of St Louis and Marie Dominique Gros of Our Lady of Sion. The orders share the preferential option for the poor, expressed in the constitution of Sion as 'the rights of minorities, of the poor and of all who are marginalised in our society'. Since then, sisters of the two congregations have met to deepen personal acquaintance and explore shared and unique traditions and rituals.

The two congregations arranged a joint pilgrimage to celebrate the two hundredth anniversary of the Turquestein Pact, on 23 June 1997. The Sisters of Sion had initiated a search for Turquestein in 1950, the Holy Year, located the spot and built the altar in 1953-4 to commemorate the discovery. On the altar they inscribed the date of the pact, the date on which they located the place and also the date of the joint St Louis-Our Lady of Sion visit. Gabrielle Mary O'Connell, who researched the history of the altar, described her first affecting sight of it in *Link* of autumn 1997: 'that altar, seen by most of us only in pictures, sturdy, strongly built from the sandstone gathered from Thérèse Brek's house, cleaned of the lichen and moss of years…and bearing the new marble tablet commemorating this bicentenary celebration of our two institutions.'

Several sisters, including Margaret Anne Agnew, Anne Lynott and Noreen Shankey, have visited Our Lady of Sion in Ein Karem, west of Jerusalem. Ein Karem is in part a community of contemplatives but also a centre for biblical training and formation and a guest house for Christians and Jews to reflect in tranquillity. Marie-Alphonse Ratisbonne, brother of the founder of Our Lady of Sion, Théodore Ratisbonne, who spent much of his religious life in Jerusalem, is buried there.

24

Unity in Diversity: the International Institute

'We maintain the breadth of vision and mobility of an institute of pontifical rite, while belonging to the local Church and serving it in ways appropriate to its needs and our resources.'

Sisters of St Louis *Constitution*, 50

The decades from 1947 to 1969 were years of consolidation and centralisation when Juilly and Ramsgrange were amalgamated with Monaghan. Simultaneously the order expanded outwards – to Ghana, Nigeria and California – while maintaining its foundations in England. Hundreds of sisters worked abroad but took their orders personally from the superior general Columbanus Greene, who also appointed local superiors, and went obediently wherever they were missioned. From 1969 onwards, partly as a result of the *aggiornamento* prescribed by the Second Vatican Council and also because of changes in society, in personal aspirations and in the number of vocations, this model of leadership was gradually abandoned and the question of how the order should be structured and led (the verb 'rule' quickly fell from favour) became a subject of continuing discussion.

One of the first means of devolving power was the gradual creation of regions and the appointment of regional superiors but more recently, as the number of sisters in Europe and the Americas has dwindled, regions have become fewer. Congregations are living organisms and need to be adaptable, so the question of structure and leadership will always be a live topic. The movement to a team model of leadership was gradual, beginning when Dorothy McCloskey was superior general, 1980-1990, and especially after the general chapter of 1985. More recently, the 2003 general chapter strongly endorsed the team model of leadership: although there has to be an official institute leader from the canonical and legal point of view and also to represent the institute before the public (as at the time of publication of *The Ryan Report* in 2009) the team members, both in central leadership and in the province/regions are very much seen as equals. The chapter documents report that 'a considerable amount of [its] time was spent struggling with and consolidating our thinking with regard to this important service [of leadership].'

Team leadership, which is regarded as a 'feminine' model, more relational than authoritarian, has, like any other system, advantages and disadvantages. It is cumbersome, so decisions and directions can seem slow in coming to fruition. In theory, at least, there is safety in the team model because the members agree on decisions and 'own' them, in current parlance. The burden is spread over three, four or five pairs of shoulders instead of resting on one. Discernment is an important aspect of the process of leadership and it often takes time to reach consensus about a particular course of action. That is why the more efficient male model dominates in business, even among women, but it is a mystery why this patriarchal model dominates in the Catholic Church when it is patently inappropriate: perhaps it is simply to do with the reluctance of authority to relinquish power after millennia of holding it.

Bridget Ehlert, who has extensive experience in facilitating general chapters and assemblies, has observed that women religious tend to engage deeply with how they are governed, who makes decisions and how, whereas male religious are satisfied with a more traditional, hierarchical system. In her view men have not moved as far as women when it comes to new, collaborative leadership models. To her mind, collaborative leadership is a gift that women religious have developed and will be able to give to the Church when the hierarchy is eventually forced by the shortage of priests to collaborate with the laity (and with women). There is not yet much sign of this in Ireland but the community in Étampes that belongs to the Nigerian province operates this kind of collaborative ministry.

For the congregational leaders in the 21st century, team leadership is seen as another act of fidelity to the order's charism, *Ut Sint Unum*, whereby the congregation is led or guided in a spirit of unity rather than in the separation mode of hierarchy. Central leadership also represents the unity of the international institute, bringing together individuals from different regions and cultures. Maud Murphy, who served a term as congregational leader, thinks it's an 'extraordinary miracle that people can come together from different parts of the globe with different personalities and make a team.'

It is a challenge for the institute's model of leadership that Nigerian society in particular is so patriarchal: as Philomena McGuinness, who spent most of her working life in western Nigeria, puts it: 'There is no household in Nigeria that does not have a head.' The Catholic Church in that country has followed suit, becoming, in the words of Ann Concannon, who worked there for many years, 'even more Roman than the Irish Church'. Many dioceses were established by Irish SMA missionaries who became the first ordinaries (bishops in charge of dioceses). Bishops sometimes insist on communicating only with the provincial leader so it is difficult to maintain the team model. Even members of the community may find it difficult to look on the members of the team as being equal, especially as respect for seniority is a central tenet in many of the Nigerian cultures. The current, larger provincial team in Nigeria allows for each leader to take responsibility for specific communities and to live in the area for which she has responsibility. In this way, it is hoped that the provincial will be freed from the pressure of constant travel from convent to convent.

No less important an issue for the St Louis Institute is its members' understanding of the concept of community. Many of the older sisters in Ireland began their religious life in large communities like Monaghan and Carrickmacross. Now Rathmines is the only community that has more than twenty members. Over time, sisters moved into ministries that did not have the predictability of teaching and were not available for regular meals or prayer and as they got older some sisters felt a strong need to have their own living space. Almost a third of the sisters in the Irish region are now living on their own, although some in a cluster of apartments that means interdependence rather than independence. In England most of the sisters live on their own: this is why the mission's leader, Phil Morris, finds the idea of the Béguines attractive. In the context of society in general this development is not at all surprising: more and more people are choosing this way of life, partly a consequence of the increased financial independence of women, with as much as 60 per cent of the total population living on their own in cities like Stockholm and New York.

Now that more of the sisters are ageing, living alone will pose its own challenges. Some of the older sisters I met were opposed to the breakdown of formal community. 'Who will care for the elderly?' they asked. 'How will sisters continue to pray together?' Living alone is the ultimate step in the transformation of the congregation in Ireland from monastic to apostolic: then there was teaching for large numbers of sisters; now there are almost as many apostolates as there are active members of the institute. But if sisters are not living together, praying together, having recreation together, it will take a more conscious effort for them, firstly to stay in touch with one another and secondly to feel a part of something bigger: the region or the international institute.

Cultural differences add complexity to the concept of community. In both Nigeria and Ghana the extended family is an essential part of society and older people are always cared for at home – nursing or care homes simply do not exist. The Ghanaian and Nigerian sisters are only now beginning to experience the challenges that come with older or unwell personnel. Their cultures dictate that they all live in community, whether they like it or not, unless a sister is obliged by her ministry to live somewhere there are no other sisters. Many communities number only three or four, unless, as in Zonkwa, a community is large because there are several apostolates in the same location.

Winifred Ojo of the central leadership team says: 'In our culture hardly anyone lives on her own: even if you are working and not married you would bring a younger brother or cousin to live with you.' Even people living in rented accommodation quickly form 'families', with which they share a kind of community life.

For Stella Akinwotu, a member of the Nigerian provincial team: 'We have to adjust for our culture: you cannot move faster than your culture or you will scandalise people...Families, friends, tenants – everybody lives with others in Nigeria. Also it is not efficient for people to live on their own. Ordinary people would envy the possessions of a religious living on her own; it would seem like not witnessing, not making a sacrifice.' A challenge for the regions of the institute is to respect the different ways religious life is lived, in keeping with the culture of the country in question.

Sisters from Ireland have contributed much to other regions in the areas of formation and renewal. Mary Jo Hand, who had been a missioner in both Nigeria and Ghana, went to Kumasi at the request of the Ghanaian sisters in 1990 to facilitate the Thirty Day Ignatian Spiritual Exercise for six sisters who were about to make their final vows. She also gave a course to a larger group on the spirituality of Tony de Mello. One evening in July as she took the cooler evening air in the compound of the secondary school in Kumasi, Marie du Rosaire Diver crossed the grass towards her to ask, 'Do we have a Catherine Dunne?' The tragic news of Catherine's death came to Kumasi from some sisters in Accra who had been listening to BBC World Service.

The idea of building respect, understanding and unity by the sharing of expertise in a structured way grew out of the extended leadership meeting (ELM) of 2007. 'Mobility for mission' is administered by Fionnuala Cole from the Mission House in Dublin and the first mobility sisters travelled in 2009. The idea is that for between one month and three a sister lives with a community in another region and either 'gives' expertise by teaching or facilitation or 'receives' expertise by studying. There is also provision for the traveller to share in the ministry of the receiving community or to undertake a different kind of ministry in the receiving country. Mobility for mission was not envisaged as 'pious tourism' but a means of continuing professional development both for the giver and the recipient(s).

Cáit Gibbons was the first Irish sister to have a taste of mobility in 2009, when she went to Africa to teach English and French in St

Louis Secondary School in Kano. What comes across clearly in her account of the trip (*Seo agus Siúd*, 2009) is her sense of a discovery of a whole new world: 'Of this I had been totally ignorant, except for names of places and photos in magazines and newsletters. Many times I had stood in the crowd outside St Louis House singing "Go Ye Afar" but once the car had disappeared from view, we hurried back to our work.' The community life and dynamic liturgies of Nigeria impressed her and she considered herself privileged to have been present for a final profession ceremony in Akure Cathedral.

Some of the most frequent requests Fionnuala Cole receives from Ghana and Nigeria are for help with formation or renewal for professed sisters. Margaret Anne Agnew and Anne Murray did formation work in Akure with novices and young sisters and Enda McMullan undertook a programme on reflective prayer through art with sisters and teachers, also in Akure, which was considered a great success. In 2010 Cecily O'Flynn, a science teacher, availed of her summer holidays to spend a month sharing the life of the sisters in Ghana. She met science teachers in Kumasi and Oku, sharing experiences and expertise, and taught biology class in Oku. She visited many communities, participated in the Ghanaian regional assembly and attended the final profession of two Ghanaian sisters.

In the summer of 2011, Úna Agnew led a renewal programme and retreat for thirty young Nigerian sisters with temporary vows in Akure – she had given a course in spirituality in the same centre in 1990 – and offered spiritual direction to six sisters, something that she calls 'a rare privilege'. Finola Cunnane's ministry has been in the areas of chaplaincy, retreat work and spiritual accompaniment, and for some years she was on the staff of the retreat centre, Grace Dieu, in Waterford. Her mobility for mission took her for two and a half months to Ghana – Accra and the novitiate in Kumasi – to provide ongoing formation for sisters and work with catechetics teachers. Mary Moran, who is based in Harrow, in London, visited Ghana in the summer of 2011 and spent time getting to know every community, as well as helping with formation in Kumasi.

California has also been involved; Elizabeth McGoldrick, the region's archivist, spent some months working in the archives in Juilly in 2010. And Ghanaian Joyce Eyiah worked in various ministries in Los Angeles under the guidance of Bríd Long and Michèle Harnett.

In 2012 Bridget Nwankwo from Nigeria spent her period of mobility working with the Merchant's Quay Ireland, a daytime service for the homeless run by the Franciscans in central Dublin.

'The Spiritual Development and Origin of the Institute' is a six-week course the sisters in Juilly have twice organised for a pair of sisters, one Nigerian and one Ghanaian, that has contributed to building relationships between Ghana and Nigeria as well as between west Africa and Europe. Several sisters contributed to the programme: Máirín Barrett introduced the visitors to the spiritual heritage of the institute and took them to Strasbourg to walk in the footsteps of Louise Humann and Louis Bautain; Elizabeth Beirne and Anne Killeen taught them French and involved them in their parish ministry and prayer life (and cooked for them). The visitors spent some further weeks sharing the parish work of the community in Étampes. Two of the Nigerian sisters who did this programme, Gladys and Chinyere, subsequently settled in Étampes to work in the parish of St Jean Baptiste de Guinette.

Fionnuala Cole feels that mobility for mission is very worthwhile. Participants need to be well briefed before they go and share a process of discernment and reflection. There may be visa problems, particularly in the case of the African sisters coming to Europe, and Fionnuala feels she has to accompany her mobiles (in spirit and virtually) on a journey that may be long and complicated and involve being in a country with an unfamiliar language.

The St Louis Schools Network also builds unity by linking schools in Ireland with St Louis schools elsewhere in the world. On the day of the official commissioning of the Le Chéile schools by congregational leaders in March 2009, four teachers from Louisville Girls' High School in Ijebu-Itele, exchange partners of St Louis, Monaghan, were present in Monaghan. The visitors included Stella Akinwotu, who is now on the provincial leadership team. It was a return visit: Vera O'Brien, who is principal in Monaghan, had visited Ijebu in February 2009 with three of her staff. A bridge of care project gives St Louis Monaghan pupils the means to contribute to Louisville and to St Louis primary schools in Nigeria by fundraising and donating schoolbooks.

Anne Murray is Ireland-west Africa schools network coordinator and passionate about the links between the old world and the new. Seven teachers from Lé Chéile schools and Kiltimagh Community School visited Nigeria to see the St Louis schools in Akure, Oka and Ondo, where there is a new primary school. Caroline Curley from Kilkeel went to Ghana with Anne Murray and Enda McMullan and visited the Jubilee School in Kumasi and the school in Mampong, where the Sisters of St Louis have a presence. Ondo links with Kiltimagh; Ikere links with Dundalk; Rathmines links with Kano, so in February 2010 teachers Colette Forde and Lisa Cullen visited St Louis Secondary School, Bompai, where Isabel Morrin was the first of many St Louis principals in 1951, a list that includes Mary Connellan, Patricia Moloney, Maud Murphy, Maura Flynn and Patricia Ebegbulem. Five St Louis sisters work in the school: at the time of the visit the principal was Catherine Ologunagba, who is now a member of Nigerian provincial leadership. The transition year pupils in Rathmines developed the link and raised funding for the trip, with the help of language teacher, Barbara Capper, and there was a return visit by Nigerian teachers.

Internationality allows for greater potential for education and continuing professional development and for access to necessary funding from a wide range of sources. The intercongregational workshop held in Ijebu-Itele in 2011, on the subjects of project cycle management and policy influencing, lobbying and advocacy, drew together twenty-five participants from eight congregations: Winifred Ojo calls it 'capacity building'. The ten-day course was arranged by Uainín Clarke and Winifred of CLT and facilitated by two Dutch management consultants from a company called MDF, which is based in Amsterdam. Clearly such a training event would be feasible only with a critical mass of sisters to attend it, and the more international the gathering the better. Management is a crucial issue, especially in Nigeria, where there are so many communities and different ministries and the congregation needs to engage with government agencies and influence policy.

Again as a means of promoting unity, the institute's central and extended leadership have been conscious of the need to renew the work of the order by establishing missions that are inter-regional and in locations where there has not been a St Louis presence up to this. After a long period of discernment and fact-finding visits to Ethiopia by Phil Morris and the late Carmel Mary Fagbemi, this process led to the creation of a new intentional mission in the town of Dawhan, diocese of Adigrat, in north-eastern Ethiopia.

The Bishop of Adigrat, Tesfaselassie Medhin, gave the St Louis sisters a site in Dawhan, a brand new town that has little more than a church and kindergarten to serve the people, and Dublin-based architect Ruth Bradfield was commissioned to design the living and working accommodation for the community. She visited Adigrat with Margaret Healy and Winifred Ojo of CLT in July 2011 to survey the site. Two Nigerian sisters, Justina Ihechere and Ijanada Emmanuel, and one Ghanaian, Benedicta Boakye-Yiadom, will, it is hoped, be missioned to Ethiopia in early 2013, and CLT has invited sisters in Ireland, England, France or California to make a commitment to this new mission for six months or a year. Ministry will be community development, although, judging by past experience, it is likely that this will evolve to include education or health in some form, as well as the empowerment of women.

Two of the areas of focus for the 2011 extended leadership meeting in England, which drew together the leadership teams of all the countries of the institute – twenty three sisters in all – were interconnectedness and improved communication between the regions. 'I don't see the congregation as an Irish one; I see it as an international one,' says Ann Concannon. For a congregation like St Louis, where many of the sisters seldom meet face to face, there is a great and constant need to focus on integration while respecting diversity. On the surface, cultural differences may not be as significant as they were in the 1940s but there is still a good deal of divergence with regard to theology and spirituality, as well as leadership, lifestyle and community life.

Epilogue

Uainín Clarke, 2009

In Pauline McGovern's *God Wills It: Centenary Story of the Sisters of St Louis*, there is a photograph taken on the steps of St Louis House in Monaghan after the celebration of Mass in October 1959 to mark the centenary of the order's arrival in Ireland. It speaks volumes: there is only one sister in the foreground of the photograph, the superior general, Columbanus Greene, but numerous priests and bishops and laymen. There are several other women but they are all appendages to their husbands; these include Sinéad de Valera and Kathleen Lemass, wives of the President of Ireland, Éamon de Valera, and the Taoiseach, Seán Lemass, respectively.

The photograph records the contribution of a religious order composed entirely of women but puts women firmly in their place – at home in the convent or beside their important husbands. At the same time it is a visual representation of how closely the Catholic Church and the Irish state were intertwined at the time, and how much part of the status quo religious orders were. An important strand of Irish social and political history in the fifty years since then has been the disentanglement of these ties.

In April 2009, when the St Louis sisters celebrated the one hundred and fiftieth anniversary of their arrival in Monaghan, the situation was different. No longer was the state represented by leading national politicians. The President, who did attend, was a woman, Mary McAleese, only the second woman ever to be elected to this position. There were women and girls – and associates – on the altar at various stages of the proceedings.

In her speech at the reception in the Four Seasons Hotel, then congregational leader, Uainín Clarke, put her finger on the zeitgeist when she thanked Monaghan town council for officially recognising the contribution of the sisters to the town: this kind of recognition from a secular authority can no longer be taken for granted: 'Given the current climate in Ireland,' she said, 'to be in religious life, to be a nun, is counter cultural.' Like the other religious orders in Ireland, the St Louis Institute went from being hand in glove with the state to being counter cultural, not in fifty years but in twenty.

Uainín described her consœurs as 'women of our time, who… are seeking to find God in today's world…women of service', despite the fragility of their situation and the increasing age profile of the institute members in Europe. She admitted that sisters felt vulnerable in the world, like the three sisters who came from Juilly on a cold January morning in 1859 and found no bed in the inn. Most importantly for the future, she said that she preferred 'to look at what was happening in religious life in general and St Louis life in particular as an invitation to trust, just like Geneviève, Clare and Clémence were invited in their day to trust.'

This book begins with the Turquestein pact of 1797 that set in motion the foundation of the Sisters of St Louis in France, Ireland, England, west Africa, North America and Brazil and their modern-day associates, as well as their cousins, the Sisters of Sion. Pauline McGovern wrote this reflection for the two hundredth anniversary of the pact (*Link*, autumn 1997) but it is even more relevant today:

'We remember what it was like then, steady numbers in the novitiate, flourishing institutions at home and abroad, well organised local communities with a majority of younger, active members, a position of status and influence in Church and society. There were elements in the hundredfold which we took for granted as compensation in the past for the highly restrictive way of life that we had chosen and persevered in…

'If we could find ourselves saying, "It's good, it's working. Goodness, grace, creativity are working, the legacy of Turquestein is working…not perfectly, of course – it never did work perfectly – not as it used to work in the past; not as we might like it to work again. But it is working, surprisingly, almost unrecognisably at times…in accordance with God's word of promise."'

Uainín Clarke emphasised 'promise' at the 2009 celebrations. 'For all that will be, yes!' was how she concluded her address at the 2009 celebrations.

Yes to being counter cultural, yes to still being on the margins of the hierarchical Church, fifty years after Vatican II, yes to growing old, yes to dying out, yes to the future of the St Louis sisters being in west Africa. Yes to being part of the cycle of history, from the 18th to the 21st century and, like everything on the planet, eventually transformed into something else.

Bibliography

Abuah, Dorothy. *A History of the Sisters of St Louis in Ghana, 1947-2002*. University of Cape Coast, Ghana, 2002 (unpublished BA thesis, Department of History).

Agnew, Úna. *The Mystical Imagination of Patrick Kavanagh: A Buttonhole in Heaven?* Dublin: Columba Press, 2003.

Agnew, Úna. 'My Way to Spirituality'. Gesa E. Thiessen. *Theology in the Making: Biography, Contexts, Methods*. Dublin: Veritas, 2005.

Barrett, Máirín. *Words to Live By*. Dublin: St Louis Institute, 1992.

——————. *Mère Thérèse de la Croix*. Dublin: St Louis Institute, 1984.

——————. *The First of the Ancestors: Joseph-Louis Colmar 1760-1818*. Dublin: St Louis Institute, 1997.

Colum, Mary. *Life and the Dream*. New York: Doubleday, 1947.

Commins, Miriam. *St Louis Charism: the Irish Dimension* (*Link*, Autumn 1990). Dublin: St Louis Institute, 1990.

Corish, Patrick. *The Irish Catholic Experience: a Historical Survey*. Dublin: Gill and Macmillan, 1985.

Ebegbulem, Patricia. *Stop Trafficking in Women and Girls: A Handbook for Schools*. Lagos: Committee for the Support of the Dignity of Women, 2011.

Fitzsimons, Kitty (ed.). *Reflections: Clochar Lughaidh Muineacháin*. Dublin: St Louis Institute, 1978.

Hogan, Edmund M. *The Irish Missionary Movement: A Historical Survey 1830-1980*. Dublin: Gill and Macmillan, 1990.

Long, Bríd. *The Theme of Conversion in the Life and Works of Abbé Louis Bautain (1796-1867)*. Rome: Gregorian Pontifical University, 1990 (unpublished doctoral thesis, Faculty of Theology).

McGovern, Pauline. *God Wills It: Centenary Story of the Sisters of St Louis*. Dublin: Browne and Nolan, 1959.

——————————. *Words for the New Millennium*. Dublin: St Louis Institute, 2000.

Ní Thiarnaigh, Eilís. *Briathar Beo Dé*. Baile Átha Cliath: Foilseacháin Ábhair Spioradálta, 2000.

O'Connell, Gabrielle M. (ed.). *Link: News and Views of St Louis Irish Region*. 1988-98.

——————————. (ed.). *Dorothy McCloskey, Superior General St Louis Sisters 1980-90*. St Louis Institute, 1991.

——————————. *The Lost Story: Kiltimagh and Balla*. Dublin: St Louis Institute, 2007.

St Louis Institute, Irish Region. *Seo agus Siúd*. 2001—.

St Louis Institute. *St Louis Online*. 2005-9.

St Louis Institute. *Musings* (monthly newsletter) 2011—.

Sisters of St Louis Education Committee, Nigeria Province. *The Grace and Task of the Catholic Educator*. Ibadan: St Louis Provincialate, 2007.

——————————. *The Art of Gracious Living*. Ibadan: St Louis Provincialate, 2001.

Acknowledgements

Thanks to the St Louis sisters in Ireland, England and France who offered me the most generous hospitality over the eighteen months I spent interviewing sisters and working in the congregation's archives in Monaghan. I enjoyed Elizabeth Beirne's *épinards à la crème* in the Villa in Juilly, a delicious queen of puddings in Newmarket and more lunches than I can count with the community in Monaghan. I also thank the sisters from the Nigerian province and the other regions – Ghana and California/Brazil – who shared their personal stories and stories of ministry with me. Everyone who spoke to me contributed to my sense of the rich tapestry of St Louis life, something I wanted to reflect in this book.

It is a tribute to the varied life stories and open spirit of the sisters I met that I so thoroughly enjoyed this part of the research for *New Horizons*.

Thanks to Nuala Cole and Dorothy McMahon in the Mission House in Rathmines, who placed the front parlour conveniently at my disposal on many occasions and who made innumerable cups of coffee for me and my interviewees.

Thanks especially to CLT member, Uainín Clarke, to institute archivist, Deirdre O'Connor and to Anne Jordan, who facilitated the writing of this book, and to the sisters who read a draft of the manuscript, correcting errors, suggesting changes and providing additional information.

Máirín Barrett, archivist in Juilly and an encyclopaedic source for the early history of the institute and its contemporary history in France, talked to me about Louise Humann, Louis Bautain and Mère Thérèse de la Croix as if she knew them personally. It was she who showed me the convent and the school, the little *salle des souvenirs* (museum) and the graveyard a short distance from the village where the sisters and Louis Bautain are buried.

This book is built on the work of previous chroniclers of the St Louis Institute. Among them are Pauline McGovern, historian and theologian; Gabrielle Mary O'Connell, historian of Kiltimagh and Balla and editor of *Link*, which reflected the doings and the history of the Irish region in the 1980s and 1990s; Bríd Long for her unpublished PhD thesis, *Louis Bautain and the Idea of Conversion*; the late Miriam Commins, archivist and historian; Dorothy Abuah, who compiled an account of the education and health ministries of the Sisters of St Louis in Ghana; Kitty Fitzsimons, who edited *Reflections* (1977); Marion McGreal, who collected a great deal of information about the recent history of the St Louis Institute; and the aforementioned Máirín Barrett. Other publications of the institute, including anniversary brochures of the Nigerian province and California region, the institute's *St Louis Online* and *Musings* and the Irish region's newsletter *Seo agus Siúd* provided valuable insights.

Finally, thanks to Terry Prone, a generous friend and mentor, and to Sean McMahon, also the best of friends, for his help.